HUNTER S. THOMPSON

An Insider's View of Deranged, Depraved, Drugged Out Brilliance

Jay Cowan

The Lyons Press
Guilford, Connecticut
An imprint of The Globe Pequot Press

One owes respect to the living: To the Dead one owes only the truth.

—Voltaire

The Lyons Press is an imprint of The Globe Pequot Press.

Thanks to Hunter Thompson Literary Executor Douglas Brinkley, Professor of History at Rice University, for excerpts used from the correspondence of Hunter S. Thompson.

Text design by Libby Kingsbury

Library of Congress Cataloging-in-Publication Data
Cowan, Jay.
Hunter S. Thompson : an insider's view of deranged, depraved, drugged-out brilliance / Jay Cowan.
p. cm.
ISBN 978-1-59921-357-6
1. Thompson, Hunter S. 2. Journalists—United States—Biography. 3. Thompson, Hunter S.—Friends and associates. 4. Cowan, Jay—Friends and associates. I. Title.
PN4874.T444C69 2009
070.92—dc22
[B]
2008045957

10 9 8 7 6 5 4 3 2 1

Printed in the United States of America

Contents

1

Beaten by Angels

Newspapers in Aspen, Colorado, have a long history of remarkable letters to the editor. Well-known jazz musician and local curmudgeon Freddie Fisher won the only award the Colorado Press Association has ever given for Letters to the Editor. But even judged in that light, another missive I read in March 1968 was wild. It began with a flourish, "Herr Editor:" and just gathered steam, discussing the writer's friend Martin Bormann and their interest in local affairs: "We were warming ourselves around the fire the other night, chatting about discipline, when I pointed out the newspaper article on Sheriff Whitmire's request for riot-control weapons."

Bormann, the infamous Nazi war criminal who was never captured, was often rumored to be living in Argentina. Or Colorado. The letter lauded the local Pitkin County Sheriff's Department for taking allegedly proactive (but clearly absurd) steps against possible riots or other subversive activity in the Aspen area. It suggested that the writer and Bormann be hired to help engineer some riots to justify the beefed-up arsenal.

It was the first of several such pieces, each "endorsing" the high Nazi principles of certain local politicians and government employees. "Aspen needs more men like this: far-sighted men who are willing to invest in the future," the letter noted near its end, and it was signed, like the others, by someone named Hunter S. Thompson.

As in many places that year, Aspen was caught in a titanic struggle, one of the great ones of our times. It was between the backroom ways things had long been done and a new, more progressive approach; between those who opposed the war in Vietnam and those who supported "my country, right or wrong"; between the conservative mind-set of old-time ranchers, town burghers, and the traditional small pond's big fish, and a wave of artists, skiers, surfers, hippies, freethinkers, drug fiends and revolutionaries; between young and old, heads and straights, leftists and right-wingers, the literal Nazis who had come from the Alps of Europe to participate in one of America's newest mountain resorts, and the freaks rolling in from San Francisco, Berkley, Ann Arbor, and the East Village.

It was a watershed period in Aspen, America, and the world, and local political tensions reflected global ones. You could hear the discussion being waged daily in restaurants, bars, living rooms, and right out on the streets. People who disagreed with something you may have been intemperate enough to state publicly wouldn't hesitate to barge out of their home, business, or a café to accost you at high volume as you walked by.

The one place that guaranteed everyone would take notice of how you felt was in the Letters to the Editor section of the *Aspen Times* and the *Aspen Illustrated News,* weekly clearinghouses for all the pent-up angst and opinions of a community of less than a thousand contentious souls who couldn't let a slight about the tidiness of their yards pass, let alone big national issues such as war and peace, communism, and drugs. The letters weren't just howls in the wilderness, because Aspen was even then a fashionable address where sophisticated people paid attention to what was going on. So, as much as the letters were honest and heartfelt protests or affirmations of whatever, they were also tiny tastes of literature and a grasping after attention and even immortality.

Being sixteen and intrigued by everything, I paid attention to what can only fairly be described as an ongoing competition in the papers, the bookstores, the restaurants, the bars, the galleries, or anywhere people met and disagreed. With these Martin Bormann letters, clearly the ante had been upped and I was impressed. There was a strong scent of genius about them. Who the hell was this guy?

I'd heard of him mainly from reading a review of his first book, *Hell's Angels, The Strange and Terrible Saga of the Outlaw Motorcycle Gangs,* in *Time* magazine. The review, which was very good, was enough to persuade me that I didn't want to read the book any more than I wanted to find out more details on the Clutter family and their killers from Truman Capote. Just knowing that these kinds of people, the Angels and the *In Cold Blood* killers, were out there was enough to trouble my sleep more than it should have. I could have lived out my days nicely without ever learning that one of the Angels liked to pop living people's eyes out of their skulls, and that many carried pliers for taking teeth from the same sort of unwilling donors.

None of it was the kind of reading that suggested much humor to me. So it was a surprise to find a very dark comedy at work in Mr. Thompson's letters. My own inclination at the time was always to go the impassioned and indignant route if I wrote to the paper: pained, persecuted, and loud, always assuming that high dudgeon was enough. But here was someone making profound points while being so sarcastic that his slyness might be missed altogether exercising a devious wit that suggested a whole new approach to dealing with injustice or whatever else might inspire you to write.

I knew Hunter Thompson had been beaten by the Angels, which seemed not just macho but poetic on the order of Rimbaud, the kind of surreal, biblical fate you couldn't invent. That he had survived was not only helpful to him personally but definitely gilded the legend. That he also, in the popular local myth, had fled to Aspen and hidden out somewhere remote in the countryside seemed to indicate that he regarded the Angels as fearfully as any rational human should, whether they had spared him once or not. It also lent weight to the local sheriff's concern that Pitkin County might be invaded by lawless barbarians come to track down the one who got away.

These letters made a couple of points about Hunter that it would take me years to fully appreciate. First, he wasn't shy about self-promotion, however indirect. By making fun of the sheriff's madness, he was also pointing out that it had been inspired by none other than himself, Hunter Thompson. These communiqués were a way of introducing himself to the community and establishing that he was somebody.

Second, Hunter was a tireless letter writer whose volumes of correspondence far outstrip the rest of his commercial output. And he always did it with one eye toward publication, a trait he sometimes mocked in others. It was, however, exceedingly shrewd on his part because that material has sustained three volumes of his Gonzo letters so far. It was also nice for anyone who got to read the letters, whether they were sent to them personally or appeared in newspapers, legal transactions, or business negotiations, as well as in the inevitable books. Because Hunter always had their historic usability in mind, the letters are well crafted and invariably entertaining.

Witness the Martin Bormann letters. I commented on them when Hunter and I first met, and then years later when some compilation or another was being considered. As a gift and a writer's lesson for me, he gave me the original of one of the letters. It was not only a remarkable collectible but evidence to me of how seriously he took even a letter to the editor, revealing a series of edits he made to nearly half of the lines in it. It also contained more than five hundred words of priceless writing, most of it centered on a scathing denunciation of a local public figure: "His letter to the editors of the *Rocky Mountain News,* published on June 17, was absolutely flawless in its logic," wrote Hunter. "I was particularly impressed with his plan to 'Get rid of the Supreme Court in Washington and get some cowboys in, instead.' Not many men in public life would have the courage to sign their names to a notion like that."

To fully appreciate why the Bormann series had me, and others, riveted, it's necessary to understand something about the context of the town where they made their initial splash. Not only was Aspen caught in that clichéd battle between the new and the old, but it was incredibly unique in ways that Hunter demonstrated he understood. That kind of insight is as appreciated in Aspen as it is in Hollywood, Washington, Wall Street, and anywhere else full of incestuous hubris and self-satisfaction.

As a former silver-mining capital, Aspen had a taste of the very high life in the late 1800s, complete with opera houses, horse racing, and fine hotels, until silver was demonetized, plunging the town and valley into fifty years of backwater quiescence. That period, especially in retrospect, turned out to be paradise for many. A difficult time, to be sure, but worth some sacrifices. Then the end of World War II changed everything when prewar plans for a ski area were finally realized about the same time high culture came rumbling back into town in the form of wealthy Chicagoans Walter and Elizabeth Paepcke.

The ski area turned Aspen into a world-class winter recreation resort. The Paepckes brought internationally renowned thinkers, artists, architects, and musicians to the valley. Within fifteen years of the end of the war, Aspen was well on its way to a renaissance that would transform it into a money-making machine and a refuge for the immensely wealthy on a level comparable with only a few other small towns on the planet. It was the new home to hundreds of postwar European immigrants who saw in the mountains of Colorado reflections of their home in the Alps, along with lodes of new money to be made in an industry they already knew something about—resorts and ski towns.

The first waves of hustlers and genuine greedheads were already arriving as well, and everything was still being run by a tight club of good old boys who didn't care to see much more change (and who could blame them?) or were too dim to grasp what was at hand. The ones who didn't get it were less villainous than those who *did* get it; the latter tried to squeeze every dime out of Aspen they could before leaving the town in ruins.

Aspen then was the kind of place where the Paepckes could be seen as saviors or harbingers of the Fall, and either side could be right. Yes, they reinvented the town for the better in many ways and would even supply you with free paint for your house, as long as you painted it the color they wanted. Just as some robber barons owned company towns, the Paepckes aspired to the same notion, but they called it the Aspen Idea and gave it a more palatable cultural veneer.

Meanwhile, business went on as you would expect at a very high-end private club. County commissioners rarely encountered a development or subdivision they didn't like, city officials were for sale cheap, and long-haired people were manifestly unwelcome and regularly harassed, beaten, and arrested for vagrancy.

The board of directors of the Aspen Skiing Corporation, which ran two of the three ski areas in the valley at the time, included some of the principal architects of the Vietnam War, including Paul Nitze and former Secretary of Defense Robert McNamara. Though it was a fabled refuge from the woes of the world, Aspen was never as completely disconnected from them as people might assume.

The flip side of the coin was why so many people kept coming to Aspen no matter what the drawbacks. There was, and is, an almost mystic energy to the place, incredible beauty in the mountains and rivers, amazing music and artists, great food, perfect snow, and some of the most interesting people in the world—in general, a miraculous confluence of the best of everything in a place so small that for a time everyone knew your name and how you liked your eggs cooked. The sense of community was so thick that it just boiled over on a regular basis, bonding people and tearing them apart in the way of any good family.

When Hunter Stockton Thompson, a defrocked southern gentleman with a wicked tongue and a long list of lusts and loathings, came careening into this scene, fresh off the front lines of some of the Western Hemisphere's flash points, it was bound to get weird, but it turned out to be an irresistible combination for the rest of his life.

After my early exposure to his writing I was dazzled and tried to learn what I could about him. It was a big surprise to me when I was in high school that my girlfriend, Marcella, sometimes babysat for him. She lived in the Woody Creek area of the county, ten or fifteen minutes from town, and Hunter did too. Woody Creek back then was very rural, betraying few hints of the elevated status as a haunt of the rich and famous it would attain over the next twenty years. At that time it consisted mostly of a trailer court and a small, rustic general store. Hunter lived up the actual Woody Creek drainage itself, several miles from the trailer court. "What's he like?" I asked Marcella after she mentioned working for him.

"I don't know. Weird. He drives a Volvo and I only see him when he takes me home."

"He takes you home?" Even then, not knowing him at all, I sensed this might be trouble. "Does he smoke dope with you or anything?"

"No. But he drinks a lot. He drives with one hand because he always has a drink in the other one."

"*What?*" We were all taking driver's ed at the time, where we were shown grim films like *Death on the Highway,* full of carnage from car wrecks; about 90 percent of them, we were told, were the result of drunk driving. So drinking and driving still seemed to me to be a serious sin. Especially when he was hauling my girlfriend around.

"It's OK. He never seems drunk and he drives fine," she reassured me, although she admitted she never told her parents about it.

I finally met Hunter when he was first trying to get a local lawyer named Joe Edwards elected as mayor of Aspen. It was 1969 and Edwards had successfully defended a so-called hippie couple who had been sitting on some steps in downtown Aspen and were busted for vagrancy by city police. As a politically motivated troublemaker at Aspen High School, I was invited to a meeting organized to determine if Edwards could be elected. I think the group wanted some representative of the youth market, even though most high school kids, including me, were too young to vote.

I was justifiably paid little attention until Hunter asked me what I thought at one point. I'm not sure what I was expecting, but he wasn't it. His speech was a low mumble that was hard to understand—a result, I'd learn later, of what he said was a speech impediment when he was a kid. Tall, rangy, and balding, I found him instantly likable because he actually seemed to care what I thought. I babbled something to the effect that I wasn't sure some of the people they considered their automatic base would necessarily turn out that way. Most of the others in the room immediately shrugged me off as too young to know anything, but Hunter came over later and pursued the idea.

"Hey, I'm Hunter. Nice to meet you. I thought you made a good point," he muttered, fiddling with cigarettes and a glass full of whiskey. He had dark, penetrating eyes and a little smile playing across his lips. He was lean and almost calm back then, wearing jeans, a T-shirt, and some kind of cargo jacket and Sorels because it was still winter. I learned later that he was thirty-one, which of course seemed oldish to me. "Why don't you think some of the local freaks will vote for Edwards?"

"I'm not sure if they'll vote at all. A lot of them don't believe in it, or don't want to take the time," I told him. "And even though a lot of them have long hair, they aren't really freaks or peace people. When I mention politics to them they either don't know what I'm talking about or they don't give a shit. And if they do, they're kind of against all the hippies coming in."

"Jesus," he grumbled, looking at me like he was seeing me differently. "You might be right. Would you vote for him?"

"Edwards? Of course."

"How do you think he'd do if we had a straw vote at the high school? Could you help us with that?"

"Yeah, probably. A lot of kids think just like their parents do, so I don't know how they'd vote. But I can talk to them." As it turned out when we actually conducted the poll, Edwards won convincingly, and it had the effect of suddenly making him credible in town, as it was assumed that the kids *would* reflect their parents' thinking.

It was an amazing experience for me. Before that, my parents and some of my teachers listened to what I said, but most people didn't, usually with good reason. But it was still encouraging to find someone, apparently important, who treated me as if I had something worthwhile to say. It was my first major discovery about Hunter as a person, and it was ultimately my most lasting.

I was kind of a rube from Wyoming, part of an actively political family. My parents moved us to Colorado in 1967 when I was still a literal Teen Age Republican who had gone door-to-door soliciting votes for whomever the Cowan side of the family supported that year.

By the time I met Hunter, I'd been transformed into a dyed-in-the-wool leftist, mostly by my homeroom schoolteacher, but also by current events. For the next thirty-five years I would have someone to talk to about politics who could really help me try to understand the art and the science and the cold, hard realities of it. "The editor of the high school newspaper is now part of our half-underground Government in Exile," Hunter wrote about me in a 1969 letter to his editor at Random

House about the political material he was gathering for his next book. The letter was later published in one of his collections.

It took awhile for me to get over trying to write like Hunter. I was actually the assistant editor of our school newspaper, *To Liberation,* and was also helping distribute Hunter and Tom Benton's *Aspen Wallposter* periodical. This usually consisted of some of Tom's more provocative art on one side (bleeding stripes on a flag background with the stars morphing into dollar signs and the words FAT CITY USA emblazoned across the lower right corner in the same dripping red as the stripes, for instance) of poster-sized heavy stock paper. On the other side were Hunter's and others' screeds on a variety of issues. In addition to accusing local politicians, by name, of being "so crooked they have to screw their pants on every morning," the *Wallposter* also contained novelties, such as lists of "treacherous drug dealers," people who would sell you bad mescaline and fake speed.

After a series of antiwar and school board–bashing pieces by me in *To Liberation,* which was included once a month in the *Aspen Times* newspaper, I was invited to contribute to the *Wallposter*. I was beside myself with pride and fear and screwed it up completely. I tried so hard to sound like Hunter even my parents called me on it. "Write more like yourself. That's why they asked *you* to do something. Let Hunter be Hunter."

It's a dilemma that confronts everyone who has ever written about Hunter and is aggressively illustrated in some of his biographies. It's like living in England for a year and ending up with a cockney accent. Bill Murray used to like to tell people who asked him how he managed to nail Hunter's mannerisms so well in the movie *Where the Buffalo Roam,* "The problem wasn't learning to be like Hunter. The problem was stopping it." I've read countless pieces written about Hunter, and only rarely do any of them avoid trying to ape him.

Failing to write well enough to be published in the *Wallposter,* I at least helped distribute it when it came out. I once spent several days helping Hunter's younger brother Jim with deliveries while Hunter and Tom Benton were busy preparing Hunter's run for sheriff. There was some concern about sending me out with Jim, and someone pulled me aside to say it would be better not to get him stoned, in case I was thinking about it. Later I learned that Jim was gay and Hunter was nervous he might do something inappropriate.

No matter what, delivering the *Wallposter* in 1970 was always an interesting experience and the kind of thing that could potentially be worth your life. Aspen at that time was growing increasingly less hidebound but was still fairly evenly split between progressives and serious rednecks. At that, it was a liberal bastion compared to the rural counties and small towns nearby. It was definitely not a wise idea back then if you had long hair (and everyone who delivered the *Wallposter* did) to be hanging out anywhere in neighboring towns like Basalt or Carbondale after dark or to go in the wrong bar or to try delivering a radical piece of artistic ranting full of pornography and disrespectful images of our government. One issue contained an image of a masturbating woman named Jilly, another had a Tom Benton alteration of a *Time* magazine cover that showed Richard Nixon with swastikas rising in his cutout eyes. The entire front of another one was a silhouette-style silkscreen of Tom's depiction of a couple making love.

"Thank god the writing isn't inflammatory," I joked to Jim as we headed away from production manager Gene Johnston's car trunk with bundles of the incendiary publication as if they were part of a drug deal. Jim just blinked at me. The cover of this issue had a brain in a set of crosshairs, and at the bottom was "THE AMERICAN DREAM." Inside, the biggest eye-catcher, after the photo of Jilly, was a headline that screamed, "Aspen Summer Of Hate 1970 . . . Will The Sheriff Be Killed?"

A dramatic excerpt from Seymour Hersh's explosive story on the slaughter of women and children in My Lai, Vietnam, took up part of one column. And in the long piece attached to the sheriff headline, Hunter once again took on prominent local politicos, including Pitkin County Sheriff Carrol Whitmire and County Commissioner Dr. Jay Sterling Baxter, who had announced that there was a "death list" circulating that called for the murders of up to eight Aspen-area public servants, including themselves.

Hunter pointed out that Whitmire was in the habit of employing this gambit about once a year to get attention and demand more money, and now he had an election coming up. "So it seemed only reasonable that this year's plot should call for a blood-bath of really lunatic dimensions, a total purge of the town's political hierarchy—and especially those few coming up for reelection," wrote Hunter in the *Wallposter*. "In the rude and cynical lexicon of career politicians, this kind of strategy is called 'Sucking for the Sympathy Vote.'"

The idea is to create a dark and terrifying "nonpolitical" problem for yourself, then use the problem to generate enough publicity to get the voters emotionally involved in your public suffering. A lower-key version of the same tactic, Hunter pointed out, is to get your wife pregnant nine months before election day. And the local twist, "promoting the notion that you're about to be killed by maniacs because you've done such a good job—is no longer considered entirely stylish in most parts of the country, particularly in urban areas where the voters are too politically sophisticated to fall for that kind of hokum," concluded Hunter.

Another piece was ostensibly contributed by Martin "Marty" Bormann and directed at Ned Vare, a recently elected counterculture city councilman. "Hunter was always the center of attention no matter where you were," said Vare in a 2007 interview for the *Clinton Recorder* newspaper. "Jack Nicholson would come by and we would just sit there. If Hunter was in the room everyone would be quiet and listen. They hung on his every word to see what he was going to do." Vare later ran for county commissioner when Hunter ran for sheriff.

The *Wallposter* story about Vare went on for a dozen stanzas and included tirades such as, "You twisted communist all covered with warts and fish eyes too crazy to see the truth right in front. . . . And you have the gall to knock Germans just because we grease our underwear to move fast through the streets & get to the bank before the Schwartzes. People like you, Vare. Ugly people. Too stupid to pour piss out of their own boots."

In the same issue, what the casual reader may not have paid much attention to was a little parenthetical near the end of Hunter's story on the sheriff, noting that the incumbent Whitmire would be facing opposition in the upcoming election from the Republican Party "(And perhaps a third Independent candidate)." In truth, Hunter had already decided to run. He had been making noise for a while about finding another Joe Edwards–style candidate to pit against Whitmire, but privately he was telling friends he might take a shot at it himself.

Though some have claimed that they later introduced Hunter to politics, he had been fascinated by it at least since writing for the *National Observer* in the early 1960s, whether he was in South America, Montana, or San Francisco. And his slant was always left leaning. Probably the single most politically galvanizing period in his life was when he went to Chicago to cover the 1968 Democratic National Convention. He saw the blood in the streets firsthand from demonstrators being whipped by Mayor Richard Daley's thug policemen and got a taste of the clubs himself for doing nothing more than marching in protest.

It was a moment he wrote about and referred to frequently after that. "I came away from Chicago shocked at what they were willing to do, and what we were up against," he told me. And it was just part of what he referred to as "the heaviest year in American history since World War II." Few would disagree. Martin Luther King Jr. was assassinated in April, two months later Bobby Kennedy was killed, the Democratic convention was the public disgrace for which the chant (and subsequent poster, T-shirt, and defining phrase) "The Whole World is Watching" was coined, and in November America went to the polls to choose between Richard Nixon and Hubert Humphrey, two of the sleaziest presidential candidates in history.

After all of that, Hunter began to devote himself to politics in a more personal manner, as if his very survival depended on it, which of course it did. Left to their own devices, the crazies of either party at that point would have happily destroyed us all. It was the beginning of Hunter's long relationship with politics at the highest level. Taking as his mantra the notion that "politics is the art of controlling your environment," Hunter instinctively recognized that he needed to do as much as he could to secure the home front he loved in Colorado first. And he had a sense that it could be done.

Given that the ragtag attempt to elect Joe Edwards as mayor had only fallen six votes short (and those were probably stolen), Hunter should have realized that he might actually be electable as sheriff when he ran in 1970 on the Freak Power ticket. But many of us knew that it was more a stunt than anything, until the very end. Hunter did little to disguise that fact, in spite of later embellishments. He liked to say that he believed, based on the Edwards's candidacy, that there was a larger constituency for radical, freak-based campaigns than people realized, both in Aspen and America. Mistaking Aspen's moods and temperament for America's is something many Aspenites have done over the years, usually to their detriment or at least their disappointment. I'm not sure that Hunter really believed what he was saying so much as he was using it for justification before and after the fact.

When his campaign turned into one of the most overcovered and analyzed elections in the history of small-town politics, it surpassed even Hunter's ambitions. And once it began to look like he might have a real chance, he got nervous and coy. When he wrote about it for *Rolling Stone* he said, "The possibility of victory can be a heavy millstone around the neck of any political candidate who might prefer, in his heart, to spend his main energies on a series of terrifying, whiplash assaults on everything the voters hold dear."

His take in private was that he began to be scared that he might actually get elected and have to perform the duties of the job. "Can you imagine?" he asked me more than once. "I'd have to be in that goddamned office taking calls about cats in trees and domestic disturbances. It's horrible. That was never the idea."

In the initial discussions that were held about his running, the intent was merely to create shock and awe, generate some press about how bad the current sheriff was, and to put The Fear into the electorate. The latter turned out to be easy and also somewhat self-defeating. Running on a platform that advocated ripping up paved streets and planting them with sod, renaming Aspen as Fat City, legalizing marijuana, and eating Jimsonweed and mescaline on the job engendered a lot of angst and resentment in the Pitkin County citizenry from one end to the other. That expanse included coal-mining hamlets, big farms and ranches, pockets of old-time miners, and numerous other outposts of the conservative, rural West: a lot more than just the semisophisticated, resort-based realm of Aspen—where most of the freaks lived.

The campaign attracted media from around the world, and while Hunter reveled in the attention and tried to fine-tune his message, others began taking the whole thing so seriously that death threats ensued. Federal undercover agents were reported to be in town, stirring their drinks with switchblades in the Hotel Jerome Bar and asking after the whereabouts of a Doctor Thompson. It sounded suspiciously like what Hunter had accused Whitmire of just a few months earlier, and everything was having an effect. Hunter was soon being accompanied by volunteer bodyguards and whisked around Aspen in a van that would spirit him from Tom Benton's studio gallery to campaign headquarters at the Hotel Jerome like some kind of celebrity or drug lord. Or perhaps the latest political rising star slated for assassination. All were roles Hunter could easily embrace.

"Out-of-town press is doing some polling that shows we're running really strong," he told me one day with more than a trace of astonishment. No one knew what it meant, because the polling was all being done in Aspen, and most of Pitkin County's voters didn't live in town. "So now we need some kind of plan, in case it happens."

Hunter had already persuaded a friend named Bill Noonan to run for county coroner after discovering that he was the only person with the power to remove the sheriff from office. Much as John F. Kennedy was said to have been told by his father to make his brother Bobby his attorney general for self-protection, Hunter became convinced he needed a cohort as coroner in case he was elected.

It's entirely possible that had Hunter run the kind of campaign he helped orchestrate for Joe Edwards two years earlier, he might have won. By the end it was too hard to try to overcome the negative press he had generated for himself, and he thought it made him look silly for trying. Talking about hiring an actual law enforcement person to run the office and clarifying certain of his stances on recreational drug usage, while only practical if you weren't joking anymore, felt like he was backsliding.

To compensate and restake his claim to being a genuine radical—and ultimately crystallize his image in the public mind for good—he shaved his already balding head completely bare at a time when everyone else was growing their hair down to their waist. He became a skinhead well before they existed as a genre and decades before the style would become a hallmark of punk. He did it as part of a bet and in the throes of a mescaline binge, but also because he was so prematurely bald that letting what was left of his hair grow long would have only made him look older, so he went the other way. And it worked, at least in terms of creating an identifiable presence and ratifying that he was "not like the others."

In the end, however, it didn't get him elected. Even though he handily carried Aspen, Hunter was beaten in the rest of the county. "When I finally lost by only four percentage points, it was the happiest day of my life. If I'd won I'd still be in jail," he wrote in his book *Better Than Sex* in 1994.

In every other respect than the vote count, he did win. His campaign completely changed the job of sheriff in Aspen, which has been in progressive and enlightened hands almost ever since. It also changed Hunter's life. In the short few months he waged his campaign he succeeded in raising his profile from that of an author with a moderately successful first book on the market to that of a shrewdly crazy, drug-gobbling political enfant terrible with a shaved head and an international reputation, even if he was mostly past the *enfant* part. His run for sheriff opened up a whole new world of subject matter for his writing, along with political contacts that would eventually rank him at the top of the lists of journalists who knew their way around and weren't afraid to let the rest of us in on it.

Writing in the extreme first person about the mayoral and sheriff's races in Aspen secured his first published piece in *Rolling Stone* magazine, eventually placing him at the forefront of a generation of scribes chronicling one of history's craziest eras. Beyond that, what really began as a lark, a political joyride, became a key part of Hunter's canonical history, at least as he willed and created it. Whether or not that was all part of the plan originally, and many of us doubted it was, you had to admire his perception and dexterity at recognizing what running for sheriff became, seizing it and making of it the next huge step in his wholly original life. The sheriff's campaign quickly catapulted Hunter out of Aspen and back into the general maelstrom of America, pursuing what would become the unholy grail of his literary aspirations: charting the Death of the American Dream.

It was an appropriately high-minded project for a man whose literary heroes were, among others, F. Scott Fitzgerald and Ernest Hemingway. It was also a potentially sellable commodity for his editors at Random House who had a multibook deal with him based on the *Hell's Angels* success and were looking for the next tome. They had already purchased a novel written by Hunter before *Hell's Angels,* titled *The Rum Diary*. He wasn't in love with the book or the idea that it see print any time soon and was actively searching for something else to sell his publisher instead.

Convinced that *The Great Gatsby* was as close to the great American novel as anyone might ever get, Hunter wanted to produce something similar, competitive, important. But he was also a self-confessed "lazy hillbilly" who now believed, based on his successes, that immersing himself totally in a story and even becoming the story himself, then writing it all in a days-long, deadline-cheating frenzy of drugs and sleeplessness was the only way to proceed. It had worked for Kerouac, it had worked for Hunter with *Hell's Angels* (the second—and by all accounts best—half of which was written in a four-day binge), and it meshed perfectly with his desired lifestyle.

During this period I stayed in touch, sometimes intentionally, sometimes not. One late night after I called a local radio station and requested "Nick Danger, Third Eye" from a Firesign Theatre Album, I was startled when it was cut off partway through and the station switched back to music. When I called to complain, the DJ, whom I knew, told me he'd received an irate call from Hunter Thompson when "Nick Danger" had barely begun, wanting to know what the hell the station was doing at that time of the night, playing some kind of low-rent comedy instead of good music when he was depending on the music.

"I told him it was you who requested it, and he said, 'Well, fuck him and tell him I said so. He should have better taste. It's not funny and you should be playing music. Loud music.'"

I was mildly shocked because I just assumed he'd like the bit, especially with its frequent drug references. When I called him on it later he told me he thought Firesign Theatre were insipid. "What about Monty Python?" I asked.

"I hate them."

"You don't think they're funny?" I was stunned.

"No. I don't think most of the English are funny, really."

"Why not?"

"It's all toilet humor."

"What?"

"Most English humor is about farts and shitting. It's all they talk about and it's juvenile. The whole fucking country, obsessed with going to the bathroom."

I thought about that when I learned he was working with an English illustrator named Ralph Steadman and then read his piece "The Kentucky Derby Is Decadent and Depraved," in *Scanlan's* magazine and wondered if he had softened his view of English humorists or if he considered Ralph potty-fixated as well. "Of course," he barked at me when I asked. "They're all demented. But he can get beyond it, when he works at it," he winked.

Though Hunter's writing included a lot of slapstick descriptions, his humor was generally more cerebral. In person he smiled a lot but rarely laughed out loud at anything. It was more considered and conspiratorial, a low chuckle just to let you know he got it. Only when he was really cranked up and pleased at an idea of his own, or occasionally someone else's, would he really slam a hand on the table and guffaw.

The early seventies were a big transition time for Hunter. He was inventing an alter ego named Raoul Duke, because, he said, "I need someone to take some of the heat instead of me, to be even weirder and really freak people out." Duke would get credit for various writings, including *Fear and Loathing in Las Vegas,* and only outlive his usefulness as a tool of Hunter's when Garry Trudeau pirated the persona for his *Doonesbury* comic strip.

Hunter and Tom Benton had also become ordained doctors of divinity in the Missionary of the New Truth, one of the original faux religions that legitimately entitled them to conduct weddings (Tom would later preside at my own wedding at Hunter's Owl Farm), bury people, and potentially receive tax-exempt status. And it was in this manner that Hunter S. Thompson became *Doctor* Hunter S. Thompson, a status that has aroused some curiosity over the years, and one that comported well with the image he was constantly constructing.

As I became more involved with local politics and various projects of Hunter's, I'd get dinnertime—and sometimes much later—phone calls from both him and his wife, Sandy. Hunter could ramble on, but there was usually a purpose. Sandy, on the other hand, seemed to call just to chat, and would do it for hours if I would. I was never sure if she just needed someone to talk to or was acting as a kind of surrogate for Hunter. But I always thought one of the reasons I got to know Hunter better during this time was because I got along well with Sandy. "She likes you," he told me. "And she doesn't like everyone." It clearly made life easier for him when he could tell her he was with me or inviting me over. It also complicated things when they were fighting and even more when they broke up.

2

The Writer as Rock Star

Because I was always a serious skier, I was particularly fascinated by the 1970 story Hunter did on Jean-Claude Killy, the great French ski-racing star.

> . . . yes, I couldn't quite believe it, but there he was: Jean-Claude Killy, the world's greatest skier, now retired at age 26 with three Olympic gold medals, a fistful of golden contracts, a personal manager and ranking celebrity status on three continents. . . . I shook my head. Killy's hard-sell scenes no longer surprised me, but finding him trapped in a beer and hotdog gig was like wandering into some housing-project kaffeeklatsch and finding Jacqueline Kennedy Onassis making a straight-faced pitch for Folger's instant-brewed.

"The Temptations of Jean-Claude Killy" was written on assignment for *Playboy*, but they spiked it. It finally ran in *Scanlan's* and was included in Hunter's first anthology, *The Great Shark Hunt*.

The story took forever and almost permanently soured his impression of ski racers. "They're stupid," he told me flatly, knowing that I had been one and was friends with many. "Or at least Killy is. He isn't paid to be smart. If we ever communicated at all, about anything, it was so short I can't be sure it wasn't just a fluke. He's so weird that he actually interrupted having sex to talk to me for half an hour on the phone, and didn't tell me about it until later. The editor hates the story. I got tired of the bullshit trying to get through all of Killy's handlers and the PR flacks and wrote about it. Killy's in America touring around for Chevrolet at all of these horrible auto shows. I haven't been kind to Chevy and I won't change it, and Hefner has been trying to get them to advertise in *Playboy* for years."

He showed me the story before it appeared in *Scanlan's,* a short-lived radical magazine out of San Francisco edited by Warren Hinckle III, who played an ongoing role in Hunter's life. I thought the piece was great, but the big thing it did for Hunter was open him up for other significant assignments, including one on the Kentucky Derby for *Scanlan's*. For the Derby story he relied, in the end and out of sheer desperation, on his already established technique of drug-aided "cramming." He finished the story in just a few days, making it more about him than anything, and it became, to his shock, a sensation. It was the first piece to be officially dubbed as "gonzo journalism" by Bill Cardoso in the *Boston Globe*. For Hunter it was like Colonel Kurtz's "diamond bullet in my forehead" from one of his favorite movies, *Apocalypse Now.*

Now he knew for sure that he could be a part of his stories, and even the central part, and make it work. The first-person participant had gotten him a book on the *Angels.* The "Freak Power in the Rockies" story had gotten him into *Rolling Stone.* And the Kentucky Derby caper had taken a total nonstory and turned it into something groundbreaking and attention getting. Other works, such as "Strange Rumblings in Aztlan" for *Rolling Stone* and the Killy piece, were intriguing readers and keeping him employed. But they weren't blazing a new trail and chasing the dragon of Literature. The Kentucky Derby story was the gateway he needed.

What it did most immediately for him was pave the way to roar off to Las Vegas, twice, in hopes of collecting some caption material for a *Sports Illustrated* piece and to write a feature for *Rolling Stone*. By unloosing his frustrated fiction powers, allowing him to create action when there was none and green-lighting him to freely interpret and render his "dark and deranging vision" of whatever event or place or time he found himself in, the marketplace had endorsed a style and genre he had created entirely and for which he was dangerously well suited.

When *Fear and Loathing in Las Vegas* came out I'd already read it in *Rolling Stone,* and I was in awe. I vividly remember laughing out loud constantly and agreeing with pretty much every thought he expressed. The Bormann letters, the *Wallposter* writing, and the *Scanlan's* pieces were all fine, and I think I would have felt the same way even if I didn't know him. I'd even surrendered and read *Hell's Angels,* surprised at how good and relatively normal it turned out to be. But *Vegas* was another animal altogether.

It was, at that particular time, much more than just a book. It was a declaration, an outrage, an event, a sea change, proof we were not alone. It was, just then in that version of America, like chewing into a live 220-volt electrical wire and draining it dry and pleading for more. Revolution was in the air, a whole new generation with a different way of looking at the world was cresting the horizon and ready to rumble, and there was nothing left to lose by letting people know where you stood. This book, in all its humor and hallucinatory rage, seemed another big affirmation of everything: that we were right, that we were winning, that we would prevail. The book can be, and is, widely read and appreciated by a succession of generations. But I think that however much readers like it, anyone who didn't read it right then and there, when it came out, will never feel quite the same impact.

Describing one of the first times he took acid, Hunter wrote in *Las Vegas*:

> I went into the men's room to eat mine. But only half at first, I thought. Good thinking, but a hard thing to accomplish under the circumstances. I ate the first half, but spilled the rest on the sleeve of my red Pendleton shirt. . . . And then, wondering what to do with it, I saw one of the musicians come in. "What's the trouble?" he said.

"Well," I said. "All this white stuff on my sleeve is LSD."

He said nothing: Merely grabbed my arm and began sucking on it. A very gross tableau. I wondered what would happen if some Kingston Trio/young stockbroker type might wander in and catch us in the act. Fuck him, I thought. With a bit of luck, it'll ruin his life—forever thinking that just behind some narrow door in all his favorite bars, men in red Pendleton shirts are getting incredible kicks from things he'll never know. Would he dare to suck a sleeve? Probably not. Play it safe. Pretend you never saw it.

There was no turning back from *Vegas,* a work that he would eventually join some of his fans in describing to biographer William McKeen, with uncharacteristic hubris, as being "as good as *The Great Gatsby* and better than *The Sun Also Rises.*" It was not only a comic tour de force but a powerful look at the warped fabric of American society as we were coming to recognize it. Beyond that, it made Hunter a celebrity. And a recognizable one at that, which was very unusual for authors. He has been described as the first rock star author. Being associated with *Rolling Stone* launched him in that direction, *Fear and Loathing in Las Vegas* made it so, and his next book, *Fear and Loathing: On the Campaign Trail '72*, set the whole thing in concrete.

Hunter, of course, liked the idea of being equated with a rock star and catered to it. He talked repeatedly about using words as music and a political tool and about "the high white notes" Fitzgerald liked in writing.

Not everyone thinks *Fear and Loathing in Las Vegas* is such a work of genius, and its effect can be subject to different moods. I reread it once in the early nineties and found it boring and dated in places. When I last reread it in 2007, I once again laughed all the way through. It was engaging and insightful and I lingered over passages I hadn't noticed before. The most famous parts, I told myself, only seemed clichéd because they had been cited, imitated, and quoted so often. Frequently by Hunter himself.

As Hunter's fame and visibility increased, I spent more time with him, at the Jerome Bar, at live music shows in town, at restaurants up and down the valley. Things were becoming more of a production with him, he seemed to require more handling, and he was inevitably late. But so was I, and I didn't have nearly as many excuses.

When he left town for the better part of a year to follow the 1972 presidential campaign, I spent part of it bumming around Europe, and the rest of it pounding nails and skiing. By the time we were both back in town, his third book in six years was coming out, *Fear and Loathing on the Campaign Trail '72*. Once again I'd been following the campaign, as had many, in installments published in *Rolling Stone*. And once again I was blown away.

There were so many things about this book to like and none to lament. While it didn't necessarily have the nonstop laugh quotient or runaway weirdness of the *Vegas* book, it was howlingly funny much more often than one would expect from political writing, being in the shadow of such essentially humorless masters of the genre as Theodore White. It provided a true insider's look at how we nominate and elect our presidents, was eerily prescient, and strangely enough, in its own doom-struck way, it provided some hope from the front line. There were, apparently, good people out there in that world and Hunter was meeting them and reporting back. What's more, one of them, George McGovern, seemed for a while to have an outside shot at getting elected president.

Unflinchingly radical and relentless, Hunter described career politicians in ways that not even H. L. Mencken had considered. He called Hubert Horatio Humphrey, the former vice president, "a treacherous old ward-heeler," and "a turnip," while confirming the kind of criminal nightmare the whole election process had become.

But many people then were still giddy with the notion that victories, and even wars, could be won. The Movement, and all those who supported it, had brought an end to Vietnam. Nixon seemed on his last legs and it really looked, even to seasoned cynics, as though it might be possible for the same people who stopped a war to incite the country to elect the best instead of the worst. We were on a roll, ran the thinking, so why not? Hunter himself *believed*—in spite of the train wreck just four years earlier, in spite of all his rational mind told him and that he passed along in his writing—and he did what he would do so often in his life and bet his heart instead of his brain, picking McGovern for an upset. Of course, it wasn't even close. McGovern lost forty-nine states and the District of Columbia. To Richard Milhous Nixon.

Hunter's unhinged but uncanny pronouncements from along the trail were, almost from the first, followed nearly as avidly as the campaign itself. And he was a rookie in the field. It helped that he quickly established deep contacts inside the various organizations, sometimes because of charm and intelligence, sometimes because people knew and liked his writing (and wanted to be written about), and sometimes because key aides and pollsters and strategists liked drugs and liked sharing them with people they felt they could trust. Once that bond was established, tongues were naturally loosened. It also became necessary for these people to keep Hunter close and pass good material to him, because he knew enough about them to end their careers and they felt they owed him for not turning them into headline-grabbing stories. They knew he never would, but it didn't hurt to stay on his good side. In professional politics, that's one of the first rules of the road.

It also didn't hurt that Hunter was willing to write things others were only whispering about. And with his natural gambler's instincts and real feel for politics, he was able to make some very astute predictions when the mainstream media was still backing dead horses.

However you get your foot in the door, you then have to execute and know your job. Hunter followed McGovern early in the primaries, well before any of the other pundits or even the voters. He helped contribute to Edmund Muskie's shockingly early collapse in the primaries with brutal dispatches describing him as doomed goods and an "Ibogaine freak" while he was still leading in the polls. And he wrote what more than one professional observer described as some of the most honest and insightful reporting on the whole campaign.

Though he will always be best remembered for the *Vegas* book, and Hunter himself called it his masterpiece, *Campaign Trail* did something ten more *Vegases* couldn't have, and that was legitimize him. Here he showed that he could apply the same fierce talents and craziness to something other than a drug-addled ramble through the weirdest town in the country, however symbolic of the sordid underbelly of the American Dream it may be. And he didn't sell out to achieve that respect, he merely wrote about the ugliest game going, up close and personal.

Now, instead of just being the idol of every druggie on seven continents, or even one of the funniest writers since Twain, he was the real deal, a thinker, an intellect, with praise heaped on him by his peers and even the masters. Tom Wolfe and Norman Mailer wrote elegant blurbs about him that he used for the next thirty years, and Kurt Vonnegut compared what he did to the advent of Cubism.

It was heady stuff, as they say, but no more than his due at that point. To his friends, including many of us in Aspen, it confirmed that we'd been right all along. He *was* good, by god. And we knew him. He was even reasonably well grounded and didn't let all the attention turn his head, and he kept a good circle of friends around with whom he didn't seem too much different. He also had a lot of the good scoop on politics and seemed to be meeting everyone. Movie stars, TV people, possible presidents. It was remarkable to be able to talk to someone who genuinely had an inside track on some of the biggest stories of the day.

Hunter made a show out of being surprised and troubled at how much his own celebrity was interfering with his life and even with his ability to cover stories. He bitched about it frequently, in person and in letters to friends during the *Campaign Trail* year. As much to let people know, it seemed, that he was actually famous, instead of to really complain. This was, after all, what he'd been seeking, and he'd never had any great sympathy for other celebrities, no matter how much he liked them. We were in the Jerome Bar one night when Jack Nicholson stopped by our table and said hi to Hunter, then went back to his own table where he was approached by every other passerby. Aspen had always had a reputation of being very laissez-faire about celebrities and I was embarrassed. "That seems really rude of people," I said to Hunter. "He must get tired of it."

Hunter didn't say anything for a minute. Then he muttered, "Don't kid yourself. Famous people want to be recognized. It makes them nervous if they aren't."

Fame was also handy for Hunter as it made it even easier for him to be the focal point of his own stories. And he enjoyed the star treatment, whether it was getting good tables in restaurants, staying after hours when the bar was supposed to be closed, or having total strangers come up to him and tell him how talented he was and ask if they could buy him a drink, lay some good drugs on him, or give him a blow job.

The women-and-sex part of fame was not something he seemed to struggle coming to terms with. As I got closer to him and Sandy and their son, Juan, it was hard not to notice a fairly steady undercurrent of fighting between Hunter and Sandy, especially when he was on deadline or stressed about something. Hunter was also growing increasingly chummy with some of the women he knew around town.

Beyond being a writer and a rising star, Hunter, when he wished to, radiated charm. Even in his youth in Kentucky he liked the girls and they liked him, and that never changed. He was, in old-fashioned parlance, a ladies' man.

Sandy, however, was about over his lifestyle by the mid-1970s and was already complaining openly to me about Hunter's womanizing, as well as his getting physical with her, grabbing and shaking her and shoving her around. He had an obvious temper, but I wanted to think he was better than that. And Sandy was sometimes hard to know how to take. Hunter knew she was talking about him and their troubles and after an outburst one day told me, "She drives me crazy because I can't reason with her. She'll be fine most of the time, but when she loses it, she goes right over the edge." He told me, as he told numerous others, that in his opinion it was because she had "eaten speed like candy for years." As can happen with divorcing couples, it became hard to believe either of them on the subject.

It wasn't like Hunter to talk too much about his personal life. He also didn't write much about relationships or Sandy or even women and sex in general, it seemed to some of his readers and critics. And he was sensitive to the matter. "What am I supposed to do?" he asked me, rhetorically.

"I'm married. I can't be writing about wild sex and orgies when I'm traveling and working. And I'm not going to just start throwing sex at home into my stories for no reason." I think it especially aggravated him to be called on this odd deficit in his writing when he clearly loved women, loved being around them and making them happy and being the gracious, never patronizing, always interested southern gentleman.

I think Hunter and Sandy were pretty monogamous for most of their relationship, but as fame increased Hunter's opportunities, and their marriage started to come apart, he became more open about his affairs. He was never the kind of guy to brag or even talk about them, but after a while, as his home life deteriorated, I think he was less concerned about keeping them a secret. And he never had to search far for company. The wives and girlfriends of some of his friends, especially the drug dealers, tended to come on to him fairly strong. And the waitresses and bar girls at the Jerome were always convivial.

One night at the Jerome, Hunter disappeared with one of the waitresses and then returned. After the bar closed and we hung out for a while, Hunter and the waitress left together. The next night the bar manager, a good friend of mine and Hunter's, asked me if I'd seen Hunter that day. I said no, that I assumed he was home. It turned out he wasn't and hadn't been all day and Sandy was calling the bar and going nuts. The manager was worried, mostly for Hunter, and tired of being bugged by Sandy, who could be maniacal about phone calls. So I finally told him, confidentially, that I thought Hunter might have left last night with one of the waitresses, and we should probably try to not let Sandy find that out.

After that, the manager's attitude changed markedly. All I can say in my own defense is I was still in my early twenties, had been drinking, and just wasn't thinking clearly. Hunter arrived shortly after that, assured us that he had just called Sandy and it was all covered. As the evening got later, the manager became loudly drunker and kept getting in my face. At 2:00 a.m. the bar closed, but a handful of us stayed on. Hunter seemed oblivious to the escalating tension between me and the manager until I finally told him, "I'm out of here. He's crazy and I don't want a scene with him."

I still couldn't figure out what the hell was going on, and as I went out into the deserted hotel lobby the manager followed me and started shouting at me and calling me out and wouldn't tell me what the problem was. Hunter appeared and watched like it was a joke until the manager, almost too drunk to stand, charged at me across the lobby and I had to put a hand on him and step aside while I yelled at Hunter, "Do something about this. I don't want to fight him!"

Hunter grabbed hold of our friend and told me to leave, he'd handle it. After he heard the whole story, the next day he said, "Well, Jesus. He's fucking the waitress, too. You didn't know that?"

Of course I didn't know that, but I learned to keep my mouth shut. I was finding myself increasingly in the middle of situations I didn't create or enjoy. For Hunter, as much as he hated fighting with Sandy, it seemed to also keep him engaged and cranked up, and he thought a lot of the stuff about the "other women" was funny.

Meanwhile, I was living with my girlfriend, Denie, and as we moved through a succession of Aspen rental apartments, Hunter began stopping by more often. Usually it was just to find a refuge in town and a quiet spot to smoke a joint, have a few bumps, watch TV, make some phone calls, and talk politics. He always needed a place in town, separate from the Jerome Bar. In fact, he needed several so that he didn't wear out his welcome with the Bentons or Semmes Luckett or me. His biggest necessity was for people who kept something like his own hours, which were almost exclusively nocturnal.

When I complained once about how overly visible I felt driving around the valley in the wee hours, he nodded and smiled. "I always feel a little weird, heading back out to Woody Creek, across McClain Flats as the sun's coming up behind me," he said. "And there's no other traffic going my way. They're all coming the other way, going to work, the Stutsmans and Vagneurs, staring at me like some kind of criminal. I just smile and wave. I think it pisses them off."

The valley was still small enough then that you could plan on knowing most of the people who passed you on any back road. They knew you weren't working any normal job if you were just heading home at 6:00 a.m. And they knew Hunter didn't have a normal job anyway.

When he wasn't stopping by our place Denie and I would join him at a bar or restaurant or drive out to Jimmy Buffett's to watch television relayed by his big new satellite dish that was about the size of a small asteroid and had to be hand-positioned by two people, especially in blizzards.

One night we went to see legendary singer/songwriter Jerry Jeff Walker play near Aspen, hanging out in his motel room and partying with him beforehand. At one point Hunter took out a big knife and began throwing and sticking it in the walls. Occasionally it didn't stick and bounced wildly back into the room. This rattled someone in the entourage who explained that everyone was a little edgy anyway, and he took Hunter aside and told him something. Hunter came back chuckling, and we all went downstairs for the show.

"They just told me that Jerry flew up here on his own Lear jet," said Hunter as we sat down. "He was getting a little restless and when they got close to Aspen he took over at the stick and wanted to land it. He put the fucking thing into such a bad dive that no one thought they were going to make it. One of the pilots managed to pull it out, and after they landed both pilots quit. So he had to go out and hire a new crew. Now no one seems to have much of a sense of humor."

It was still a great show, and I spent most of the night wandering around with Jerry Jeff and Hunter until I finally headed home around three. Just after I got there the phone rang and it was Jerry. "Is Hunter there?"

"No. I thought he was with you."

"Ahh, we got separated. He was acting weird."

"Right."

"Tell him to call me if you hear from him."

"OK. Take care."

About half an hour later the phone rang again. "Yeah, it's me," grumbled Hunter.

"Uh-huh."

"Have you seen Jerry?"

"No. He called here awhile ago looking for you."

"Oh? Well, he's crazy. Don't give him my number."

He's crazy? I thought. "OK."

"Yeah. You're sure he's not there?"

"No, he's not here. We're in bed. Asleep."

"Oh. Right. OK. Don't tell him where I am."

After the next night's show, we heard a rumor that it was really bad and that Jerry Jeff was so drunk he fell off the stage halfway through and couldn't finish.

Aspen was a remarkable place to be then. During most of the seventies, even with a suddenly accelerated growth rate, there were only a couple of thousand people in the whole county. Yet we had unbelievable cultural events and music, and it was all on such a personal scale that we got to meet the players in very casual circumstances. Some of them were starting to buy homes in the valley and perform regularly in town.

Through Hunter, I got invited to events like Jimmy Buffett's wedding in 1978. Held in an early-twentieth-century castle in the nearby town of Redstone, it was one of the biggest social events of many years, with a guest list of hundreds and incredible music. Along with Jimmy's own Coral Reefers band were people such as Glenn Frey, Joe Walsh, and Mike Bloomfield, as well as many of the best musicians in the area. It was the kind of event that seemed to perfectly symbolize the wild heights of those times, a fairy-tale rock-and-roll wedding in a mountain castle with everyone poised between their recent, easy-living, semicommunal past, and a future exploding with possibilities and strangeness, with the potential for great achievements or tragedy, at that tipping point where now, when you look back, you can see that everything was changing. Whatever lay ahead it wasn't going to be like what had come before. And for many people what had come before was, if not an entire golden age, at least a golden generation: fifteen years where lives had been lived as they should be and we had all gotten to spend time with the gods in what turned out to be a largely godless land. As we left Redstone Castle that day, I didn't know we were celebrating the end of something we would never be able to recover.

3

Life on the Farm

In 1976 the lease was up at my latest digs in Aspen, and the little caretaker's cabin at Owl Farm next door to Hunter's house was available because the current tenant was leaving. It would have been a real score under any circumstances. But with Hunter offering to take money off the rent for any work I did, it was way too good to pass up.

So Denie and I moved out to Owl Farm and began living about fifty yards away from Hunter, Sandy, Juan, a big Doberman named Lazlo, a mynah bird named Edward, and a growing flock of peacocks. Sandy was perhaps five foot two, hair the color of her name, with a tinge of unrehabilitated hippie to her. She was trim and busy, laughed a lot, and you could see some residual craziness in her glittery eyes; how else to explain being married to Hunter? Juan was only seven or eight when we moved in, with jet-black hair and features that were a fair cross between Hunter and Sandy, with some random Korean thrown in. Hunter liked to claim his own grandfather was Korean.

My cabin was a small, early-sixties-style shack with a recently added squared-log living room with a vaulted ceiling. Where the old roof met the new room were panes of glass, and there were also skylights in the new roof. We eventually got over the surprise of hearing loud screeching that wasn't Hunter's, followed by thumping that sounded like sheep on our roof, then looking up to see the unearthly features of big peacock faces staring in our rooftop windows. But it freaked the shit out of visitors for as long as I lived there.

The Farm was one hundred and forty fairly flat but ascending acres lodged between two small ridgelike mesas on either side. There were two houses on the Farm, a large collapsed barn, and an old abandoned cistern. A gully ran just outside our back door, carved into the red earth coming down from red-rock cliffs a mile or so up behind the houses. It had obviously been scoured by water at some time and then further dug out with a backhoe.

"This was a dairy farm years ago before Stranahan bought it," Hunter told me when I asked about it. George Stranahan was Hunter's friend who had sold him the property. "Back up above where the irrigation ditch runs across the high end of the property, they had big snow melt one year. Some beavers built a dam, and then they had a cloudburst rain. The dams held the water all pooled up until they broke, and a flash flood came down that blew the farmhouse here and everything else all the way to Woody Creek." That was across the road and down another five hundred yards. "They said they found wheels of cheese floating in the Roaring Fork River for days afterward."

Hunter's house was, and is, unimposing. Its low-slung ranch style wasn't the suburban definition of the term but the genuine article. Sided with peeling brown channel lap, diligently functional and haphazardly modified by him over the years, it was larger than it looked because it had more depth than was readily apparent and a full basement. There was a deck on the front and a glassed-in utility porch on the western end of the house. To the left of that Hunter eventually appended a kind of crude, rough-hewn log garage that looks worse than it may sound. But for twenty years there was no garage at all, so he liked it once there was.

Everyone usually entered through the main front door in a spot amidships of the home on the front deck. Past the screen door was a thick wooden door, often locked, with a metal slot in it like at a speakeasy. The living room was . . . busy, decorated with large, custom-made stereo speakers and a couch and several heavy chairs in the vicinity of a stone fireplace. Hunter's personal chair was a stout wooden thing with wool blankets draped over it like the master's throne in a Canadian hunting lodge. He would settle himself into it every once in a while but rarely stay for long. And when he leaped up he would almost invariably stumble over Lazlo, their huge Doberman pinscher with a heart of gold, who was always taken by surprise, as was everyone, by Hunter's sudden outbursts or lunges.

For a while a snarling boar's head pointed upward from the lazy Susan in the middle of a round table in front of the fireplace. A stuffed cobra that I bought for him in Thailand resided on the mantle. A shark's jaw and other exotica and trinkets, such as a long, sharpened steel lance decked out in feathers, were positioned here and there. Hunter used to like to go in a certain shop in the Denver Airport on his way home from assignments or speeches and buy some primitive piece of weaponry/art that was usually fairly expensive. It was stuff he liked and thought would interest visitors and friends, and he used it as a way to indulge himself with something that he couldn't snort, smoke, drink, or otherwise make go away, and would often be the only evidence he had that he was actually making money. All the rest of it went to paying an unrelenting stream of bills.

To the immediate left of the front door, and also straight ahead, were full floor-to-ceiling bookshelves with a collection of baseball caps hanging from them. In the middle of the shelves on the left was a doorway into the kitchen. The living room was a reasonable size, and the kitchen area was nearly its equal. The kitchen was always the heart of the house, long before people took to describing it as some kind of postmodern "salon."

There was never anything fancy about the kitchen, its accoutrements, or the attitude it usually hosted. The first thing you saw was a wall of pine cabinets straight ahead as you walked in, above the stove and sink and dishwasher. A high counter ran partway down the middle of the kitchen, a continuation of the counter that included the sink and stove and described a square U as it ran along the southern wall then turned to extend about eight feet down the center of the room. After Sandy left, that counter always held Hunter's typewriter, folders, notes, paper, cigarettes, cocktail, and so on. He sat at a stool there when he wasn't up pacing or rummaging through cabinets or arguing with the big TV in the corner. On the other side of the counter was a couch, also facing the tube, and a big, old, seldom-played piano against the wall that adjoined the living room entrance area.

For years a birdcage holding Edward the mynah sat near the refrigerator against the back wall, which held two doorways. The one on the left led to the stairs into the basement, the closed-in utility porch, and a storeroom/office beyond. The right doorway led to a bathroom and the master bedroom in the back of the house, behind the living room.

The most noticeable feature of the infamous kitchen was that it was papered from stem to stern as if there'd been an explosion in a note factory. Several pieces of art clung to the wall adjoining the living room—pieces by Tom Benton and Paul Pascarella and a Ralph Steadman of Bob Dylan bearing a cross—along with changing galleries of photos of wives and girlfriends. But most of the rest of the kitchen—walls, cabinets, stove vent, refrigerator, windows, shades, backsplashes, drawer handles, and more—were all covered with pieces of paper with something scrawled on them. Many were lists, perhaps memorable or just the most current, but Hunter was notorious for his lists.

Often this literal wallpapering consisted of clips from newspapers or magazines, and quotes, either Hunter's own or attributed to a TV show or event or a book or author he liked, done in his inimitable large, melodramatic scrawl, which was a cross between Ralph Steadman's hand and that of a practiced book signer. "There are many rooms in the mansion . . ."; "There Is Some Shit We Will Not Eat"; "When the going gets weird, the weird turn pro"; "The Heart Of Darkness"; "It never got weird enough for me"; "Buy The Ticket And Take The Ride"; "I Am Not Like The Others"; and so on.

Some were changed out regularly, others stayed until they were curled and faded. Sometimes they were written on blank typing paper, sometimes on yellow legal pad sheets, sometimes on hotel stationery from around the world: Key West, Las Vegas, Washington, Hollywood, Zaire, Saigon, London. In sum, it looked not unlike the nearby Woody

Creek Tavern has for years—so thoroughly festooned with stuff that you can't remember what color the walls are, much less find them.

This style of decorating continued down the basement stairwell where there used to be a motley gallery of panels from the Sunday color *Doonesbury* cartoons that featured Duke. Sandy loved them but Hunter didn't. I always liked Garry Trudeau's work and was amazed the first time I commented on them in the house and Hunter just scowled. "He hates them," Sandy said, rolling her eyes.

"Why?" I asked.

"How would you like to be made into a cartoon?" he bristled, "have people pointing at you. 'Oh, there goes Uncle Duke,' with fucking bubbles over your head." He also didn't like the uncanny similarities between the cartoon strip drawings and his home, and even my cabin next door where Zonker lived for a while as the caretaker. It was a year or more after moving to the Farm before Sandy told me Hunter thought someone close to him was feeding Trudeau detailed information about him, and that he worried it might be me. Eventually he decided it was someone at *Rolling Stone* who knew him and Trudeau well.

The largely unfinished basement held the hot water heater, other infrastructure, and lots of junk and boxes. The main attraction of the basement was the War Room, a finished den where Hunter could go to the mattresses, hunker down and write in solitude (back when he still did that occasionally), meet with people in private, and so on. Truly, it was his office rendered as a bunker and then largely ignored. But it was always locked and no one, not Sandy, not me as the caretaker, not Juan, was allowed in there without his express invitation. And it had its own exterior entrance/exit in the form of a set of steps down into the ground where an old coal chute had been.

Carpeted in red with a desk, file cabinets, gun safe, and a big brown couch, it was a guy's room, where Hunter could make deals and stash things that he didn't want his impressionable and very bright young son to see. I met him there fairly often when he'd call next door and ask me to stop over, but not wanting to wake Sandy or Juan, he'd let me in the back way. This was where I first met CBS newsman Ed Bradley, whom I admired a lot and who was afflicted by such a bad nosebleed for the occasion that he had Kleenex sticking out of both nostrils.

Eventually Hunter also tacked a back deck and hot tub onto the house. The immediate grounds down to the jack-leg wood fence along the Lenado road were meagerly watered and sometimes mowed, then used for setting off explosions and shooting at targets and random pieces of found objects and junk sculptures Hunter scattered around. On his deck right by the front door for many years was a large metal sculpture of a bat, the flying rat kind, that I considered one of his most enviable possessions.

A circular gravel driveway led up to our two houses, circumnavigating a couple of big old cottonwoods in the process. The peacocks, when they weren't out pecking around in the yard or landing on my roof like an alien invasion, divided their time between roosting up in those cottonwoods or congregating around their wire-mesh and hay-lined cage at the far eastern end of Hunter's front deck. They served as reliable alarms for any vehicle that pulled into the driveway, screeching like pheasants that have been set on fire. This would bring out Lazlo who would bound up and stare eyeball to eyeball at the driver through the car door. He was so imposing he never had to bare a fang, nor do I think he could have if he tried. But most people who didn't know him, and even some who did, stayed in their cars until someone came out to greet them.

The farm theme continued inside where there was frequently a cat, and as long as Sandy and Juan were there, Edward the mynah bird. Edward loved Juan particularly and would call after him, the way he heard Sandy do. Around Hunter, on the other hand, he always seemed jittery. Probably because Hunter would slap the cage if Edward wouldn't be quiet, or squawk back at him in menacing tones. At some point Hunter made an audiocassette tape of himself and Edward and played it when he got bored or wanted to annoy guests. It was allegedly of him banging on Edward's cage, which was covered with a blanket, with his hands and fists and finally a fire extinguisher. After that he yanked off the blanket and foamed Edward with the extinguisher.

The tape pissed off pretty much everyone he ever played it for and I think most of us assumed it was just another prank, unfunny as it might be, and we'd look at Sandy or Juan for some kind of sign that he hadn't really done this. But either they weren't paying attention to him anymore, or they'd just shrug and stomp off. They didn't think it was funny either.

If the presence of so many critters lent credence to the idea of Hunter's residence being a farm, perhaps so did the occasional element of apparent cruelty toward animals, which is not uncommon in ranches of the West. Hunter's ambivalent treatment of animals was troubling. A lot of it seemed to be for effect, but you could never be sure, and I always wondered why he wanted that particular effect. Granted, it was shocking and outraging to most people, which was the point. But if he wasn't really tormenting innocent animals, then why try to make people think he was? Just to see what he could make people believe, perhaps?

A column he wrote for the *San Francisco Examiner,* later published in his book *Generation of Swine,* about essentially torturing a red fox that he caught trying to eat his peacocks was also carried in one of the local papers and provoked a huge outcry. He immediately maintained it was only an allegory, but the question remained: what purpose was the column supposed to serve? It wasn't a good story, it wasn't funny, and it made you think badly of the writer. Paul Theroux and others have done this and been lauded for it, but as a literary tactic it can never be expected to be greeted warmly. Hunter tried it again in 1991 by publishing a short, legendary story he had circulated among friends for years called *Screw-jack*, attributed to Raoul Duke.

This sick little tale kept some of the violent tone of the red fox episode and added sex with a cat to the mix. "I lifted him up to my face and kissed him deeply on the lips. I forced my tongue between his fangs and rolled it around the ridges on the top of his mouth. I gripped him around his strong young shoulders and pulled him closer to me. His purring was so loud and strong that it made us both tremble."

The influences for such a piece are many, ranging from the ever-pressing need to be original and bold to his ongoing fascination with the life and work of William Burroughs. And good writing, which the story displayed, even in the service of bizarrerie, is still good writing.

I wasn't sure how to reconcile his sometimes strange attitude toward animals with the fact that he unfailingly took such good care of his peacocks. With all the regular turmoil and commotion and gunfire going on around Owl Farm, I couldn't understand why they stayed. And every once in a while, one would finally wander off. But mostly they hung in through thick and thin, and I finally realized that they probably thought of all the screaming, shooting, and general cacophony as just the sounds of more of their screeching flock. When the stereo would be on, *LOUD* with the doors open, Hunter yelling, traffic rumbling by on the road, and the peacocks chiming in at their highest decibels, it was like the literal definition of Bedlam.

While I think Hunter wanted Owl Farm to be a mountain version of the life he loved in Big Sur, where he had lived for a time before he fled to Aspen, his ultimate interpretation of farm life in the Rockies was extremely skewed, equal parts *Animal Farm,* funny farm, "Maggie's Farm," and Walden Pond with guns.

Still, all things considered, Denie and I managed to settle in pretty nicely. In addition to our regular day jobs, we had a list of Farm duties that offset some of our rent. These included picking up essentials in town (red boxes of Dunhills at The Spice Shop, food for Lazlo and Edward at the pet shop, the occasional case or two of booze), the mail from Doris at the old Woody Creek post office, responding to the less-important phone calls and correspondence, and looking after everything when Hunter and the family were gone. I also made sure the aging septic tanks got pumped, dealt with skunk invasions, trimmed the yard area around our place as often as possible with a weed eater, shoveled the snow off the roofs and satellite dish, and made sure the red, three-hundred-gallon gasoline tank was kept filled.

The latter was the kind of thing that could occasion an urgent series of notes from Hunter. One I kept is dated 4/6/79 and consists of a newspaper clipping with a story about the Senate agreeing unanimously "to allow President Carter to ban home gasoline tanks and other forms of fuel hoarding." That paragraph was circled in red, along with a later line in the story that read: "Those who have already installed such tanks could be ordered not to use them." Hunter had scrawled between the two highlighted sentences the word "Jesus!"

The next note was on L'Ermitage hotel stationery from Los Angeles. "Let's call the Co-op & order a full tank of their best gasoline for my red tank—which we should move to some safer location at once. OK. H" By "safer" he meant less visible.

A third note in this series is from Denie telling him, among other things, "Also you have 300 gallons of gas at Owl Farm!" His note across the bottom read: "Cazart!—how do we work a sharing plan? Let me know . . . H."

Life at the Farm was never dull and had distinct elements of Dylan's lyrics to it: "he hands you a nickel, he hands you a dime, he asks you with a grin, if you're having a good time." Certainly Hunter's farm life, after being filtered through his relentlessly gonzo prism, wasn't the sort of pastoral gig most people might imagine. The challenges presented to a quiet country gentleman and man of leisure were endless.

While some agrarian efforts on the land might have seemed appropriate as well—a nice garden, say, or an alfalfa crop—the only things that ever got planted while I was there were . . . more problematic. The previous tenants in our cabin, in fact, had a garden directly behind their house, but it had lain fallow for several years. Once, when we had been gone for a while, we returned to find that the person who had been house-sitting for us had engaged in some horticulture as well. There in the garden area were ten rows, about twenty feet long, of perfect little pot plants sprouting eagerly out of the soil.

Hunter had been out of town also, and by the time he returned some of the plants were over a foot tall and robustly healthy. We were still debating what to do about them when Hunter showed up at our door and asked what the hell was going on. "Are you out of your minds?" he asked, as we stood surveying the plot.

"We didn't do it," I said.

"I don't care who did it, we could all get busted." For all of his love of drugs, Hunter tried hard to never be involved in anything but their consumption. He was fascinated by drug dealing but wanted no part of the potential legal fallout from being involved in the trade. "They're on my property and it could get seized. I could lose it all."

"Oh," I replied. "Well, that's not good. But they're not that visible."

"No, unless the guy filling the propane tanks sees them, or someone working on the phone poles on the road, or someone who wants to hike up behind the houses. You have friends over all the time who'd just have to look out your back window. And I don't trust most of your flaky friends anyway," he grinned.

"Thanks. But you're right about the plants. We'll get rid of them." It hurt to say it, because now that they were there, growing and even thriving, I had visions of not having to buy pot for years. Maybe even making some money.

"Well . . . you know I'd love to keep them, but it'd be crazy. Don't do anything drastic yet, let me think about it," Hunter mumbled, and went back to his place.

The next afternoon I came home to find several people with large video cameras taking pictures of the garden, and I went inside and called Hunter. "Yeah, it's a BBC film crew," he said distractedly. "They're doing this rotten goddamned thing about me for television. That stupid fucker Steadman set this up and I forgot about it."

"You did not!" I could hear Sandy in the background. "I've been reminding you for days!"

"Yeah, yeah. So you say. It's still a horrible idea," he groused.

Though he seemed to court publicity in his every act and deed, Hunter liked to pretend that interviews and photographs were never his idea, but that his agent or wife or publisher was demanding them. He didn't want to appear to scramble after the spotlight or celebrity but to seem to have it foisted on him. And just to reinforce the point, his usual way of dealing with any impending and irrevocable appointment with people who mattered but he didn't know, was to binge for days beforehand and not get any sleep at all. Often he simply refused to get out of bed for them. And if he did he was not a lot of fun. If he wasn't largely incoherent the chances were good he'd be in a really foul mood. Since he was still making sense this time, I figured he was in the pissed-off stage, but it didn't sound that bad.

"You think it's smart to have this on film?" I asked, carefully.

"They said it would just be close-ups and they won't say where it is. Just somewhere around Aspen."

"Well, that's good. Then I'll get rid of everything right after they leave."

There was a pause while he considered this. "Yeah, I suppose that's wise."

One year, Owl Farm did end up producing the only cash crop I was aware of during Hunter's tenure there. I was once again away, as was the Doctor, but I was told that guerilla growing tactics were employed with much greater discretion than before, and the old cistern turned out to be a perfect drying chamber. I came home to find a few plants still hanging from my cabin's rafters. But Hunter and I never got anything from the deal, which, due to our careful vigilance, never reoccurred.

Beyond the agricultural aspects of the Farm were other distractions. Hunter once fought rancorously for a couple of years with a neighbor I'll call Fat Fred to avoid butting heads with his lawyer. Fred was widely hated for moving in and promptly rerouting Woody Creek where it flowed through his property, with no permission or right to do so. In the West, you can mess with a man's woman before you can mess with his water. And that was just the beginning of Fat Fred's rumored transgressions, which also included his alleged mistreatment of some exotic pets as well as his girlfriends and wives.

On the other side was Hunter firing shots in Fred's vicinity—at a porcupine, said Hunter; at Fred's ranch, said Fred. It was all capped by the poisoning of a trout pond at Fred's, which he accused Hunter of but which turned out to be the accidental handiwork of Fred's own son screwing up with pesticides.

When Hunter's downstream neighbor, actor Don Johnson, married Melanie Griffith at their home, hordes of paparazzi swarmed into the area and above it in helicopters. Police were called out when some photographers alleged that their helicopter had been fired on by security people at Johnson's. After further investigation, suspicion settled on Hunter, but no charges were ever filed.

Another neighbor, television producer Tony Yerkovich, who created *Miami Vice* and then bought the property next door to Hunter, once planned to build a home on a major elk corridor through his land until Hunter rallied other Woody Creek residents in protest.

Hunter's across-the-road neighbors, on the other hand, were not stars and were easier to live with. His response was to frequently fire guns in their direction. Not intentionally so much, but because they lived downhill from him, behind occasional targets, and far enough away, he assumed they were safe.

"See that black box up there?" he asked me one afternoon, pointing at a phone pole straight out in front of his house alongside the road.

"Yeah?"

"There were two guys out there all day putting that up. I think it's some kind of fucking eavesdropping device, so I'm using it for target practice. Think you can hit it?" he asked, handing me a .22 caliber Olympic target pistol. The box wasn't more than fifty yards away and I popped it a couple of times and handed the gun back. He never did hit it, and the bullets went arcing off toward his unsuspecting neighbors.

The location of Owl Farm was occasionally a problem. Agents from the Secret Service one day notified Hunter that he wouldn't be able to leave his home for several days without first contacting them. You can imagine how well that went over. He found out that President Bush the elder and Margaret Thatcher were coming to Aspen, and Bush would be staying near Hunter's at the home of the ambassador to the United Kingdom, Henry Catto.

Hunter flipped. After calling half a dozen lawyers and using his old friend and local sheriff Bob Braudis for a reference, he finally got the Secret Service to back off, but he remained "a person of interest" throughout the state visit, which turned out to be where Bush and Thatcher agreed to the first invasion of Iraq known as Desert Storm.

Other days the problems were more prosaic, such as a neighbor's helicopter coming in for a very rough, out-of-control landing and cutting the power lines to the area. I ran out to see what had happened and found the owner/pilot climbing shakily out and thanking god he hadn't crashed. I told him not to be too thankful, because Hunter was right in the middle of the big Oklahoma-Texas annual football game with heavy bets on every down and was now without any electricity. This was quickly followed by Hunter storming out in our direction, yelling and cursing and demanding to know when the electricity was going to be fixed. The neighbor headed off to call the power company, and Hunter stomped back to his car and drove down to the Woody Creek Tavern.

In 1993 the telephone company U.S. West was burying new phone lines along the road in front of Hunter's house when the crew killed some trees, broke an irrigation pipe, and ended up having to dig up the road. So he confronted them in full throat. "They don't have the right to destroy this land," he was quoted as telling a county engineer named Hensley who was summoned to the scene, along with phone company people, a deputy sheriff, and a reporter. According to a newspaper account,

> The county and U.S. West approached the incident cautiously after Thompson's secretary called with a message that included the words "trees," "mad" and "guns." What piqued Thompson's ire as much as the dead trees was that the phone company was upgrading the lines all the way to the near ghost town of Lenado. "Do you mean to say that every time some homeless person moves into a shack, U.S. West thinks it has to provide phone service?" he asked Hensley. The affirmative answer prompted conjectures about evil real estate plots and conspiracies to increase development in the area, and Thompson retreated to his home to "gather some reinforcements" among his neighbors to bolster opposition to the project.

What else could a poor man of the land do? As he wrote for one of his *San Francisco Examiner* columns, later included in the book *Generation of Swine*: "I am a good neighbor on most nights, but not in the calving season. Writing is a hard dollar, but it is a lot better than reaching up inside a maddened cow and grabbing a breeched calf by the legs." The piece ended with:

> It was good to be home—but when I got there the phone was ringing. It was George, my neighbor from the Flying Dog Ranch, about five miles up the hill. He was having trouble delivering his calves, he said, and he needed an extra hand.
>
> My heart filled with hate, but it was clear that I had no choice.

"Should I bring rope?" I asked.

"No," he replied. "We'll use a chain—just slide it over the fetlocks and pull."

It seemed weird, but George knows cattle, and I am after all a farmer. I got in the Jeep and drove up the road.

Not every day, of course, was filled with sitcom material. Hunter and Sandy finally got around to splitting up while we were living next door. It all came to a head one day when I got a call from Sandy saying that she and Juan had moved out while Hunter was gone. She didn't say where she was but insisted on giving me her phone number, while expressly forbidding me to tell Hunter. This is not the kind of situation feuding couples should put friends in, nor one any sane friend should accept.

When Hunter got back he was livid that Sandy had taken Juan, who went willingly, and that she wouldn't tell him where she was and he couldn't contact her. Tom Benton, Semmes Luckett, and a couple of other friends came out to the house right away and attempted to track down Sandy and help Hunter. When Tom found out I knew where Sandy was, he came over immediately. "If you know something you better tell him, because he's really crazy right now," he told me, literally wringing his hands.

"I told Sandy I wouldn't. Do you want to call her and ask her?"

"No, no. Because if you give me her number, I'll give it to Hunter. You should probably deal with him directly on this," he said, and we walked outside to where Hunter and a couple of other people were standing by the big cottonwoods in the driveway. He was sweating and fuming.

"Do you know where she is, and you haven't told me?" he yelled.

"I don't know where she is. I have a phone number for her and she asked me not to give it to you."

"You better decide right now who's side you're on! If you want to still have a place to live after today, goddamnit, you better give it to me!"

He was clenching and unclenching his fists, and Benton and someone else said, in unison, "Just tell him. She'll get over it."

"How would you feel if it was you who had asked me not to tell her something?" I yelled back at him.

"I'm not going to fucking argue with you! You don't have the right to keep something like this to yourself."

I looked at him and looked at Tom and walked over and gave Tom a slip of paper with her number on it. "She didn't say I couldn't give it to you."

They never did reconcile, and it was probably best for both. Later that night, after Hunter had talked to her and worked out something that made him feel better, we went into town to the bar, and I drove us home after closing. Often as quick to forgive as to get mad, he rarely apologized, he just became good old Hunter again and acted like nothing had happened. As he stepped out of the car and thanked me for the ride, I said, "Look, I'm sorry about earlier. You know I'm on your side, a hundred percent, always."

He smiled. "I know. But don't you mean a thousand percent?" and walked off chuckling. "I'm behind him a thousand percent," was what George McGovern had so famously said about supporting his first vice presidential pick in 1972, Thomas Eagleton, only days before dumping him.

Not long after this, Hunter's girlfriend, Laila Nabulsi, moved to the Farm. She worked on the hugely popular television program *Saturday Night Live* and he'd met her in John Belushi's dressing room when his marriage with Sandy was already collapsing. Laila is of Palestinian heritage and she was young, beautiful, smart, and energetic with a great sense of humor—a perfect match for Hunter who seemed happier than he'd been in years. She was much closer to my age than Hunter's and we became friends and she brought new energy and charm to the Farm.

"We had a pretty good family life, it wasn't all just craziness," she remembers now. "I was with him for quite a while, off and on, and we visited his mother whom he hadn't seen in a while, had Christmas with his brother twice, and traveled all over, to Florida, Hawaii, Europe to see Ralph. We were pretty normal in a lot of ways, and did things together that I don't think he really ever did again after that."

In 1979 my parents moved from Aspen to Sun Valley, Idaho, and had only been gone a few months when I got a call that my father was very sick. By that evening, the Sun Valley doctors were saying they didn't know what was wrong, but they didn't expect him to survive the night. Hunter immediately put me in touch with Dr. Robert O. Morgen, his physician and one of the best in the business. Dr. Morgen talked to dad's doctors and recommended that we move him immediately to Salt Lake City via air ambulance, which he arranged. In the end, dad died of cancer within a couple of weeks. But Hunter did everything he humanly could to help me the whole time. Maybe it was because he'd lost his father very young, or maybe it was just because he was in a position to help a friend.

A couple of years later Denie and I were married at the Farm, under some Mongolian tents in the field above the houses, on a bright blue day in September with all the leaves changing on the surrounding hillsides. Before the ceremony, performed by Tom Benton, Hunter had us come to the house, and while Laila helped me pin on a flower, Hunter poured me a wineglass full of vodka, and I drank it without ever feeling it. Later, when we drove out to the Snowmass Club for the reception, Hunter thought we should arrive trailing the traditional clattering of cans. So for the last hundred yards of the drive he had brought out a huge, old, empty hot water heater and attached it to the bumper of my car with a chain.

A few years after that I was back living at the Farm for the second time when my marriage ended. Hunter was a good friend then as well. "You know you can't stay mad at women just because they're trouble sometimes, right?" he asked me earnestly, after about a month had gone by. "Don't stay around the house and sulk. It doesn't help. I know these things."

4

The King of Fun

One night while we were watching a *Nightline* show on military recruiting irregularities, Hunter told me how he had first gotten into drugs. "It was at Eglin Air Force Base where I really went off for good," he chuckled. "At eighteen or nineteen I wandered into a recruiting office half drunk and passed the vocational test with the highest scores they'd seen and went straight to the Flight Training School wait list. I figured out that it would take two and a half years at least to get flying." So he opted for sports editor at Eglin after being sent to various high-tech training schools.

"Understand that at this time this was the hip thing to be doing—enlisting—going to special schools," he stressed, with one of his sly grins. "It wasn't just the New Dumb back then who were joining," and he tilted his head at the TV. "I joined trying to straighten my life out and become a real citizen. And then I got down there and saw how twisted and corrupt everything was. People selling off entire rooms of copper wiring and every scam you could imagine. I was the only honest one around—just a dumb kid—and then I fell in love with the base dentist's daughter and discovered speed. Her father was a colonel and I was writing a column everyone hated and working two jobs. She knew about speed because he had it, and all of a sudden I could do two jobs, and her, and it was great. Nothing was ever quite the same after that."

He felt it was particularly apt that the military had introduced him to drugs. And given his fondness for the Beat Generation, drugs fit in well with the lifestyle he imagined for himself: a writer and adventurer in Kerouac's footsteps, doing dope, drinking, and "tear-assing around the world, looking for the shit," as they say in *Apocalypse Now*. Hunter liked action from early on, and when nothing else was happening, good drugs could fill in. Even when something *was* going on, the drugs were still a nice way to amplify anything, turning it into a challenge, a scene, and possibly a story.

No matter what else he was known for, Hunter S. Thompson was first, last, and always an iconic symbol of drug use in a society that still regards many of his favorite forms of them as felonious. That may have complicated his personal life, but it also helped make him successful. He was fond of saying, "While I wouldn't recommend a life of drugs and alcohol for anyone else, it has worked for me." Of course in the end, that was debatable. The rampant substance abuse was a double-edged sword for Hunter, fueling both his rise and fall.

Even before they completely overran Hunter's life, drugs had become a major pain in the ass for him. You would have thought, for instance, that he'd have been arrested constantly, every time he left home. And to hear him tell it, he was. But if you took him at his word or anything close to it in his writing or knew his habits well, you knew he never really got in trouble for even a tiny fraction of what he could have.

There are many possible reasons why he wasn't busted more often, but one of them had to do with the difficult distinctions between myth and reality, between fiction and nonfiction in Hunter's writing and his life. Even those who enjoyed getting high as much as Hunter did frequently found themselves wondering how much of what he wrote and claimed about his drug use was true and how much was just legend-stoking and a highly creative imagination.

While Hunter weighed in on that issue himself, he did little to ultimately clarify it. He loved the exaggerated and fictional elements of his writing, even when he wasn't writing overt fiction. But when it came to important stories and political pieces, he tried to be very clear about what was obviously invention. Still, there was a strong sense of, "Fuck 'em if they can't take a joke," to what he did in a tradition that many have noted dates from at least Jonathan Swift and Voltaire.

The whole issue of what was real in his writing and what wasn't sometimes created serious trouble for him, as revealed in letters published in his book *Fear and Loathing in America.* The August 1975 issue of *Esquire* ran excerpts of the *Washington Post's* Style-section writer Sally Quinn's new book, containing an unfortunate misquote of Hunter in what was an otherwise friendly piece. The completely unsourced quote was that he had said, "at least 45% of what I write is true." Considering that he was then working as an influential political reporter and receiving much attention and money for it, this was potentially ruinous. As Hunter wrote to his attorney Sandy Berger, "Shit, *nobody* would pay a writer for 55% lies—not even in the Style section of the *Post*."

Hunter pointed out that he had been asked frequently about how much of his *Fear and Loathing in Las Vegas* book was true. "And for reasons that should be perfectly obvious I usually reply with a figure ranging anywhere from 60% to 80%," he wrote to Sally Quinn.

To Sandy Berger he observed, "I've mentioned various percentages. . . . but always in very vague terms and always to confuse the issue of fiction and/or non-fiction in a book so potentially incriminating that I'd never claim it was 100% true."

The matter of adrenochrome in *Fear and Loathing in Las Vegas* is a prime example of the kind of thing that caused even serious drug abusers to raise eyebrows.

> "What is it?"
>
> "Adrenochrome," he said. "You won't need much. Just a little tiny taste. . . . That stuff makes pure mescaline seem like ginger beer. You'll go completely crazy if you take too much."
>
> "Where'd you get this?" I asked. . . . "There's only one source for this stuff. . . . The adrenaline glands from a living human body. . . . It's no good if you get it out of a corpse."

Because I couldn't always trust what Hunter told me, I asked Tom Benton if the drug really existed. Tom didn't know, though like most of us he assumed it didn't. "If it did, he never offered me any," he said, sounding both hurt and relieved.

We all knew it didn't exist and Hunter finally admitted as much. But what he loved was that it had to come from the adrenal gland of a living human being. That was enough to discredit the whole idea, but it also lent it some very bent intrigue. You wanted to believe no one would even countenance, let alone advertise, that kind of thing. But you also wanted to know what it was like and if you could handle it.

This is where writers always have an advantage, as well as a presumptive guilt, regarding anything they say in public, to their closest friends, or even on paper. Because they are, after all, *writers,* and part of what makes them that is the ability to spin a good yarn regardless of how true it is. They're good at lying, and people tend to expect them to exaggerate their stories or invent them altogether. And those people often include editors who do not hesitate, when copy is dry, to tell their writers, "Write, for Christ's sake!"

Hunter had the added justification of saying that he might take liberties with the truth but only for dramatic effect or when it was to keep from being arrested. "Only a fool would claim some of these things are true," he told me more than once, "whether they are or not."

With his report during the 1972 presidential campaign of candidate Edmund Muskie ingesting a bizarre drug called ibogaine, he maintained that he clearly labeled it "as a fantasy (or a 'rumor')," employed to make a point about Muskie's increasingly erratic behavior. The piece, later included in *Fear and Loathing on the Campaign Trail '72,* caused huge repercussions.

> I immediately recognized The Ibogaine Effect—from Muskie's tearful breakdown on the flatbed truck in New Hampshire, the delusions and altered thinking that characterized his campaign in Florida, and finally the condition of "total rage" that gripped him in Wisconsin.

Further on he elaborated on an incident in Florida:

> There he was—far gone in a bad Ibogaine frenzy—suddenly shoved out in a rainstorm to face a sullen crowd and some kind of snarling lunatic going for his legs while he tried to explain why he was "the only democrat who can beat Nixon."

This was the same kind of style that had set *Fear and Loathing in Las Vegas* far apart from almost everything that came before it, and it wasn't just his so-called gonzo approach to first-person participation. What really defined it at that moment in time was its active focus on drug use. It wasn't the barely coded lyrics of *White Rabbit* or *Sgt. Pepper's Lonely Hearts Club Band;* it wasn't poetic howls by Allen Ginsberg or Lawrence Ferlinghetti; it wasn't William Burroughs's jangled, postmodern mysticism; or the blurry photos of *Life* magazine covering Timothy Leary. It was frontline reportage of using these substances and recording the results out in the world at large, often at events designed to make the experience unusual to the point of being totally unique. And it was funny.

The latter was a big deal. *Vegas* wasn't a clinical study, and it wasn't an intellectual treatise à la Aldous Huxley's *The Doors of Perception* and *Heaven and Hell.* It also wasn't the chronicling of broken dreams and shattered lives, the tragic addicts' journals that were the primary record of drug writings prior to Hunter's. This was outrageous, alive, hysterical, and even inviting. Why *not* take acid and go to the Super Bowl or to a DAs convention in Vegas? And why not be proud of it, or at least happy about it? Skulking around like a pervert, doing your drugs in back alleys and dark rooms might have been a legal necessity, but it didn't have to be an attitude. For Hunter there was no shame in what he was doing. He enjoyed it and knew lots of others who did as well, and he chose to write about it in that context.

And he did, warts and all. He never flinched from describing the downside of the experiences. That was part of the formula that everyone in the drug culture understood. Those who didn't pursue an active drug-based lifestyle still appreciated the humor of how things could turn on you instantly even in normal times, not to mention when you're wandering around ripped to the gills in circumstances where that could have real consequences.

But the primary stroke of genius behind the *Vegas* book, beyond his editors' allowing it to be printed at all, lay in Hunter's doing something no one else was doing at the time and doing it exceptionally well. He not only discovered an original niche in the writing industry but managed to create an ongoing market for himself by his virtuosity, craziness, and zealous commitment to his discipline. The drugs, not the writing.

Hunter knew he couldn't afford to come across as inauthentic when chronicling his alleged exploits, unless it was in the service of comedy and deliberate exaggeration. Therefore, it behooved him to keep fully abreast of the trends in the field, as it were—to stay involved and out there as much as possible to avoid committing some terrible gaffe that every freak in the country would call him on every time he stuck his head out the door.

There was no dearth of people willing to assist in his research, whether by providing the materials or the companionship or both. To many of his followers, this had to seem like the ultimate perk of Hunter's lifestyle. No matter where he went, twenty-four hours a day, he would find people who were only too happy to supply him with drugs in exchange for spending some time in his presence. Way too many of them, in fact. The stages where he delivered his speeches were always littered with more joints and pills and packets of powders than anyone in their right, or wrong, mind would have ever considered consuming. Even Hunter.

This syndrome is, in fact, a major danger for many stars. John Belushi, who was a friend of Hunter's, had a bodyguard the last year or more of his life whose job was to get him to work out more and to keep him away from drugs and from the people who wanted to give or sell them to him. It was, of course, an impossible task, and everyone knows the result.

Laila Nabulsi was a very close friend of Belushi and his wife's, and like everyone around Belushi, adored him. So did Hunter, who also talked about how genuinely crazy he was from the first. I once told Hunter that I really liked a bit Belushi had done on a *Saturday Night Live* show when Hunter had been backstage. It was a weather report for paranoid shut-ins, and it ended with such a maniacal and lengthy display of hail storms and other heavy weather that Jane Curtin tried to cut in twice while Belushi thrashed around, throwing sugar cubes into a fan and glasses of water in his face. "I swear to god, Curtin," he glared at her and raised his hand the last time she tried to stop him, and she flinched as though she thought he meant it. Really.

"Yeah," Hunter smiled. "He was running about three minutes over by that point and everyone was hysterical with fear that he just wouldn't quit. He came running back into the dressing room right before the bit and was stuffing rocks of coke in his lower lip, like it was chewing tobacco. He was completely out of his mind."

"No." I squinted at him. "You couldn't do that. Your gums would start bleeding, you couldn't swallow or talk. Your whole damn mouth would be numb."

Hunter just arched his eyebrows and shrugged. "You'll have to tell him that," he said, talking around his cigarette holder. "It seemed to work. You liked the bit."

I never got the chance to ask Belushi about it, even though he was in Aspen and at Owl Farm not long before he died. Things got so wild at Hunter's that Belushi fled and had to be picked up on the road nearby by strangers in the wee hours of the morning. Hunter asked me the next morning if I'd seen John. "He's a monster," he mumbled over the phone. "He left here like some kind of rabid animal and—*WHAT?*"

I could hear Laila in the background, saying "Don't yell at me! You drove him off, and you call *him* crazy!"

"Yeah, well he is, but who cares? Not me. I didn't tell him to leave. He just ran out of here like he'd snapped."

Hunter and John could do that—dart out of a house in an unfamiliar place on a back road and count on the kindness of strangers who would know who they were, pick them up, and understand that they had some kind of situation on their hands. The rest of us would just get arrested or run over.

This is a nice perk, up to a point. Hunter liked (indeed *required*) companionship, and if it was with people who wanted to turn him on, so much the better. But he was far from being indiscriminate, because that kind of thing can backfire in a hurry. Not only are drugs always a weirdness magnet, but you're dealing with strangers at potentially their worst. They're high on who knows what and you have no way of knowing how they handle it. You can't even tell that about some of your best friends. "One of the things you learn, after years of dealing with drug people, is that everything is serious," Hunter wrote in *Vegas*. "You can turn your back on a person, but never turn your back on a drug—especially when it's waving a razor-sharp hunting knife in your eyes."

What's more, Hunter didn't just want to avoid the real losers, he craved *good* company, engaging and stimulating, stylish and presentable enough to at least not attract too much attention or turn hinky if things got truly weird.

Believe it or not, for many years Hunter was one of the stablest people you could do drugs with. That may seem a bad commentary on the choice of other people available. But in spite of the *Doonesbury* image and his own somewhat manufactured persona, Hunter prided himself on not being an obvious stoner, whether he was on acid, smoking pot, speeding his brains out, tooted to the max, or working on his fifteenth tall whiskey and ice. Or, frequently, all of the above.

He talked about disliking people who couldn't handle themselves, period, but especially out in public. No one likes to have to explain why their friends are nodding out and drooling all the time, or beady-eyed and jumpy, or red-eyed and giggly, or slack-jawed and slurry. For more than a few people, including Hunter, a big part of getting high had to do with how you handle it. That was his challenge, to test his limits and ability to function, "to keep your head when all about you are losing theirs," though that may not be quite what Kipling had in mind.

In a time when everyone was doing drugs, or at least everyone *we* knew, it was no different than if they had all been racing motorcycles or trying to pass their bar exams. Lots of people wanted to be the best at what they did, even if what they did was just being crazy. It's an evolutionary instinct, that drive to be the bravest, the boldest, the ones everyone recognizes for their prowess, because they're better or stronger or more willing to take it to the limit.

Hunter not only had that instinct in almost everything he did, but he liked to be acknowledged for it. We were both at a mutual friend's one day in the late 1970s when the friend cracked open a moving box full of top-of-the-line Colombian blow. The box was one of those tall brown cardboard ones normally used for big lamps, but lined with plastic, and the coke was just heaped in there, not bagged up or anything. We were in an upstairs room looking out over the lower living room where Hunter was sitting with his back to us. I reached into the box and grabbed a rock the size of a softball, probably six ounces of pure flake and fragile as glass and handed it to my friend and said, "Toss this to Hunter." He shouted at Hunter and lobbed the rock down to him.

Hunter turned around, recognized what it was immediately, and caught it in one hand just a foot or two above the floor. "You crazy fuck!" he bellowed. "What if I'd missed?"

"You didn't," said my friend.

"That's shag carpeting!" he said, looking at the floor in horror. If he'd bobbled it, the rock would have shattered into dust and been mostly absorbed by the carpet, no matter how long anyone snorted and chewed on it.

"We have faith in you."

He smiled up at me knowingly. "Yeah. Either that, or you've been doing too much of this," he said, eyeing the rock and moving over to a nearby coffee table with it.

Hunter told this story to people for years because he loved everything about it: the trust implicit in throwing him something like that to begin with, that he caught it, and that it was a rock that huge, at least ten thousand dollars' worth of some of the best coke in the world, something most humans would never see.

Like lots of us, Hunter just lumped all of this under the label of a good time and took onto himself the role of the King of Fun. He never talked a lot about why getting high was so much fun. But there is at least one sound theory behind why so many adventurous and talented people like drugs as a challenge to begin with, and why that "fun" gene tends to propagate.

I got an issue of *Natural History* magazine in the mail one day in the summer of 1990 with a big peacock on the cover. Since I'd spent years living around Hunter's peacocks at very close quarters, I was curious to read about them, but I had trouble finding the story. That's because it was titled, "Kung Fu Kerosene Drinking." Normally that alone would have immediately attracted my attention, but I was looking for the peacocks and this title didn't seem to fit. Yet there they were, explained by a small headline under the title that read: "Our eager consumption of toxic chemicals may stem in part from an animal instinct gone awry."

I came to think of this groundbreaking paper by Jared Diamond as the peacock theory of drug abuse. And since Hunter kept a flock of peacocks and was also one of the most interesting drug abusers I knew, I always associated him with this theory.

What it amounted to was a more broadly applied notion by an Israeli biologist named Amotz Zahavi stating that females of a species might be attracted to apparently deleterious male traits, precisely because they constitute handicaps. Both Diamond and Zahavi were fascinated by why a bird of paradise or a peacock, with clear impediments such as an enormous tail, would use these handicaps as advertisements for themselves in their mating displays. According to Diamond's article, Zahavi proposed that these flaunted flaws, "constituted valid indicators that the rest of the animal's genes must be good precisely because those traits themselves impose handicaps. Any male that has managed to survive despite such a handicap must have terrific genes in other respects."

Diamond then wrote, "I think Zahavi's theory can be extended to human abuse of chemicals and to displays for gaining other benefits besides sexual ones."

Obviously, many aspects of taking drugs could be seen as simply creating challenges for yourself. Enough acid or toot can vastly complicate even simple acts such as speaking, so getting anything done at all feels like an accomplishment and can also provide huge entertainment for an inordinate length of time. The theory also offered an explanation for the massive consumption Hunter favored and the seemingly unwritten rule for half the people I knew, including Hunter, that anything worth using was worth abusing, no matter how bad it made you feel or act.

That's where the kung fu kerosene drinking came in for Diamond, as a symbol of many kinds of substance abuse. Certain Indonesian kung fu adherents of Diamond's acquaintance drank kerosene as a regular trial of their strength. "Only a really robust person could get through that test," he noted. The same might be said of daily killing a bottle or two of whiskey and snorting coke until your sinuses bleed. Lesser men would admit defeat and slink away.

I've known a number of heroic bingers and hard-core, long-term users of everything. But I don't think any drank and snorted coke in any greater quantity or more consistently, for longer, than Hunter. This is one of those rock-and roll kind of records there would be heavy competition for, it would be impossible to judge, and the prize is an early death. I was routinely stunned by Hunter, who would start drinking shortly after rising, usually in midafternoon, then begin snorting coke and smoking both cigarettes and dope shortly after that. He never seemed to have much trouble eating, which I took to be a southern thing, since you couldn't force-feed most binging cokeheads with a muzzle loader.

For years off and on Hunter would happily ensconce himself at the Woody Creek Tavern bar, drinking, snacking, surreptitiously tooting, reading newspapers, glancing up at the TV in the corner and talking to the bartender and anyone else at the bar with him. Eventually he would roll home, do some work, watch some sports, shoot at something, curse all the bill collectors and underpaying editors, write a hundred notes and faxes, stomp around the house in a fit about something, then get strongly into the dope and booze and finally lurch off to bed around sunrise. By that point, the quantity he had imbibed of everything all told would be very hard to guess. Those actually trying to keep track or pace—an astonished girlfriend or journalist, say—were usually so far off their game less than halfway through a typical Hunter day that there was no hope of ever conducting a really accurate audit, though many tried.

In sum amounts for the alcohol, I know by the late 1970s he was downing one to two quarts of hard liquor a day, plus beer. In his prime, you could watch him keep pouring it down and barely miss a beat. I just figured he was a serious mutant. "I drink and smoke like a fish swims," he liked to say. "I don't even notice it."

His day started with Coronas or Heinekens when he'd first get up around 3:00 p.m. until he had some food and settled his stomach, then it was on to the big tumblers of Chivas or Wild Turkey, with more beer chasers. If he was at the Woody Creek Tavern, there could be frequent rounds of Biffs (Bailey's Irish Cream in a shot glass with an Irish whiskey floater) or shots of Chartreuse for anyone within range. Wherever he was, the flow of booze continued apace throughout his waking hours.

Hunter started drinking young and probably for the reason many of his peers in Kentucky did, because it was the accepted custom for real men in that part of the country. That, and wanting to imitate the writers he admired, was good enough for Hunter. In the end, as was the case with all his idols, the liquor was Hunter's worst vice.

A maintenance bump or two every fifteen or twenty minutes out of the black Deering coke grinder he always kept handy amounted to at least two grams a day (and much more when he was really binging), at anywhere from seventy to a hundred dollars a gram. That won't sound like much to some hard-core users, but Hunter never did huge gag lines. His were, surprisingly, more modest, but there were lots of them throughout his day. And he rarely saw a day without coke for thirty years unless he was asleep. His total lifetime cocaine tab had to have approached two million dollars. *Just for the blow alone*. And that's part of the point, really. Coke has long been a way of getting powerfully high while also strutting your success and money.

For Hunter, a conservative estimate of his coke consumption would be in the hundred-grand-a-year range, which would mean closer to three million dollars total. Of course, he probably didn't actually spend that much, since people frequently comped him. Hunter could be generous in return, but that gets expensive and didn't happen often. He could also be difficult about paying his drug bills. With new sources, he sometimes considered a gram here and there to be a bonus for getting to hang around with him. For sources he valued he tried to stay caught up or they'd shut him off. But he always had enough options to leave himself some wiggle room.

Because of the long hours he frequently kept, it's hard to even guess at how many cigarettes he smoked a day. His notorious Venturi Tar-Gard cigarette holders were supposed to get rid of the worst toxins, but he frequently spread the tar in the holder from previous smokes on the next cigarette. "I can quit any time I want to," he used to tell me, not even flinching at the cliché. "My mother did it when she turned seventy. Just stopped and hasn't smoked again since. And she's in good shape. No worse for the wear. Christ, she's seventy. So I know I can do the same thing." It never happened, of course, maybe because he never reached seventy. I'm sure three packs a day of Dunhills or 555s (or even Marlboros in a pinch) would have been a fair average for him, throwing in those times when he slept for twenty-four hours.

He once told the columnist Bob Greene, "Smoking has been good for me. I have been smoking five packs of cigarettes a day for twenty-five years, and I'm in perfect health." This possibly inflated estimate of his own consumption and physical well-being was occasioned by a letter he'd written Greene when Greene had endorsed a spray for nonsmokers to use on smokers.

"The idea of the can," wrote Greene, "is to squirt it at people who are smoking cigarettes in public places—elevators, buses, etc.—where they are not supposed to be smoking. When the button on top of the can is pushed, a wet, harmless, lemon-scented spray comes out, extinguishing the cigarette and splashing the face of the smoker."

When Hunter first read the piece he went ballistic. "That Nazi water-head! If anyone ever sprays me with anything they'll fucking regret it."

To Greene he wrote, "Bob—I noticed your column in the Rocky Mountain News regarding Paul Wright and his anti-smoking spray cans . . . and I thought you should know that us degenerates have sprays, too," in reference to his plan to respond to any dousing with his own Mace or pepper spray. "The first time Wright spends 40 minutes retching with pain and fear on the floor of some ill-chosen elevator, he might have second thoughts about his Carrie Nation trip."

Greene ultimately called Hunter. "I asked him why he was endorsing such a filthy habit," he later wrote.

"What filthy habit?" Dr. Thompson said. "Is smoking cigarettes any more filthy a habit than sweating? Now sweating is a filthy habit. Do you sweat? Then you're imposing your filthy habit on me."

When Greene noted that the antismoking spray was very harmless compared to Hunter's Mace, Hunter replied, "That's the whole point of it. There would be no point in carrying around a spray can unless it was dangerous. My can is very dangerous. If it wasn't, it would be useless."

Eventually Hunter explained that he preferred to smoke English Dunhills because American cigarettes are "full of scum and perfume."

Greene then noted that Hunter said the scum and perfume didn't make them unhealthy, just bad tasting.

No showdown ever developed between Greene's publicly endorsed lemon-mist spray and Hunter's Mace. But Hunter had established in print the levels of his own nicotine consumption and the reasons why his preferred cigarettes weren't American, along with his willingness to use tobacco the same way he used drugs and words, in as confrontational and provocative a manner as possible. And he viewed it as his duty to stand up for his and every smoker's rights—another long and weird battle that he would lose.

Many of Hunter's days had add-ons and specials to this standard daily menu of nicotine, alcohol, cocaine, and herb. Some hallucinogens were always nice, a little acid or mescaline, some mushrooms or peyote. Any upper was welcome from a line of crank to moldy old white crosses, along with whatever else he found in various stashes or was brought by visitors, including big bowls of red Lebanese hash, capsules that could be PCP or MDA or DMT, and any kind of Peace pill, Truck, Milltown, or Tossed Salad he could find.

It wasn't quite this brutal in the early days, but by the late 1970s he was into a severe daily rut of this level of intake. Almost as amazing as the drugs and alcohol was the food. He liked to stay supplied with continuous rounds of it—huge breakfasts, snacks, meals, side dishes, deserts, fruits, whatever—throughout his waking hours. It was easy if he was at the Tavern, but even at home he managed, as long as someone was willing to help or there were groceries on hand he could work with, barbecue being his preferred format. Along with all the alcohol and other liquids came tall, endless glasses of cranberry juice. "Good for cleansing the system," he'd insist. Also acidic enough to scour ships, even when not being used as a side for hundred-proof whiskey.

It was like watching some whole new extreme form of the species, casually but voraciously inhaling fuel and stimulants on a level, and in combinations, heretofore unimagined. Yet you got used to it fairly quickly. There are just people out there who defy all the norms and vibrate along like some sort of wild, half-sprung generators, thriving on what would kill mere mortals. Hunter was one of them.

He described the physical evidence of his own room at one point in *Fear and Loathing in Las Vegas*. What may well have been hyperbole at the time soon became very real.

> No, these were not the hoofprints of your normal godfearing junkie. It was far too savage, too aggressive. There was evidence, in this room, of excessive consumption of almost every type of drug known to civilized man since 1544 A.D. It could only be explained as a montage, a sort of exaggerated medical exhibit, put together very carefully to show what might happen if twenty-two serious drug felons—each with a different addiction—were penned up together in the same room for five days and nights, without relief.

By 1988 I had been through a lot with Hunter on the drug front. I'd seen him be brilliant and funny and charming while on every conceivable combination of drugs. I'd partied just as hard, had fun with him, and admired his control and poise. But I'd also seen him be the opposite of all that, so often that it was no longer fun or even tolerable most of the time.

He never seemed to have many problems with psychedelics. "Feed your head," he wrote in a letter to *Rolling Stone* publisher Jann Wenner once, stealing from Jefferson Airplane, then adding "& starve a habit; that's what I always say." I never saw or heard of him pulling an actual freak-out. Any time I did hallucinogens with him it was entertaining, a form of what he called "verbal ping-pong" combined with betting on television shows and letting the music work its magic. We didn't get outside that much, which was my preferred locale, except to drive around a bit, either maneuvering from one person's house to another or going up the road at Woody Creek just to see what the night and countryside held: the glowing buds on serviceberry bushes that seemed to float unattached in the air, sudden white wings of swooping owls in the headlights, the wails of coyotes, and stars so close we had to shield our eyes from their light. There was always lots of laughter and inarticulable wisdom that nevertheless seemed shared.

Acid has an energy component all its own, as do psilocybin and mescaline, and it's always important to try to direct it toward something fun instead of overly deep or heavy. Having several people around was always good with Hunter. We tripped by ourselves more than once, but were usually glad when someone else made an appearance. As with many drugs, Hunter could get easily distracted by sex, or the possibility of it. But my experiences with him were never the lunacy of *Vegas* or other writings. He was usually less antic than normal, more reflective, less verbal, and clearly enjoying himself instead of raving. All of this, of course, depended on the environment to a large degree, and whether he was using other substances in combination.

We once went out to Jimmy Buffett's to watch some event on satellite television, and Hunter and I didn't come on to the acid we'd taken until we'd been there for a little while. When it was time to leave, several hours later, we had ridiculous trouble getting out of Buffett's driveway, and alternated between debilitating laughter and genuine mortification when someone had to come out from the house to help us. Twice. After that I tried to drive us back to the Farm the regular way but missed an important turn, and we ended up deep on a dirt road into the mountains before either of us sensed something was amiss. Smoking a couple of joints and drinking dry whatever resources Hunter had did nothing to help, but it kept us amused. Running out of liquor did add an element of urgency to Hunter's situation, at which point I redoubled my efforts to focus, lost money betting on where alternative roads would take us, and finally got us back out onto the highway after logging about fifty extra miles when we were less than ten miles from home to begin with.

Hunter's relationship with marijuana was on again, off again for years. He pretty much ridiculed it before going to Saigon in 1975 on assignment and encountering what he liked to claim was the first pot strong enough to make a believer out of him. We'd had killer Thai weed in Aspen for years, as well as other strong exotics from around the world and just over the hill. But, typically, Hunter had to go to Vietnam to be persuaded there was powerful herb in the world. From then on, he smoked pot regularly, depending on what he needed to do and what other drugs he was taking. But it certainly didn't even make the top-ten list of the substances he had abuse issues with.

Even though downers and opiates might have suited him better than the speed and coke he loved, Hunter never displayed much fondness for them until the later years of his life when he took them regularly and heavily for serious pain. Any time he had to spend in hospitals was a horror show, first because he was a prima donna, and second because there were rarely enough painkillers in the pharmacy to keep him quiet.

I went to the Aspen Valley Hospital to see him several times, once after he kneecapped himself while playing paddle tennis. It was, admittedly, a nasty injury, self-inflicted when the follow-through from his big serve took the heavy wooden racquet straight into his own knee with the force of someone trying to chop apple wood. But the yelling and moaning and scene that ensued would have convinced you he'd had his leg ripped off at the hip and was dying.

In the hospital he was inconsolable, howling and pressing the nurse's call button every few seconds, ranting into the intercom for more painkillers, sending people to find the doctors, and hollering out into the hall. "If I can't get some *GODDAMNED MEDICATION* in here soon, I'll start destroying things and sending out for my own drugs!"

"I can't stand pain. Not even to be around it," Hunter told anyone who would listen. He even admitted as much in print occasionally but then covered himself by saying, "I hate pain, despite my ability to tolerate it beyond all known parameters." It was a level of tolerance unwitnessed by any of his friends, in front of whom he never hesitated to go all to pieces when hurting. Our longtime mutual friend Monty Chitty said for years, "They never made diapers big enough for Hunter Thompson."

The day Hunter died I talked to Tom Benton about it, and we speculated on how much pain he was in, trying to recover from various ailments and surgeries, and whether that might have led to the suicide. "But was he really hurting that much?" I asked, because I thought he seemed like he was getting better.

"You know him," sighed Tom. "He couldn't stand pain, even a little. He'd get a splinter and start hollering for the morphine."

When Hunter had been in the hospital for the knee injury, his personal physician, Dr. Morgen, was frank with us. "We can't give him enough narcotics to kill the pain because he has such a high resistance."

"Why?" I asked. "He doesn't do opiates." He didn't then.

"No. It's not because of the other drugs he does. It's the drinking." Morgen knew both Hunter and me well by then.

In April 1978 Dr. Morgen wrote a letter that Hunter gave me a copy of and loved to carry around and quote from. It began by saying: "Dear Hunter: I was certainly pleased that you did proceed with selected laboratory studies on April 4, 1978, and am delighted with the results which, for all practical purposes, were completely normal." The words "completely normal" were underlined by Hunter.

"Even my doctor is astounded. I should have been dead by twenty-seven," he'd gloat, sounding an old refrain, "but here I am in my forties, a medical miracle." Of course, his quoting from the letter was selective. This third paragraph didn't get much play in Hunter's version of the story:

> As pleased as I am with the normal laboratory studies, it alters my opinion little, if any, regarding your general health and the presence of chronic liver disease. I feel the former is suboptimal [an understatement] and the latter a virtual certainty. You may recall that I informed you, and have done so in the past, that such tests of liver function may remain within normal limits until the very advanced stages of chronic, slowly progressive liver disease.

For Hunter's paddle tennis injury, Morgen told us, "We can't give him the amounts of painkillers he's demanding."

"Why the fuck not?" shouted Hunter. "I'll sign a waiver. I'll take full responsibility. And I'll also hire a whole new medical team and change hospitals if you can't get me some fucking relief and do it soon!" he threatened with the kind of heat that caused his face to purple and his words to come out in literal spits while he flailed around in random acts of rage. This usually produced results, and they'd eventually pump him full of painkillers just to shut him up.

Otherwise, the only time he really liked any form of downer was after coming off a long, high-speed day or series of days when he needed sleep and couldn't get it any other way than by gobbling a handful of Valium or Thorazine.

In 1982 Hunter agreed to try rehab in order to save his relationship with Laila, who was by her own admission obsessed with thinking that he was going to die of an overdose as John Belushi had. After a lot of dickering in which Hunter insisted he would only go if there was a facility located on the ocean somewhere, they found one in Florida where an old friend met him at the airport, took him to the clinic, and paid for everything. He didn't stay, of course, and Laila has spent a lot of time in the last quarter-century wishing she had gone with him and thinking that maybe if she had it would have helped.

I don't think it would have. Eventually, along with Deborah and Tom Benton, I was asked to participate in a couple of interventions with Hunter during the latter half of the eighties. This was not something anyone took lightly, and I never even thought about attempting it with anyone else after that.

For starters, it wasn't as if any of us were the kind of sterling examples of abstinence who could easily get away with that kind of gig. It was our opinion at the time, arrived at from a keen sense of necessity, that our firsthand-users perspective should have lent us some credibility. But none of us wanted to formally intervene. We doubted it would work, and we were right. Though both efforts were well-motivated attempts to get him to take care of himself, they were nevertheless disastrous.

Hunter had a hair-trigger temper and didn't suffer most people gladly, let alone fools, or those he thought traitorous. You can imagine how well he took to being told he needed to get a grip on his drugs and drinking from friends who usually stood shoulder to shoulder with him while consuming, and most of whom he hitherto trusted.

"What gives any of you the goddamned right to come in my house and tell me what to do?" he stormed around in his kitchen at our first session. "You think I can't handle my drugs? According to who?" And he looked straight at his girlfriend at the time, Maria Khan. "You think you have any idea what my life is like? I've seen all of you more fucked up than I ever hope to be and never told any of you I thought you had a problem!"

There may be no human more scathing than a bright, articulate alcoholic in a bad mood, especially when cornered. We tried to tell him that he was letting a lot of things get by him and missing opportunities and deadlines because he was so wasted all the time. This particularly applied to his college speaking engagements, where he usually insisted on being fucked up, late, and occasionally belligerent. Sometimes he was so tardy and incoherent that audiences turned hostile, mutinying and demanding their money back. We were all worried about how he was going to pay the bills if he couldn't even keep it together to do the speeches any more.

But he didn't care. "I can do those speeches in my sleep and no one would know the difference. And I make more deadlines than any writer in the business! Do you have to write fifty filthy columns a year?" he asked, glaring at me. "Don't tell me my business. I don't tell you yours, and you can be goddamned happy for that! Why does this have anything to do with you?"

"I asked him to be here," said Maria.

"I love you. You're a good friend," I said, and it sounded so lame I just stopped. Then I said something completely off the point and selfish. "I'd kill for just one of the opportunities I see you pass on every day. I'd give up an arm for your life." I think I had in mind a free rafting trip to Africa he'd just turned down from someone because he couldn't get off his ass and out the door.

He turned on me and yelled, "And have you ever considered that maybe I'd give an arm for your life?"

No, I hadn't, I told him at equal volume. "I think that's bullshit. You sit around here in a stupor and can't write anything, and then say you hate fish-wrap journalism. But you can make more money with one story than I can make in a year. Why would you want my life? You're the best at what you do and it matters. Or it should."

"I've been doing this for twenty fucking years and you can take my word for it, it doesn't matter. I don't give a shit what you think my life is like, or what any of you think. You don't know. You have no fucking idea. And this isn't love, it's some kind of stunt. You should be careful. None of you know what kind of mistake you're making here." He glared and pointed at us with his cigarette, pacing like a caged tiger, sweating, swearing, and spilling his drink. But there was no way to argue with him and no real reason to want to after awhile. Everyone knows that if you don't desire change yourself, no one else can force it on you. Especially not if you're someone like Hunter.

He staked out his territory on this matter as early as 1974 when he lashed out in a letter to the editor of the *Village Voice* about a writer, Brock Brower, who described his own "Walking Nervous Breakdown," and implied that other writers such as Hunter were on the same bad trip. The letter was later published in *Fear and Loathing in America.* "How would Brower feel if I flipped his coin in print and included his name among those writers who had inadvertently joined me on the long slide to terminal brain damage from drugs?" asked Hunter. "Which may or may not be true—and I frankly don't give a fuck either way—but if the day ever comes when I decide to publicize my own failure & blame it on drugs, I hope I'll have the grace to ride that rail alone, like I started."

After awhile, his natural energy was overwhelmed by the chemical surrogates and increasingly devoted to finding and doing more drugs, or obsessing over the latest way he was being screwed or any distraction or detail that would divert him from having to do the writing he was assigned.

Not that he stopped writing, regardless. He wrote compulsively, every day, but most often in the form of long faxes, letters, and notes. This seemed to give him far more satisfaction than books and magazine stories and was much easier to do while relentlessly fucked up. It didn't pay very well, initially, unless he managed to scare up a good sucker bet or an old debt someone owed him. But he did eventually employ his correspondence to produce several books, the last of which is not upon us yet.

Though he had shrewdly and hilariously focused on drugs to create a literary classic with *Fear and Loathing in Las Vegas,* Hunter also had the sense to not go to the well too often with the genre. He continued to use drugs as a leitmotif, a backdrop, for most of his best work. His assessment of Edmund Muskie's coming out of a bad primary loss in Florida in the 1972 campaign was one of the most widely quoted of the year: "He talked like a farmer with terminal cancer trying to borrow money on next year's crops." But the description of "Big Ed" as an ibogaine freak was even more devastating and funny. It was also guaranteed to be unique.

Not all of his drug references and parables were funny or outrageous or used for background. There were very serious and sober moments when Hunter put them to work as stirring and original reference points and metaphors for times that could understand them all too well.

"The big market, these days, is in Downers," he wrote about the early seventies in *Vegas*. "Reds and smack—Seconal and heroin—and a hellbroth of bad domestic grass sprayed with everything from arsenic to horse tranquilizers. What sells, today, is Whatever Fucks You Up—whatever short-circuits your brain and grounds it out for the longest possible time. . . . Uppers are no longer stylish. . . . "Consciousness Expansion" went out with LBJ. . . . and it is worth noting, historically, that downers came in with Nixon."

It was only when he started his "Hey Rube" column for the ESPN Web site in the early 2000s that he seemed to finally jettison most of the druggy baggage and revert to his beloved sports writing, leavened with the occasional political barrage and lots of betting and odds making. He was focusing on producing some relatively easy new material while also continuing to exploit his old stuff for collections. Much of his earliest writing consisted of travel-based stories for the *National Observer* and for small outlets in the eastern United States and Puerto Rico in the early 1960s. In addition to being pre-gonzo these also had virtually no references to drugs, though he always mentioned drinking. Obviously this was because drugs were a less-prevalent force in his life and in the popular culture of the time as well.

By the new century Hunter wasn't visibly throttling back his own drug consumption except when health issues forced it, but he certainly understood that under the Bush regimes, publicly leaning on his drug use could be even more dangerous. It was an artistic, political, and lifestyle dilemma that in the context of a creeping New World Order would bother him during the rest of his career. Everyone was veering radically to the right, while everything he had fought for seemed doomed, relegated to a quaint, hippiefied past that was not only naive but, according to the new arbiters of taste and morals, horribly wrong and so out of tune with the prevailing ethos of greed and power as to be thought completely irrelevant.

Hunter couldn't surrender to that "rising tide of scum." On the other hand, there was ample evidence that his drinking and drugging and preoccupation with tortured weirdness wasn't producing consistently great writing. "Hey Rube" would often lurch back into the old, trackless meanders that echoed his personal confusion and confirmed an inability to complete anything longer than a thousand words. His heart and mind clearly weren't always in it.

As Hunter's physical problems mounted, so did the pressure on him to address his substance abuse. His bad back and hips and deteriorating insides began dictating how many drugs and how much drinking he could tolerate. During his lengthy back surgery process he reportedly lapsed into violent alcohol withdrawal seizures that had to be alleviated to not risk his life. During some of these periods and his growing dependence on painkillers, more lucidity cropped up in his writing. Sometimes he was almost straight, and sometimes the drugs were less conducive to Ritalin-style pyrotechnics.

Even under continuous assault from himself, his steel-trap mind was still quicker and sharper than most peoples'. He had always been noticeably different, not like the others. In the *Las Vegas* book he said, "I felt very obvious. Amphetamine psychosis? Paranoid dementia?—What is it? My Argentine luggage? This crippled, loping walk that once made me a reject from the Naval ROTC?"

That walk was because one leg was longer than the other. But now all the legitimate physical singularities just seemed like further indications to the rest of the world of how disabled he was from drugs and booze. The image that he'd once worn proudly had become a haunting, a portrait of Dorian Gray in reverse, a creation that he was becoming. The thoughtful pauses he had always employed because he was really listening and thinking now seemed to require quick intervention by interviewers, afraid Hunter hadn't heard or couldn't speak. Limps and lurches born of legitimate injuries and surgeries made him look dissipated, old, and feeble, as an eightysomething instead of a sixtysomething.

He was fully aware he was being mocked by people who neither knew nor respected him, and condescended to by some who did. In his increasingly rare public appearances he was liable to be treated like a sick old man, a doddering drunk who could go all Peter O'Toole at any minute, losing the thread of what he was saying, trailing off into his trademark low mumble, leaving everyone wondering what to do next. It wasn't so much that it actually happened, as that everyone feared it might, and he could recognize that fear in others and their attendant coddling or dismissal.

The only time there seemed to be any fun left in his role as the King of Fun was when he was so far gone, at the end of a multiday bender, that all the angst and frenzy had departed along with most of his cognitive abilities. It was never hard to tell when that point had been reached. A permanent loopy smile would stitch itself across his face; his tongue would stick slightly out between his lips and teeth, Michael Jordan style; his eyes glowed but failed to really focus; and he would stumble without trying to disguise it and not even bother to bellow at whatever had tripped him up.

There was a point where he became a kid again, or a prekid, the one before he cared who people thought he was, before the liability of a big-time mind had made itself apparent. It was then that he seemed to achieve the refuge he was always seeking, arriving at a place where he no longer had to think or act, where he muffled that troublesome intellect and didn't feel compelled to explain himself or anything else anymore to anyone.

5

The Craft

Many critics maintain that Hunter's best work was compressed into a six-year period from 1967 to 1973, during which he produced three books that many would have been happy to call a career (and that some feel he did): *Hell's Angels, Fear and Loathing in Las Vegas,* and *Fear and Loathing on the Campaign Trail '72*. Bill McKeen, chair of the journalism department at the University of Florida, who teaches Thompson in his classes and is one of Hunter's biographers, agrees. "The first three books are classics of a kind, and Vegas was the epitome. There was good writing after that, but I don't think anything as good as those."

The actual amount of writing time spent on the trio, in total, would be hard to calculate, but it could be rendered into weeks, and not a lot of them. That's because of Hunter's technique of saving much of his writing for the deadline and then binging on words and drugs until it was done. He originally devised the method in a wild panic to finish the last half of *Hell's Angels* when he locked himself in a motel room in Oakland for four days and ate speed and jammed.

He soon applied the same approach to magazine work and life in general. And it was the fact of the magazine deadlines that made possible the edgy urgency that ran through his work then and the ultimate existence of the material at all. Consistently filing the stories for *Rolling Stone* that would later become the *Vegas* and *Campaign* books not only kept Hunter's bills paid, more or less, but gave him the copy he needed for the books.

Where those magazine stories and the "lashing together" of the books took a lot of time wasn't in the writing, but on the research end, as well as with the actual carving out of finished text. The latter developed into an excruciating and protracted process for Hunter and everyone around him. And the live-the-part style of reporting, for all its glamour, was also exhausting and time consuming. Hunter spent a full year of constant travel on the 1972 campaign trail, broken up only by periods of hunkering down in Washington, D.C., a place full of people he found generally contemptible but just warped enough to keep him interested.

By 1973 Hunter had been on the road for most of the past ten years and he was getting tired of it. He liked holing up at the Farm and maybe escaping to somewhere warm for a while during the long winters. But he still needed work to cover his bills. In spite of their critical acclaim and ultimate impact on American literature, the three books he'd written by then were not bringing in major money.

Hunter blamed some of this on bad marketing skills and sloppy management by his publishers, and some of it on the fact that his work wasn't exactly designed for mass appeal and no one was making movies out of it. Yet. So he was compelled to keep taking assignments and indulging in "fish-wrap journalism" that included most magazine work and definitely *Rolling Stone,* which he regarded as little more than a glorified newspaper. Nevertheless, from the beginning, Hunter's feature writing held to a consistently high standard that made it vivid reading, usually about compelling and important subjects. If they seemed to lack significance, he would find or create it.

Two important aspects of Hunter's craft were with him from the very beginning. The first is that his writing was consistently smart. He had paid close attention to the writers he admired and how they did what they did. Much of that was self-taught, which is far more difficult than it might seem. Most people know what they like when they read it. But they rarely know why the writer is able to deliver it. Hunter used to brag about having copied whole chapters of Fitzgerald and Hemingway in longhand to try to get a feel for their rhythm.

Hunter also chose smart topics more often than not, something else that's harder to do than it may sound. But most of all, he was always very, very smart himself. Truly smarter than anyone else I've ever been around, and usually hands down the smartest guy in the room. When his brother Davison spoke at Hunter's first memorial service, he said: "Even at eight or nine, Hunter was already off-the-charts bright." I think that summed it up, right to the end.

He was also funny. Funny to talk to, funny to be around, and a very funny writer, another difficult accomplishment. He knew a lot about humor and thought about it carefully and was able to put it on paper. It had to come as a big surprise to anyone paying attention after his *Hell's Angels* book. *Fear and Loathing in Las Vegas,* announcing the arrival of a major new voice in American humor, wasn't the follow-up most reasonable people were expecting.

Hunter's wit and brains helped create a naturally aggressive and original voice, ensuring that the writing always "leaped off the page," as one of his personal editors, Greg Ditrinco (now the editor of *SKI* magazine), describes it. "You couldn't *not* read it," says Greg, "it was just so strong." There were no tricks or gimmicks to it. He simply used words others didn't, as if they'd been invented especially for him, with an honesty and vigor that made most other writing seem worn out and kiss ass.

His hand with often brutal descriptions was so powerful it worried even him sometimes. A 1973 letter to Jerome Grossman, a political activist in the Eugene McCarthy and George McGovern camps, was later published in *Fear and Loathing in America* and confessed something few other people would ever hear. "One of my continuing fears is that a combination of rampant ego and fun with the language might result in the flaying of innocent people. . . . but I try to be careful, and a backwards glance at the evidence leaves me feeling pretty clean."

The fact that all three of Hunter's first books had grown out of magazine assignments meant that every magazine assignment was a potential book. Whether it would become the entire book, or just a portion of it, was his frequent dilemma. In continuing to pursue his Death of the American Dream angle, he was confronted with an abundance of material. To complicate matters further, he wasn't sure how much more journalism he wanted to do if he could be writing fiction or screenplays instead, for a lot more money.

Still, when a story struck his fancy and he thought the expense money adequate, he was hungry enough for action and attention, and pleased enough with his position in being able to go after both at will, then he would do it. He'd already traveled a lot (South America, the Caribbean, all over America) by the time I met him. Now his interests had honed in on big sporting events and anything that promised fun and a frolic in the high life.

It was as if, after the Hell's Angels experience, being on site for the riots during the 1968 Democratic convention in Chicago, and losing a race for sheriff in Pitkin County in 1970, he'd had enough of being bludgeoned and beaten. After that his choices were more likely to reveal the rot and corruption behind the great American facade from the inside instead of from the trenches. He went to the America's Cup yacht races in 1970 and got banned from the premises for trying to paint "Fuck The Pope" on one of the boats. The campaign trail consumed all of'72. In '73 he went to write about the Super Bowl, but never made it to the game. He still wrote a good story. There was shark hunting in the Yucatan in '74, which anchored another book, and the Ali–Foreman fight in Zaire in '75, where he never made it to the bout. This much-speculated-on incident has been blown up into a fateful mistake that marked the beginning of the end of Hunter's "real" writing career, and that's silly. His intention, many people forget, was to watch the fight with the president of Zaire, and when that fell through, he didn't feel like there was any original angle to be had by sitting ringside with several hundred other journalists.

After Zaire, assignments continued much as they had. He arrived in Saigon on the eve of the American withdrawal in '75 and wrote about it for *Rolling Stone,* then dropped in on the '76 campaign trail with Jimmy Carter, wrote about that, and dropped out again. Most of his stories were true road shows, and not all of them made it into print. Such is the way of journalism. When they did, which was usually, the writing was sharp and entertaining, sometimes even inspired and lasting.

He also discovered that he could be great without ever leaving the Farm, something that pleased him not only because he was tired of constant travel but because his expenses for it often outstripped what the magazines would cover. Running for sheriff was a prime example of something he could do at home and provided stories that facilitated his future role as one of the country's most astute political writers.

One of Hunter's best pieces written from home memorialized his recently vanished longtime associate and brother in arms, Oscar Acosta, in "The Banshee Screams for Buffalo Meat" in *Rolling Stone* in 1977. By the time this major piece came out, Hunter had been languishing long enough to attract the scrutiny of some columnists and critics who were wondering when his next book would materialize and what had become of one of America's shining talents. Some of his magazine stories were well received, others were being called increasingly self-indulgent, with no payoffs. It had been four years since his last book and Hunter had begun making regular college speeches that paid decently but were too often disasters, where he once again spent more than he made.

When I read "The Banshee" one morning at home on Owl Farm I went out and bought a bottle of Dom Perignon and took it next door. Sandy was in the kitchen and smiled at me. "He doesn't really like champagne, but I think he'll appreciate that, and I'll help him with it. Why don't you just take it on back to him."

It was early afternoon and Hunter was awake but still in bed. I waved the copy of *Rolling Stone* at him and said, "Welcome back."

"Yeah?" he asked.

"I think this is the best thing you've written in a while."

"Oh? Well, thanks. Yeah. I liked it but you never know."

"You don't have to drink this," I said, handing him the champagne. "But Sandy might like it."

"No, no. Come on, let's have some," he grinned, popping the cork, taking a swig from the bottle and passing it back. He rarely failed to show his appreciation of someone appreciating him, which is an admirable trait.

I still think that single piece was one of the best things Hunter ever wrote. It brought together so many themes he loved and revealed a particularly fine hand with a eulogy—tender, troubling, funny, and honest where it needed to be. Maybe that's why he always thought himself so well suited to write the obit for the American Dream.

The story resonated profoundly for me and made me laugh. I don't know that it did that for everyone, but Hunter got good feedback on it. While it didn't immediately lend itself to anchoring the next book, it did generate movie interest, which was what he'd been seeking, and it excited him. Jack Nicholson had recently helped Jim Harrison sell his *Legends of the Fall* novellas to filmmakers for something like $1.5 million, and that got Hunter's attention.

By that time, in the late 1970s, Hunter had developed a keen interest in the Florida Keys, where he had friends and contacts and could be close to the kind of action he loved: the ocean, the boating, the fishing and sporting life that had so beguiled Hemingway; the drug smugglers and dope dealers of south Florida who were already legends and persons of interest for Hunter on multiple levels; and the ongoing Cuban boatlift that was overripe with possibilities.

Spending time in Florida got Hunter out of Aspen in the winter, put him close to a lot of good material and drugs, and meshed well with several different story ideas he was pursuing. Since his days in the Caribbean he had liked locating stories in the area. His early novel, *The Rum Diary,* still nagged at him as unfinished business with a great premise. From that, in one form or another, he derived the inspiration for *Cigarette Key* and *The Silk Road,* both of them prospective novels that could turn on a dime (or a hundred grand) into treatments or screenplays. For the sake of authenticity, he'd insist with a crooked smile, immersing himself in the local culture was a must.

It was also as good a place as any to write a treatment and prospective screenplay for what became *Where the Buffalo Roam,* the movie starring Bill Murray and Peter Boyle, based very loosely on "The Banshee Screams for Buffalo Meat" story. Oscar Acosta was a Latino lawyer and activist also known as the Brown Buffalo.

Hunter talked quite a bit about how much he was and wasn't making on his various projects, and even gave me a copy of the contract for this one to show me how treatments and screenplays were being written and paid for. Because he was receiving, in installments, a hundred thousand dollars for the movie rights and a screenplay, he felt unusually flush and as though he was finally approaching the level of material success he deserved. Some accused him of selling out cheap. But Hunter viewed it as easy money with a nearly limitless expense account that would allow him to comport himself as a man of means among his friends and peers: the artists, movie people, and big-time drug dealers who lived like wild gods.

Increasingly, Hunter was growing more bound up in the rituals and mannerisms of his writing process than in the actual production of sustained trains of thought on paper. The movie did nothing but accelerate this trend toward composing in brief, but always lively, bursts. What he was doing for the film consisted mostly of comments, ideas, short scenes, quotes, and riffs of dialogue, along with compulsive revisions. It seemed made to order for him. I began to suspect that he liked the Hollywood form of writing as much for its short-attention-span pacing as he did for its prospective riches.

He was also starting lots of projects, in the manner of movie moguls, but not finishing many and none willingly. We began several, one of them when I started talking to him about Baby Doc Duvalier in Haiti, where I spent some time, and his business trafficking in the blood and body parts of his citizens. Blood was becoming a much-in-demand commodity for the rich who stored it in case they needed transfusions. I speculated about what might happen if some disease were to attack our blood supplies. We decided it might lead to a kind of industrial vampirism, with professional ghouls hired to vacuum the blood from unwilling donors. He said, "We'll call it *The Day the Blood Ran Out,*" and he waved the treatment in front of people for several years to no avail. This was just the way Hollywood seemed to work, he concluded, and it kept everyone busy, if only in turnaround.

Hunter, meanwhile, grew as tired of the movie deadlines as he did of the journalism ones. Part of this was simple economics that any drug dealer or longtime editor could understand. In the dope world it's called "fronting" and is always a mistake, because no one wants to pay for product they've already consumed. In Hunter's case, and that of many writers, there is an inclination to spend the advance—from the publisher, the movie company, whomever—and then not want to have to deliver the goods. Especially if you feel you've been had for cheap, as every writer always does, particularly the good ones.

Another part of what was becoming a legendary difficulty to work with on Hunter's part was the knowledge that too much of what he was doing lacked any real story line or natural attraction for him. It was his standard complaint, and it was hard to tell if he just didn't like the stories he was considering, or if he couldn't see an effective way of involving himself as sufficiently in them as he wanted and needed.

The Hunter style, even before it was fully gonzo, was rigorously first person. Beyond that, it quickly became participatory, in the manner of George Plimpton and Tom Wolfe, only more so. It was the continuation of the New Journalism notion that "the only way to write honestly about the scene is to be part of it." The writer as a combatant was not entirely new, but the writer as the main focal point of the story was, except in the cases of celebrity autobiographies. Hunter had maintained a narrative throughout *Hell's Angels, Vegas,* and the *Campaign Trail* book, even when it wasn't easy, and there had always been a larger purpose, a broader story. But now his writing was growing so self-centered it was becoming a trap. It was a great style, much beloved by other writers, because it seemed easy and followed the central dictum of writing what you know. But being so self-involved was actually difficult and sometimes a detriment to the story, if there even was a story.

Nevertheless, the gonzo genre, however unintentional, turned out to be a stroke of genius. "Of course, it became the Gonzo breakthrough piece, but at the time I thought I was finished as a writer," Hunter wrote in 1990 in *Songs of the Doomed* about the story "The Kentucky Derby Is Decadent and Depraved."

> At first I was typing, then I was just ripping the pages out of my notebook, because I'd worn myself down to the point where I couldn't think, much less write. The magazine was holding the presses. . . . I thought it was a disaster. But then just days after it came out, I began to get calls and letters from all over the country saying what a fantastic

breakthrough format in journalism. I thought, Jesus Christ . . . I guess I shouldn't say anything. In a way it was an almost accidental breakthrough—a whole new style of journalism which now passes for whatever Gonzo is . . . accident and desperation.

Only a few artists of any kind have ever developed their own genre so successfully with such a stranglehold of originality and talent that they were the only ones thought competent to pull it off and everyone else was just a pretender. William Burroughs often said that no one else should even try to write like Hunter because it can't be done.

If for Marshall McLuhan the medium *was* the message, and if for many artists their process is integral to, and sometimes indistinguishable from, their art, then so was Hunter's gonzo methodology, such as it was. It was also self-limiting and wide open for self-caricaturization. If Hemingway had seemed only to be imitating himself at the end, what was Hunter doing every time he wandered into some drug-addled digression that ate up two pages of a major feature? He was fast becoming a prisoner of his own game, enjoined by myth, laziness, self-absorption, show business, and addiction. He had pursued the rock star dream and was suffering the rock star syndrome.

He was not only strung out on coke and alcohol, but he was in love with the lifestyle, the characters, the literary position he had created for himself, and the possibilities that seemed so inherent and accessible in employing drugs for his art. At first he didn't really self-medicate to improve his writing as too many writers have, whatever their prescription of choice. He used drugs to improve, or seriously alter, the moment, to have fun and stay interested. Dropping a little acid or gobbling some speed was always guaranteed to change any situation.

Coke and booze were different. Though he had once denounced coke with regularity, it eventually became his chief obsession. And whereas amphetamines had once provided him with the kind of stimulation that he could channel and use constructively up to a point, coke never really did that. It always promised greatness, and in the right dosages, combinations, and circumstances it could be used productively for a very limited and tenuous time. But mostly it was far more of a distraction than an aid.

At a certain point, not fully discernible at the time, Hunter seemed to begin to believe that the great writing, the inspiration, and the very words themselves may have their origins somewhere in the drugs and the bottle rather than in him. Or at least he suspected that some of his genius derived from a perfect balance between himself and the drugs and could be as elusive as a great golf swing. That way lies madness, of course, and I think he taunted himself with the terrible prospect that his best powers weren't entirely within his own control. He may not have fully believed it, but the mere possibility was enough to do damage and to provide him with a career-level excuse to keep drinking and drugging.

In a *National Observer* piece about Hemingway in 1964, published in *The Great Shark Hunt,* Hunter foreshadowed his own eventual doubts. Charley Mason, a pianist Hunter met in Ketchum, Idaho, related having asked Ernest once what it took to break into the literary life. Hemingway told him, "There's only one thing I live by—that's having the power of conviction and knowing what to leave out."

Hunter noted that Hemingway had said as much before, "but whether he still believed it in the winter of his years is another matter. There is good evidence that he was not always sure what to leave out, and very little evidence to show that his power of conviction survived the war." Hunter, like all young lions, sensed a weakness at the core of his heroes and contemporaries.

> Fitzgerald fell apart when the world no longer danced to his music; Faulkner's conviction faltered when he had to confront Twentieth Century Negroes instead of the black symbols in his books; and when Dos Passos tried to change his convictions he lost all his power. Today we have Mailer, Jones, and Styron, three potentially great writers bogged down in what seems to be a crisis of convictions brought on, like Hemingway's, by the mean nature of a world that will not stand still long enough for them to see it clear as a whole.

This was what people like to call "wisdom beyond his years," and was especially telling because Hunter in 1964 wasn't yet consigning himself a place among these giants and wasn't being as consciously autobiographical as he would become. It was a simple assessment of the life he was trying to lead, long before it became as overcomplicated as Hemingway's and Fitzgerald's had by worlds not of their making or choice. This was especially difficult for people who, for a while, seemed so perfectly bred for their moments in time. If Papa and F. Scott had been the ideal chroniclers, via fiction, of the prewar years, Hunter was equally well cast for the 1960s, 1970s, and 1980s.

But of course the chaos of progress, or at least advancing time, has never been static. By the late 1970s, Hunter was already sensing that his time, the time of drugs and music and revolution, had passed. In one of his most celebrated quotes from *Vegas,* he wrote as movingly about the actual, almost literal, cresting of that wave as anyone has ever written about the end of anything, with all the wistful pain and premonition that is at the heart of great tragedy and downfall:

> And that, I think, was the handle—that sense of inevitable victory over the forces of Old and Evil. Not in any mean or military sense; we didn't need that. Our energy would simply prevail. There was no point in fighting—on our side or theirs. We had all the momentum; we were riding the crest of a high and beautiful wave. . . . So now, less than five years later, you can go up on a steep hill in Las Vegas and look west, and with the right kind of eyes you can almost see the high-water mark—that place where the wave finally broke and rolled back.

In the end, drugs and the drug culture were such a fundamental part of Hunter's existence that it was almost impossible for him to forsake them, just as it was for Hemingway to have to confront a life in which he could no longer womanize and drink. Hunter spoke for, as well as to, the drug culture, and it wasn't an obligation he wanted to shirk.

Regardless of his own health, and any question about how well the drug themes continued to play, Hunter was reluctant to depart too much from what had been so successful for him and had seemed to stand for something: a time and an aggressive position within that time that meant "there's some shit we just won't eat." Hunter didn't want to abandon the good fight and principled stances at a time when the whole world seemed willing to do that on a whim.

What happened to Hunter and his writing at the hands of coke and booze isn't at all dissimilar from what happened to his idols. "I'm not sure I'm qualified to comment firsthand about the deterioration of Hunter's writing," says editor Greg Ditrinco. "But maybe with some of these guys, it's a little the same. When you're a good writer young, it might be hard for your writing to mature, and you keep going back to what worked to begin with." A lot of what afflicted Hemingway and Fitzgerald, as well as Hunter, was trying to keep up with a young man's game after they weren't still young. "Taking that many drugs is a young man's sport," noted Greg. So is fishing for giant marlin, partying like a Kennedy, or hanging out in war zones. And no one stays young forever. But for some, much of life can become a battle to do just that.

If, as Hunter felt, Hemingway had written his own epitaph in the story "Big Two-Hearted River," and Fitzgerald had done the same with *The Great Gatsby,* then Hunter's extended suicide note began in *Las Vegas* and ended in *The Kingdom of Fear*. But it was probably best summarized in "The Banshee Screams for Buffalo Meat." Maybe that's why he felt no need to write the real thing when he shot himself.

Many elements were in play for Hunter in the late 1970s and early 1980s. He had Laila, he had Owl Farm, and he had a career that was taking him where he wanted to go. But he could never make enough money to keep up with expenses, let alone get ahead, and there was an increasing air of desperation about his enterprises. He was hard on his friends and family, and most of us only put up with it because we knew he was equally hard on himself.

Or at least that's what I told myself. All of his friends dealt with the issue at some point, especially those he called on for help with his writing. I'd watched him politely filch good material and quotes from people he knew for a long time and sometimes felt that our mutual friend Tom Benton supplied some of his best inspiration. Tom, being older than Hunter and far wiser than me, never attached much importance to the assistance he provided. He never pointed out, as the rest of us might, that a great line in something had actually been his. And he rarely made the mistake of answering a desperate deadline summons when Hunter needed to file a story and was out of ideas.

That was left to Hunter's longtime aide-de-camp, Deborah Fuller; whoever his latest paramour was; whatever friends might find themselves in his lair at the time; and me, situated conveniently next door. Though he liked to flatter people by soliciting their input, he was very picky about whom he'd really listen to, and that made those he chose feel special.

Which was good since the process was often torturous and thankless, except for seeing a line of yours in print. Frequently, no matter how well intentioned or good an edit was or a suggestion for some wording or even an idea for a whole chapter, section, or column, it was like wrestling an alligator to get him to listen. He thrashed and churned, lashing out with his formidably toothy critiques and judgments, protecting his voice and whatever there was of his story line, guzzling Wild Turkey and tooting up every few minutes, and yet still lapsing almost comatose for such extended periods that you didn't know if he was thinking or passed out upright with his eyes open. But there was always an editor on the other end of the line, pulling out his or her hair and trying to decide how to fill the big void in their publication in the next twelve minutes if the final and irrevocable deadline wasn't met.

It wasn't that Hunter defied editing, failed to understand the need for it, or felt his writing was untouchable. He intuitively understood the demands of editors, to a point, and worked with them long and regularly for the desired effect. Eventually he even came to rely on them too much to pull together competing themes and topics, to bundle and package his buckshot notes and rootless scrawls, to give form and intimations of substance to wild rants and disparate yearnings. But he rarely became so tired and bent that he would easily let go of the power of a particular word or sacrifice his hold over what he wanted to be sure everyone knew was his inimitable style and presence.

6

The Process

I hate writing. It's pure hell and I wish I didn't have to do it.

—Hunter S. Thompson, Boston University, 1978

I'd rather mine coal than go home and write that article. But I have a choice of that or a job. And after doing it for twenty years, I'm probably unemployable.

—Hunter S. Thompson, University of California-Davis, 1979

When asked to give honest advice to another writer, Hunter could be brutal. That alone identified him as a natural editor. He didn't mind providing a blurb or even a foreword for work he liked. But he never really wanted to critique or edit anyone else's material, let alone that of a friend, because he knew that nothing good could come of it. He tried to tell that to almost anyone who ever asked him to read something of theirs. He could have lied, but I think he believed that honesty was his thing, a big part of what he did, and that to do less would make people wonder when they could trust him. I know he believed that his friends, especially, deserved the truth. But being blunt and, worst of all, right about someone's bad writing is hard on anyone, and it may have done permanent damage to his relationship with several people, including Oscar Acosta.

I only learned that later, after he'd already had some exposure to my writing in the local newspapers. Politely declining to use the piece he had asked me to write for the *Aspen Wallposter* in 1970 may have been one of the last polite things he wrote to anyone in that position. After that, he felt the nicest way he could deal with something he didn't think worthy was to pretend it never existed, unless he was pushed by someone he couldn't ignore.

Such as me. In 1982 I wrote a story about the ugly collapse of Big Oil's billion-dollar oil shale enterprises in western Colorado, not far from Aspen. I was still trying to get something published at *Rolling Stone,* and the oil shale debacle seemed like a great story, but my piece was rejected and I couldn't figure out why. After listening to me bitching about as long as he cared to, Hunter told me to give the story to him and not get my feelings hurt later.

It came back with a piece of Hotel King Kamehameha stationery attached with nine notes written on it, corresponding to pages in the text where he'd made other comments. What he had to say wasn't that bad, but for years after he would hand me copies of other things he'd been given by friends. He wanted me to see that no one was spared. His first suggestion on my oil shale story said, "needs one <u>human</u> example." He had hoped that for a locally based story like this, I might have gotten some interviews with some of the thousands of abruptly displaced employees, along with a few quotes from the brass that didn't come off the same AP wire everyone else used. This was such an obvious point that I'm sure it pained him to have to say it. But I wasn't very successful just walking up to pissed-off oil workers and asking them how they felt. And I knew I also needed to talk to the people calling the shots, whose names or positions would give the story some clout. But they didn't need to talk to me, and wouldn't. If as a reporter I couldn't come up with a way to get access to the people who mattered in a story, Hunter intimated, then I probably needed to write about something else.

He didn't give up on me, though, and in his almost paternal efforts to shepherd my writing he'd sometimes give me the edit notes for pieces, especially ones I'd helped with. Though some may think that big-time writers hardly get edited, Hunter was *always* edited, relentlessly and exhaustively, for reasons of space and potential litigation, as well as taste and coherency. In 1983 he passed along the original notes and edits of his feature for *Rolling Stone* on the Roxanne Pulitzer divorce trial in Palm Beach, called "A Dog Took My Place."

This was a story I'd provided proofreading for, suggestions, and out-loud laughter that he always took as a good sign. It was also one he never found himself fully satisfied with, and that he'd asked me for my thoughts on while he was writing. It sounded tailor made for him at the time, combining wealth, sex, perversion, and the law into another seamy American tale.

> Big names in the mud, multiple sodomies, raw treachery, bad craziness—the Pulitzer gig had everything. It was clearly a story that a man in the right mood could have fun with. And I was in that mood. I needed a carnival in my life. So I decided to go to Palm Beach: whoop it up with the rich for a while, drink gin, drive convertibles, snort cocaine and frolic with beautiful lesbians. Nevermind the story. It would take care of itself. It was ripe in every direction.

"The Nature and Fate of the Rich" was just one of his subheads that sought to put things in a properly significant perspective. But he never really got comfortable with the essential frivolousness of the case. So he spent even more time than normal researching, writing, and rewriting to compensate, to try to find the meat and the relevancy, to make the story shine. Ultimately, though, his conclusion in print summed up all his feelings about what was widely described as his "coming out of semiretirement" to cover the trial. "The judge had made up his mind early on, and the rest was all show business, a blizzard of strange publicity that amused half the English-speaking world for a few months and in the end meant nothing at all."

In addition to his illuminating progressive edits on the piece, in the form of two heavily scrawled upon galleys, what also sticks out is the quantity of margin notes he attached to the finished and published product, detailing the ways in which it had not come out as he wished. This after-the-fact tinkering would have seemed pointlessly obsessive if it wasn't for the fact that the story, like all of his, would later end up in an anthology where he could make the changes he wanted.

For Hunter, the editorial process was usually only half about the actual writing; the word choices, length, flow, and so on. The other half of the battle was always legal, with major skirmishes over what a given magazine's or publisher's lawyers would allow him to say. The Pulitzer story began and ended that way. He wanted the lead quote to come from Roxanne who was a fan of his and spoke openly with him about the case.

"I can't afford to lose," he quoted her as telling him. "They'll run me out of town and I'll wind up on some street corner over there in West Palm." On one of his early edit pages that line is annotated with, "lawyer cut no proof." Written on the opening page of the final published version he gave me was: "all opening quotes deleted by R. S. lawyer." Several section heads are also marked with a slash or an X and the words "lawyers change."

Even his big, synopsis-style headline under the title that he often used to precede his stories, and for which he was famous, wasn't rendered to his liking. This one started: *Notes from the Behavioral Sink and Other Queer Tales from Palm Beach . . .* He crossed out "from" before Palm Beach and wrote "of." The published version continued: *and Wild Lies and Relentless Perjury . . . a Fishead Judge Meets a Naked Cinderella . . .* He struck the first "and" and the subsequent two "a's", substituting "The" both times, to read "The" Fishead Judge and "The" Naked Cinderella. The headline concluded: *Dark, Dark Days on the Gold Coast, Long Nights for Animals.* He crossed out the second "Dark" and added four running periods at the end.

Hunter was obviously choosy about his words, just as surgeons or mechanics are particular about their tools, and they were gathered into his work in a layering process. He put the basics on paper in his unique voice from the start, then added the details in subsequent drafts, coming up with new titles, quotes for arresting headers, deletions and additions where necessary, and so on. The two versions of his galley edits he gave me of the Pulitzer story reveal more about his approach. They are on oversized paper sent from *Rolling Stone,* with a single formatted column down the middle of each. This allowed Hunter to cut and paste (literally, back then), changing the order of the sections multiple times.

For his first forays into a story, Hunter took what he called "practice runs" at it, banging out several thousand words at a go just to get in the right frame of mind and into the flow—to "limber up." Often whole chunks of those riffs remained as the core of the structure, while he figured out how best to organize the final edifice.

Getting the headers right was always very important to him, and he toiled on this one. He still didn't have a title he liked by the time he filed the story. On the first page of the first galley he wrote, "Pulitzer vs. Pulitzer: Nightmare in Palm Beach," then crossed it out and scribbled in what would be the ultimate title, "A Dog Took My Place," a line he had used in an earlier work. This became the object of a pitched battle when the lawyers immediately quashed it for fear of lawsuits from the Pulitzers over intimations of bestiality. "Intimations?" he fumed to me. "That's all anyone down there talks about, is fucking their pets!" Eventually he created a fictional scenario for the title's derivation that pleased everyone, but he didn't forget or forgive the lawyers for their numerous transgressions.

He also has a note on the same page about "Veblen Leisure Class quote?" crossed out, some minor word changes, and various experiments in subheaders: "Let The Trials Begin" crossed out, and "Let The Season Begin," also crossed out. Further along he splices in another descriptive dash, adding "lines of palm trees" to a sentence. Then, at twenty-five paragraphs into the story he makes another addition.

"The very name 'Palm Beach,' long synonymous with old wealth and aristocratic style," and here he had crossed out "had come to be thought of as a place" and substituted "was coming to be associated with berserk sleaziness, a place where price tags mean nothing and the rich are always in heat." The paragraph is already very strong, and "berserk sleaziness" just adds the final flourish.

The story was another dead-on dissection of the American privileged class in one of its smarmiest and most outrageous settings. The prose pushed the envelope for the time on writing about bizarre sex and the "savage rituals" of the superwealthy. It's genuinely brilliant, with some of the funniest things he'd written in years, even though at first blush it wasn't the kind of story you'd normally find Hunter doing, as he wrote at the outset:

> Divorce court is not a prestige beat in the newspaper business. It is a cut above writing obituaries or covering the Rotary Club, but it is basically a squalid assignment. . . . The trials are tedious, the testimony is ugly, and the people you meet on the job tend to have incurable problems.

Hunter's biggest accomplishment with the piece is that right from the beginning he's able to frame the story as a deep brooding on the nature of the rich, accomplished by relating all of the demented craziness so fluidly that it's impossible to put down. He owns the story from the start. In abbreviated form, or random quotes, it rings as true as anything he ever wrote.

In totality, however, it took on the most noticeably troubling tics of his work by that time. The first two sections are rife with several different ways of saying the same thing. Taken cumulatively it has real impact, but you also begin to notice the parts that seem as if he couldn't decide which metaphor or anecdote or stray musing was the best, so he threw them all in. Admittedly, making a cut would be hard to do when they're all so good. It was typical of Hunter, for whom a lot of anything was never enough. Like many writers, he often decided he'd include everything and let an editor decide what should go. Sometimes they had the same trouble he did and included it all. So he wasn't without codependents in his occasionally bloated creations.

Different sections of the story are switched about regularly in the various drafts, and he cuts as often as he adds, if only to demonstrate that he wasn't entirely oblivious to the constraints of space. Whole sections that caused apoplexy in the legal staff, but that Hunter insisted in his margin notes were vital, are rendered in italics in the published version so they can be construed as conjecture or hearsay or even fable.

William F. Buckley Jr. had been the first to point out that Hunter appeared to be afraid of, or uninterested in, writing about sex, so Hunter was endeavoring to include more in his stories. For the Pulitzer trial he could write at length about it with a good excuse. And it seemed to usher in a new era, wherein he romped in the porn industry with the Mitchell brothers, who produced adult films and owned the infamous O'Farell Theater in San Francisco, and ruminated on feminist porn in *Playboy*. Sex, in the gonzo world, had to be as twisted as everything else.

The Pulitzer case was not, in the end, Hunter's Pulitzer Prize winner, but it was one of his last truly great magazine features and definingly transitional. After eighteen days of immersing himself in the atmosphere of the trial (while rarely actually going into the courtroom), then writing about it and editing it for weeks, he was once again seriously disillusioned with the continued viability of journalism as his medium.

It was hard to know when he was just looking for excuses not to write and when he really felt like he had to be careful not to keep imitating himself. As he had for more than ten years, he groused that he was a sideshow himself at the trial, which greatly complicated his life. I wasn't the only one who thought he protested too loudly.

As most of his reviewers and biographers, including William McKeen, have noted over the years, what had once seemed so original in Hunter's writing was becoming repetitious and, against long odds, clichéd. He was reusing his best bits and growing increasingly self-referencing. When the columns were cherry-picked and made into the inevitable book, having so many of them side-by-side heightens the visibility of the repetitions. Certain words, such as *weird, atavistic, twisted, hideous,* and so on, got trotted out to excess in the columns that make up the bulk of *Generation of Swine* and *Hey Rube*. Key phrases were employed so often they should have carried trademark labels: "how long, oh Lord, how long," "it never got weird enough for me," "How much weirdness can you take, brother, before your love will crack?" "Buy the ticket and take the ride," "when the going gets tough, the weird turn pro," "a dog took my place," "the hog is in the tunnel," "the fat is in the fire," and many more. There was a kind of Vonnegutian air but without the intentional fatalism to the deliberate repetitions, as when he frequently used, "that is all ye know, and all ye need to know," which he adapted from Keats.

The regularity of his references to the book of Revelations was ultimately off putting, and there were numbers of other quotes he couldn't quit. "Genius round the world stands hand in hand, and one shock of recognition runs the whole circle round" was used repeatedly and attributed variously to Art Linkletter or Herman Melville. He also loved mentioning that no one believed Thomas Edison until he managed to harness electricity, comparing that to the way Hunter felt his own genius was neglected. He especially liked it because Edison was a known early cocaine adherent.

These kinds of redundancies aren't uncommon in writers and are probably only aggravating if you make a study of their work or immerse yourself in too much of them at any one time. There was still plenty of fresh writing in between the recycled lines, but it was hard, even for Hunter himself, to avoid a feeling that we'd all been down these same roads too many times. Overall there was a palpable casting about in his writing for the important stuff, for the big fish, for the well-told story that would eclipse everything else.

This wasn't at odds with how he viewed good writing. In a 1968 letter to Tom Wolfe, published in *Fear and Loathing in America,* Hunter was fairly specific about his tastes (and they never really changed): "I don't know about you, but in my own mind I value peaks far more than continuity or sustained efforts. Those are for caretakers on the killing-floor. Mr. Fitzgerald spoke in terms of 'the high white note,' which explains it pretty well—at least as far as I'm concerned. That, in fact, is the theme of the book [*Fear and Loathing in Las Vegas*] that Random House is finally forcing me to write."

In short, if the good parts of your writing were *really* good, if they soared, then the earthbound rest was acceptable. When he began doing columns regularly in 1985 and I was frequently called over to help on deadlines, he lived by a rule he first shared with me years earlier. "It's all about the lead, especially in something as short as a column. But even in a magazine story, you want to make sure you have them by the short hairs from the start. If they've bought the book, they'll probably read it, even if it doesn't grip them right away. But for a column you have to grab them immediately. That's all I really care about. I want to do something they won't read anywhere else. Get a couple of graphs like that in, and you don't have to worry so much about the rest."

His very first column at the *San Francisco Examiner* was a big deal and he wanted to be sure he made a statement with it. He was also actively developing his latest persona, Gene Skinner, at the time. Searching for inspiration he asked me over right after I'd returned from a trip to Montana. I figured he was just fussing over a few words or sentences, but he didn't have anything at all and the deadline was imminent.

Magazine editors tend to give writers shadow deadlines, well ahead of when they actually need them. Hunter had sussed that out long ago and was an expert at waiting until the real "drop-dead" date. And even that could get pushed back to the final proofing stage, called bluelines, if they respected you enough and needed your work desperately to accompany already-commissioned and delivered illustrations and fill an otherwise giant hole in the periodical.

With books, real deadlines seemed to Hunter not to exist at all, regardless of the wording in his contracts. As he wrote to his agent, Lynn Nesbit, in 1971, "I tend to work only as hard as I think I have to work—and what gets me in gear is a serious deadline & people screaming at me on the long-distance telephone about specifics—like, 'We must have the ending to Chapter Seven by Friday, or the printers are going to sack the whole goddamn book.'"

Newspapers, however, are a very different breed. They are relentlessly ravenous and there is a very quick and immutable deadline beyond which the presses stop for no man. For many in the writing business, newspapers are a daily crunch. For Hunter it was only weekly, but even that would become onerous and sometimes impossible. This was only the very first column, and not even he wanted to initiate the project by missing the first deadline altogether. They were giving him a thousand words, a lot for a columnist, and paying him a dollar a word, which wasn't terrible at the time, and he needed the money.

I walked into his kitchen to an air of grumpy gloom and handed him something I thought he might find funny. Not for the column or posterity but just because he liked getting odd things from people. It was a bright yellow flyer that was handed out in Yellowstone Park on the heels of a visiting Frenchman's having been mortally gored by a buffalo after getting way too close to it trying to take pictures. It bore a fairly crude illustration of a buffalo skewering a man with a camera, along with the words:

> WARNING
>
> NEARLY A DOZEN VISITORS HAVE BEEN GORED BY BUFFALO THIS SUMMER.
>
> Bison can weigh 2000 pounds
> and can sprint at 30mph,
> three times faster than you can run.
>
> All the animals in the park are wild, unpredictable and dangerous.
>
> Stay in or near your car and do not approach wildlife.

I thought it was almost classic destiny that this French tourist, whom news stories said had been warned by his countrymen that America was a barbaric land with its West still full of cowboys and Indians, had been killed by a buffalo. Back home they would be saying, "We told him so," with big Gallic shrugs.

While I was sure Hunter's first column would contain some fairly pointed political insights of national interest, couched in whatever piece of personal turmoil and weirdness he could generate, that wasn't what he was thinking at all. In fact, he wanted to distance himself a little from politics and move on in the realm of fiction with more things he could write from home instead of on the road. On September 23, 1985, Hunter's debut column hit the stands accompanied by a big front-page banner. The title of the piece was "Buffalo Gores a Visitor." The lead graph read:

> My friend Skinner was trapped and mauled by a rogue buffalo while traveling to Wyoming to visit his ex-wife on Labor Day. Nobody knows what happened. On the front seat of his 300 h.p. aluminum-body Land Rover, found three days later in a roadside rest area near the Montana state line, authorities found a yellow printed "WARNING" notice from the U.S. Dept. of the Interior saying: [and here he quoted the flyer I'd given him].

The piece continued in that manner for three more paragraphs, loaded with skewed details lifted from my life, then veered abruptly off into other areas, all of them on a list of potential future ideas for his column. I was flattered to once again be misrepresented in some of his writing, even if it was as some component of Skinner, his new thuggish, mercenary, alter ego.

In what would become standard operating procedure for many columns to come, at way past the eleventh hour Hunter had finally taken the material he had at hand—essentially a list of pitches—and grafted a startling lead onto it and turned it in. I was happy to have played a part in it, he was happy that it didn't come out anything like I thought it might, and I tried to learn from the example. He gave me handfuls of copies of the story along with the edits and notes and letters connected to it to facilitate my education, and a handwritten cover note reading: "Dear Jay—one of these days you may figure out the brutal simplicity of writing like a professional (see above). If not, call me when you get work. Good luck." And he signed it.

The headline was catchy, the lead was great, and the premise original. That's the trifecta right there. Willie Hearst, the *Examiner*'s owner and scion of the Hearst publishing empire, sent Hunter a letter the next day saying: "Dear Hunter: The first column was a tour de force. The whole thing read like one continuous idea. The first sentence was a masterpiece. Best Regards, Will." This wasn't long before Hunter demanded the removal of his first editor and was at serious odds with Hearst over expenses.

The buffalo portion of the column became a small, quirky vignette in the latest fashion of an old Hunter habit. Though these tangents often went nowhere, they were intended as excerpts from a world at large with which most people would be . . . unfamiliar. And they were usually entertaining no matter what. He was still parading his command of the language and sportswriter's skill with adjectives, while piling on the details that he loved and felt were intrinsic to his, or anyone's, work.

He spent several days a few months later obsessing over how to drop the right names in his column when he wanted to mention power-brokering Washington, D.C., restaurants and clubs. You can't afford to position yourself as a savvy political insider and start referring to some place that no one hip or powerful has been in for months. When he finally came up with a consensus on Duke Zeibert's restaurant, the name showed up in virtually every Washington-based column he wrote after that.

On the other hand, it didn't occur to him to be as precise in other areas. In that debut *Examiner* column he also wrote: "According to hoof-prints taken at the scene, the beast chased him for 2,000 yards across muddy pastures and razor-sharp mesquite bushes and finally ran him down and pinned him like a dumb animal against a rusty hurricane fence." The humor is what counts and never mind that there is no mesquite within five hundred miles of Yellowstone Park.

He told me on a few occasions that what he looked for in writing and what I looked for were sometimes different. When he first talked about Robert Sabbag, who had written a book called *Snowblind* and some stories for *Rolling Stone,* and said he admired his work, I assumed it was because Sabbag was creating good, first-person, frontline accounts of using drugs and traveling in the cocaine culture of South America. It was something no one else was doing, especially without sounding like bad imitations of Hunter. But Hunter told me, "What interests me most are the words, some of the things he says, the way he uses the word 'flourishes,' for instance." Another line he mentioned was when Sabbag summed up how combining coke with quaaludes made him feel: "There is order in the universe." It was short and perfect and he identified with it immediately.

I used to bristle a little at his thinking me completely insensitive to the finer subtleties of writing. But it was Hunter's way of saying that he wasn't always who I, or others, thought he was. There was a

Dylanesque quality to it of sometimes insisting that his motivations and tastes weren't always political, or druggie, or whatever other slant we were expecting. It happened frequently during the editing process for his *Examiner* columns. He wouldn't so much belabor the difference in the way he looked at things and the way I or Maria did. He would just choose a different slant or tone or entire way of proceeding from what we were envisioning, and often enough that it sometimes seemed intentionally perverse.

These situations only occurred because editing the columns was often tortured, late at night, when Hunter wasn't always bringing his A game. David Burgin, the *Examiner*'s editor at the time, a fellow Kentuckian who had worked with Will Hearst to hire Hunter, clashed early with Hunter on editing. One of the last things Burgin wrote Hunter ended with, "Have a strong day. Stop yelling—It ain't worth it. And remember your voice. Best, David." An amiable, smart, and well-written editor named David McCumber replaced Burgin as Hunter's editor and worked with him for years on various projects.

"Publisher Will Hearst decided somebody more expendable than the editor of the newspaper should handle Hunter's column, or that's the impression I got when he ominously invited me into his office to discuss being Hunter's new 'control,'" wrote McCumber in his eulogy for Hunter in the *Seattle Post Intelligencer*. "When I said, 'sure,' Hunter burst out of Will's bathroom, fell to the floor, did ten push-ups, then grabbed two tumblers, filled them with scotch, jammed one into my hand, shook the other hand, and the hog, as he would say, was in the tunnel. He would write the column for five years, three of them with a little help from me, and the best of them would make a book, *Generation of Swine,* that sold a quarter million copies in hardback."

Sometimes even the last resort of patching together the random notes and recent clutter in Hunter's kitchen/office failed to produce anything even remotely palatable to Hunter or McCumber. At this point, facing the withdrawal of the column and his resulting lack of payment and the wrath of Hearst, Hunter would sometimes succumb to a proxy.

A few times when Hunter was so wasted and tired after days of being up, Maria and I had to create big chunks of columns from whole cloth, with only Hunter's mumbles and gestures and orphaned sentences to go on. David did what he could to assemble the mess on the other end, but Hunter hated these episodes and never let anyone forget it. Usually if he was too fucked up he would finally admit defeat and pull the piece rather than allowing someone else to write it for him.

Even attempting to suggest a way he might say something—after a lapse of an hour or two in any input at all as the clock ticked down and he nodded and drank and mumbled—was enough to send him in the other direction entirely. Yet he also loved writing by committee, if it was his hand-chosen and carefully directed committee. It was viable for good material (he once described himself to Tom Wolfe as "a natural word-thief in every way") and for sparking his own imagination, and he could endear women and repay other friends by using their suggestions, quotes, and even names in the finished product.

After Sandy departed the Farm and Hunter moved his office from a back room into the kitchen, he usually enjoyed talking to a constant parade of people throughout his work hours. And when he wasn't writing he listened far more than he spoke, staying engaged and current with everyone in attendance. Even when he *was* writing, he liked it to be participatory. He just never appreciated people thinking he might be predictable or that his work was easy.

One of the results of having his office in the kitchen was that it made an ongoing spectacle of him writing. For most of his early books and articles he liked to go solo and cram. At the Farm he would lock himself in the basement War Room at deadline time, or at least disappear into the back beyond the "public" rooms of the house. By the late 1970s, however, he seemed happiest in a room full of people and chaos, with constant input, on-site editing, phones ringing, faxes screeching, and at least one TV and some music blaring, whether from his big home stereo or his traveling Nakamichi. He craved instant feedback, musician style, and of course loved being the center of attention as a sort of performance artist. Later he became enamored of hearing his own writing read aloud to him.

I thought this seemed like a gruesome affectation, but I wasn't immune to the allure of being asked to read. He said he found it useful for cadences and flow, to know if the writing, old or new, stood up to the oral tradition and sounded natural and unforced. I couldn't help but wonder if there wasn't a part of him that also wanted the reader to recognize the real musicality of his words. In a letter he wrote to Viet Cong Colonel Vo Don Giang in Vietnam in 1975 (later anthologized) he first mentioned, "I'm not an especially good typist, but I am one of the best writers currently using the English language as both a musical instrument and a political weapon," and he wasn't abashed about how cocky that might sound.

I probably would never have tried reading his stuff aloud on my own. But one day in the early 2000s I ran into Hunter and Ralph Steadman at the Woody Creek Tavern. Hunter was especially jovial and invited me to their table where Ralph, in his full regalia of multipocketed fishing vest crammed with various pens, inks, and sundry devices, set up his video camera while Hunter told me about Ralph's latest project. "He wants to publish a long version of *The Curse of Lono,* with some of the cuts to my text restored, and a lot more of his original drawings that they never used. He's crazy, of course." Ralph frowned.

"You've talked about this before," I said. "It seems like a good idea."

"Maybe," Hunter replied. "I've been having people read the chapters out loud, to see how it sounds all these years later. I've been surprised. It holds up pretty well. I don't know if we want to go back and add anything." Given his original anger over the editing of the book, this was a surprising, though I think accurate, assessment about what critics, if not me, had come to think of as one of his lighter and lesser works.

Ralph glared at him. "But it's such a waste. They didn't have room for so many of the drawings. And you were furious at the cuts they made to your story."

"Well, let's see. Do you want to read a chapter for us?" Hunter asked me. I don't do many readings because I have a voice that offends me. But this was Hunter asking, it was Ralph's video, and I knew the work well. I'd been in Hawaii while it was being researched and present for much of the writing and editing back in Woody Creek with Hunter and Laila. I'm still fond of Hawaii and I get to spend some time there.

"You can even pronounce some of these fucking names, can't you?" Hunter grinned, and Ralph looked happy again.

So off I read and it was actually revealing, as well as fun. And funny. I realized right away that something Hunter watched for was how others read his funny lines and how the reader as well as the listeners reacted. Several of us were at an outdoor table, and the chapter flowed very well and drew laughs every few lines. I don't think I stopped smiling for most of the reading, much to Hunter's delight. Several times he'd ask for a comment, based on some expression or inflection in my reading, and I'd tell him some story I'd heard in Hawaii that related to his own, or mention people we both knew and how they were doing. Like all good storytelling, reading out loud is a throwback to the tribal art and I understood clearly and suddenly why it fascinated him.

Once again, I had sold Hunter a little short. What I took to be mostly an indulgence was actually self-serving in a much smarter way. Hunter used readings to find out what was funny, what was touching, what flowed, what worked, and what didn't. You could hear it in a reader's voice, see it in the eyes and lips, and tell it by the reaction of the rest of the audience. It is also about the only way you can get an inkling of how your writing is actually understood by someone other than you. Plus, it pleases people to be asked to read and may teach them something about your work, which is all win-win if the writing can stand up to it.

During this period toward the end of his career, Hunter seemed to be learning something from his original writing again. While it was often convenient to plunder his own past for new collections, I think he began wallowing a bit there and enjoying it. Works such as *The Rum Diary,* his first book-length fiction, now struck him as less juvenile than when he first produced them.

He was so unhappy with *The Rum Diary* when he first sold it that he later bought it back from his publisher rather than have it released. Eventually, though, it was published in much the same Hemingwayesque form as it was originally written and met with some success and good reviews. I enjoyed it a lot, in spite of never being a big Hemingway fan. Shorn and focused, *Rum Diary* made you realize that Hunter could do it, just as Picasso's early work let you know he was a classically trained painter. It also contained the most completely drawn, full-depth characters Hunter ever created, making me wish he'd done more of that later on. Toward the end, he gravitated back to that style. Gone were some of the overheated descriptions, the outrageous side stories and guitar solos that had so long marked his style. His sentences were shorter and crisper, not just in the resurrected old material but in the new stuff as well: most of the connective and retrospective writing he did for *Kingdom of Fear* and the last year or so of "Hey Rube."

For his entire career, Hunter wanted to write novels most of all. And many will say that he wrote several besides *Rum Diary*. The *Vegas* book is often referred to as a novel, though that begs the question of how much journalism, or autobiography, a novel can tolerate before the format is being abused. The same holds true for *The Curse of Lono*, as well as "The Banshee Screams for Buffalo Meat," "Fear and Loathing in Elko," and other stories.

I once asked him, before *Rum Diary* had come out, why he was so determined to write a novel. "I've made so many comparisons between fiction and nonfiction, I have to see what it's all about," he said. "I'll have to box myself in. It's like announcing a duel. After it's public, it's hard to back out." And why didn't he write any more true novels after *Rum Diary*? Maybe he just never really had to. Hunter was able to use fiction and satire to get at truth and reality in everything he wrote. And I sometimes felt that the real burden he wasn't able to manage, after the first three books and the withheld *Rum Diary*, was a true narrative arc throughout an entire book of wholly original material.

With nonfiction subjects, a story line will usually suggest itself for an article; for a book, if there's a common theme, then great. But Hunter's collections are just anthology-style, greatest-hits assemblages that don't have to contain any overall story line. Given his troubles even finding good story lines for his articles, having to invent one completely, and then sustain it for a novel, was perhaps, by the last twenty years of his life, more than he could deliver. And just "lashing together" all of those "high white notes," he eventually realized, wasn't quite the same thing.

7

A Man of Letters and a Life of Notes

J—
I'm down in the hole where I belong—come on down the back-stairs + check in before getting into the Lord's business—because this is, as you know, the Lord's day.

Doc

To most sane people, and nonwriters, Hunter's shocking tonnage of correspondence would seem nothing short of possessed. He generated so many notes on everything, from needing lightbulbs to finding the best hotel room in Las Vegas to quotes from movies and newspapers, that it was a serious task just to store it all. His basement was full of boxes and file cabinets crammed with an amount of paper only an arsonist could love.

Hunter's edit notes alone are frequently as extensive as the writings they accompany. And his often handwritten letters to friends, lovers, family, associates, peers, editors, creditors, politicians, lawyers, and so on are so plentiful they have constituted multiple volumes of his canon so far, barely making a dent in the numbers of them out there.

It says much about Hunter that he not only wrote constantly in one form or another, but he was so self-aware, and just plain cocky, from an early age that he kept copies of nearly all of it. This started well before computers or home copier machines, meaning he carbon copied everything beginning in the mid- to late 1950s up until about 1975, not an easy nor inexpensive task—but one full of plans and expectations, and he was right. And once good copiers became available he really went to town replicating everything he ever laid pen or typing fingers on, always mindful of his estate and books such as this.

Of course those he communicated with via his notes and letters generally kept them as well, often even when they were excoriating, because they were so classic, well written, funny, and handwrought. What has been described, even by me, as Hunter's "scrawl," is really more artistic than that word implies. He wrote fluidly, with an actual technical passion, and demanded the best instruments for each task (certain sizes of Sharpies, usually, in his preferred metallic gold and silver when signing books), whether autographing glossy book covers, annotating his galleys, or just issuing edicts, complaints, and to-do lists. When he had the room, and he often wrote on yellow legal pads so he *would* have the room, his words were crafted in a large, flowing script given to showy outbursts, with lots of exclamation marks, question marks, and underlining. He frequently employed variations of editing terms and odd abbreviations, along with demonstrating the same tendency his published writings had to capitalize words whenever he felt so moved. It was also easy to tell when the long hours and cumulative drugs had begun to take their toll, because his penmanship tumbled a bit, literally sloping down the page at times, and the content got fussier and more repetitive. These were red flags to most of his editors and friends, who took what followed with larger doses of salt and patience than usual.

The repressed painter and illustrator came out in Hunter when he wrote by hand, and I have numerous samples of his and Ralph Steadman's bold inscriptions that aren't easy to tell apart. It's difficult to conceive, in our computerized age, of the fact that Hunter wrote like this *daily*, when he was conscious, and often at lengths of up to several thousand words just in notes and letters. Every day. It's tough to grind out this equivalent of a dozen double-spaced, twelve-point-type pages daily when all we have to do is tap it into a computer and hit "Save." He wrote a lot of this by hand and never stinted on the words.

It was hard not to see some of this as a substitute for the real writing he needed to be doing. On the other hand, he ultimately made money from it, as he always suspected and planned. And the world received widely spread samples of his writing-as-art everywhere he went.

Denie and I once got a fifteen-page handwritten note in blue and red ink on yellow legal paper dated 3/26/79, getting us caught up with him after his return from somewhere. It contains fifty-four separate, numbered items in alternating colors, ranging from "My Bank of Aspen acct. is about $3000 overdrawn" to ".44 Magnum from Dick Goodwin" to "Jesus—this a list to end all lists—& I think we need 3 (three) Xerox copies for the permanent record—I have a tab at Aspen Copy Ser." This one list alone could be published as is and it would be longer than his infamous *Screw-jack* book, and at least as entertaining.

Dave Burgin at the *Examiner* got an eleven-page barrage in September 1985 that Hunter describes at the outset as "a maze of memos—a working paper of sorts." It reflects Hunter's decline through its course, tracking a clearly worsening temper, and concludes with, "Okay—how's that for a no-frills memo? The next one is going to cost you a dollar a word, plus expenses. Which is as it should be. If you wanted golf you should have stayed in Orlando. See you soon HST"

As many epics as he composed, Hunter also excelled with short quotes and snarls affixed to whatever paper was at hand. He gave me examples that include "CHASE ATTACK KILL EAT" lifted from a documentary on Bengal tigers and spread over an entire page of *Rolling Stone* stationery; "Open door & scream—I'm 88% deaf" on L'Ermitage stationery; and "The Longest Hour" slashed across Las Vegas Hilton stationery also splattered with phone numbers and other miscellany.

Others that he'd pull off the wall and thrust at me when he thought I needed inspiration include things such as, "Musical chairs for keeps—But where do the losers sit?" and "You're only safe as long as I'm right." Many of the musings are intended as subheads for somewhere, a genre he was considered a genius in even by longtime editors: "Amortizing the Doomed or Who Gets the Bill for The Casualties? or more to the point: Who Pays it?" Another says: "Bring me the head of C. R. Dunne or This is the Jimmy I knew."

Hunter also jotted down memorable quotes incessantly, either for use later in a story or just to stick on a wall. "God created all men—but Winchester + baseball bats made them equal. Evil Knevil [*sic*] ABC Evening News 6/16/78" and "There's a small percentage that want to see death—but not all of them—most of them are pullin for you [*sic*] E Knevil," occupy one piece of paper I have.

Story, book, and film ideas were also frequent subjects of his doodling, and you could almost feel the bumps of coke, swigs of whiskey, and puffs of pot he'd be taking as he composed them. One I have was done in red Magic Marker and blue ink: "Fear + Loathing in a place you'll never know. Last Dance. . . . (?) etc" is carved across the top of one page, followed by: "1978 will be the year of Ali—first Spinks in February (Vegas)—then Norton 'next fall' in some foreign country. one-year That means a <u>six-month</u> commitment—Dec '77 through Dec '78. articles for Jann—one book for Silberman." Here an arrow points to the next page topped by a line reading: "Articles—$15K + $30K total $45K then, all expenses by HST."

He was lining out his upcoming year with plans to center it on Ali's fights by writing several articles for *Rolling Stone,* then turning them into a book for Random House: "$100,000—book advance—book to cover entire period, from <u>now</u> to Miami to Vegas (Spinks fight), then back for the Main Gigs—Pd. training camp Arum—OK/book, Dr Freddy Pacheco, Hal Conrad, Angelo Dundee, The Art of Boxing—a camera-eye look at Ali preparing for the END—but first Spinks + then Norton for the final $12 million." He appended one last cryptic line in red to the whole memo: "Shamberg film 7. also."

One three-foot long, taped-together scroll of a list he made for himself and me consisted of L'Ermitage and *Rolling Stone* Dr. Hunter S. Thompson National Correspondent stationery with numerous to-dos relating to his divorce from Sandy and the movie *Where the Buffalo Roam*: "Call Pierre inre deed + Arum for divorce specialist, Call Jack inre Director, Clean out bank acct."

Another piece of lined paper is headed "Sunday Dec 4'77 WC [Woody Creek]" and is the text of a telegram to John Belushi at his *Saturday Night Live* address in New York trying to arrange security for himself while he was in the city on a speaking engagement. Part of it reads:

```
Urgent inre your call
Sunday nite. Confirm $400
per hour security fee if
repeat if you can meet
TWA #156 arriving JFK 5:33
Monday, then get me to
NYU for my 7:30 speech
then to a TV
set by nine for Miami
Baltimore game.
```

Telegrams were one of Hunter's preferred methods of communications before everyone had fax machines. They lent a properly glamorous note of old-line reporter style to important communiqués, and he liked the format in general.

I had dozens of notes left on my doors and windows over the years so that he didn't have to wake me in the middle of the night when he was up and working and in case he retired before I rose. Many were similar to one I saved on plain, unadorned typing paper lettered in green saying, "Jay call or come over—I slept for 33 hours—OK. See you later. H"

Most notes and lists he wrote to me were of a business nature. A two-pager dated 5/31 and done on the Woody Creek Rod & Gun Club letterhead refers to the apportionment of water rights being leased from a neighbor. "If anything weird happens, call me at the beach," it instructs at one point, then ends by finalizing an arrangement with me: "in/re watering trees, etc: One week taking care of the water should be one week free rent, ok? Yeah. . . . don't let all the trees die . . ."

For several years, Hunter's cat would move in with me when Hunter was gone for any length of time, occasioning more notes: "Jay Is Walter over there with you? . . . I haven't seen him for too many days—I just figured he'd adopted you, for continuity's sake— . . . Let me know today if you have him . . ."

When the subject was more personal he tried hard to be polite. On a piece of *Rolling Stone* paper with his National Correspondent header and the time of 4:25 a.m., he wrote: "J/D . . . Inre: dinner—I forgot that tonight is Fight Nite. . . . + I've been preparing all week for the action. —Can we have dinner some other nite? Let me know. H"

He could also be demanding, especially if I was late returning some piece of hardware or a movie tape he needed. "J I need the RF/Video cord off the Betamax TONITE—please bring it over to the house when you get back or leave it outside yr. door—so I can pick it up TONITE Thanx H"

Two colorfully hand-done and clearly urgent notes early one morning were typical of his responses to any upgrades or repairs to my house that I might plan without his consent. Or even with it. On plain white paper the first one read: "Jay" in huge green crayon, followed by red crayon: "Carpet? Check with me before you install any carpet at my expense. HST" The next one, placed somewhere else in case I missed the first one, was also in red and green written on yellow Mayflower Hotel stationery from New York, with essentially the same message. I got the point.

Even the most mundane things he dealt with had humor in them. In a note asking Denie to check on his insurance coverage for rental cars he finishes with "so why don't you ask the Aspen Agency if they are covering me, or if the Lauderdale Rent-a-Car is responsible for anything that happens to me or the car, or anything I may or may not crush by accident. OK HST"

A telling instruction to me is written across a typed note on a *Playboy* magazine memo pad from someone Hunter had worked with there: "August 29, 1978, Hunter: Here, from the lady herself, is something to remember her by. While the wit may not on first glance appear competitive with that of, say Dean Swift or young Vetter, what did they look like in Argyle socks?" It was signed with an indecipherable slash and, alas, I never saw the picture. Hunter drew an arrow pointing to the signature and he wrote: "Arthur Kretchmer —send a note to Arthur, telling Rozanne Katen to get in touch with me via Bob Bookman at ICM in BevHills inre: pursuing her film career. H"

The line between notes and something more is blurry in Hunter's work. Some short pieces carried a lot of punch. After reading a lengthy spy novel I'd written, he gave me an intro to an agent, Bob Datilla, by calling him in the middle of the night to say that I'd be sending the manuscript. Datilla was naturally grumpy about the hour. I'm not sure how good my book would have had to be after that, but it wasn't good enough. Even so, it was a nice gesture on Hunter's part. The cover note he gave me to accompany the book was written on Woody Creek Rod & Gun Club stationery: "Aug 10 '85 Dear Bob—Here is the spy novel I mentioned on the phone the other night. If you sell it, I'll expect the normal finder's fee. I'll call in a few days—my life has turned weird since I saw you last. Thanks, HST *—sorry I woke you up"

A memo Hunter sent to Gary Hart's campaign manager, Bill Dixon, was typed on Jann Wenner's Brannan Street letterhead.

> 2/8/85 Dear Billy, ["Dixon c/o Gary Hart" is handwritten in] I understand you have a project for 1988. What is it? And how can it make me even more powerful, rich and famous than I already am? I have, as you know, elected the last two presidents. And I don't mind going for three (3). . . . When I saw Paul Kirk on 5th Ave. the other day he slapped me on one of my trailing jowls & called me a dumb bastard because I didn't invite him to Elko. Jesus! How could I have known the difference between Burke and Kirk? I tried to explain this to him, but he slapped me again & started talking about Billy Carter. Fuck those people. I love power, Billy, but mainly I love rock & roll. . . . Maybe we should just zoom off to Jamaica, Billy—hire some fat boys and scare up a case of amyls. Just you & me old sport; we know what's happening. Death to the weird, eh? Let them eat shit and die.

Famous literary feuds have gone on through the centuries, and Hunter has included some of his own in his various collections of letters. One of his most wicked and ongoing disagreements was with cartoonist Garry Trudeau. As I've mentioned, Hunter always loudly complained that he hated being in *Doonesbury* even though many people were convinced it ultimately helped fuel his fame and make him more money. He was asked more than once during college speeches about Trudeau and told the audience at Brandeis University, "I'd like to break his kneecaps for five hundred bucks."

In 1979 I was handling Hunter's mail while he was out of town and in between assistants. One of the batches I picked up included a personal postcard from Trudeau, dated 6 June 1979. On the image side was a photo of a desktop with an antique typewriter and a newspaper folded over on top of it, a bottle of Michelob, some panels from *Doonesbury,* scissors, a pen, an open ink bottle, a box of Starboard Tack matches, some paper clips, and an ashtray with a roach in it. I thought it was clever.

On the other side, Trudeau's address was printed on the card and he had handwritten the rest in black ink. The gist was that as "an interested party," he "nearly puked" reading the script for *Where the Buffalo Roam,* calling it a "piece of shit," and saying that however much Hunter had been paid for the rights it wasn't enough. He ended by lecturing Hunter that if he wanted to ruin his own reputation he should at least have the integrity to do it himself.

Hunter called later that night to check in and I read him the card over the phone while holding it away from my ear. "That crazy shithead!" he roared. "What the hell has come over him? Is he out of his mind? Why in the name of Christ would he think he has anything to say about this, or anything else? I'll fuck Jane Pauley and we'll see how he likes that, the slimy little leech!"

Then we moved on. When he got home he gave me Trudeau's card to keep. He didn't want it around. Along with it was a copy of the letter he sent Trudeau on his Rolling Stone National Correspondent letterhead dated June 20, '79.

Garry Trudeau

You silly little fart. Don't lay your karmic nightmares on me, and don't bother me with any more postcards about your vomiting problems. The only other person I know who puked every time he said the word "integrity" was Richard Nixon.

And what lame instinct suddenly prompts you to start commenting on my material? You've done pretty well by skimming it for the past five years, so keep your pompous whining to yourself and don't complain.

If you must vomit, go down to Morty's and use that special low-rent stall they keep for lightweight Yalies who steal other peoples' work for a living.

But don't worry, old sport. You'll get yours. . . . and in the meantime, feel free to call on me for professional advice at any time. I'm not like the others.

Sincerely,
HST

Hunter, in addition to generating staggering amounts of correspondence, also received wheelbarrows of it, much of it truly deranged. In the mid-1970s he started using his assistants to screen it but not so thoroughly that he'd miss any of the adulation, which was copious, or something with a potential story idea. As a result, I began to actually respond to the kinds of letters previous screeners had ignored. This wasn't always a good idea. But it did interest Hunter occasionally, as with a letter dated Feb. 27, 1979, and sent from a prison in Georgia.

Hunter wrote my name across the top and several notes throughout its closely packed five pages. The writer had run various porno businesses in Denver and Kansas City, he said, and unwisely neglected to pay bribes to the proper people. Now he wanted to trade his freedom for what he claimed was information about members of a sex ring in California "who pick up young hitchhikers and trick them into going with them to a very remote and well-guarded spot and then sexually abuse-torture and murder them. . . . These people have been doing it for 9 years I know of. They have killed several hundred young boys and girls." He had been turned down by everyone from the state cops to the FBI and was hoping that Hunter could write it up for publication but warned "I need to talk to you face to face before you go poking around in this." Hunter had underlined that part in red and written "indeed" by it. He was clearly intrigued and at the end, where the writer said, "One other thing—you don't get prime information from saints, they don't know anything," Hunter had written "yeah" and then: "J what do you think about this one?—should we look further? My feeling is negative, but . . . H"

In retrospect this could easily have been legitimate. It talked about snuff films the perpetrators were making that the writer had seen, and the timing was such that it could have related to convicted serial killer Charles Ng and his atrocities that were discovered a few years later. Frankly, it scared the shit out of me, and when Hunter had qualms it gave me all the reason I needed to agree with him, and he passed on it. There were plenty more where that came from.

In some of the first letters I waded through, I found people who wanted to get together with him to discuss what was behind the series of bizarre cattle mutilations going on around the West; girls living on weed and *Amanita muscaria* mushrooms in Breckenridge, Colorado; mountains of fan mail that sought to connect on whatever weird level possible; random pieces of writing, more or less in his style, with names such as "The Continuing Saga of Dr. Iguana"; requests for his writing (gratis) from such exotic publications as the apparently completely fictitious Jupiter Express in Kamloops, British Columbia; weird clips and extracts and copies of stories from all over the world, often about drugs from people clearly on them; raves beginning with a variation of "Having just read [fill in the blank] for the zillionth time, I thought I should drop you a line"; potential political candidates seeking his wisdom and/or endorsement; Xeroxed warnings that the American military was composed of nothing but drug addicts; business proposals that included writing collaborations with unknowns, art exhibits, collections of his material published by unknown presses in the hinterlands, drug deals, merchandising, and stories about how weird and fascinating the correspondents were; several asking if he was aware that someone was making a movie about him starring Bill Murray; and one from a vague California "presidio" that signed off with, "I gotta close before they find out," etched in a pathological scribble alone on the third page of a feverish rant.

Another one was from someone convinced that the recently elected president, Ronald Wilson Reagan, was the anti-Christ, because the number of letters in his name translated to 666, and because his first act as president was to receive a gift of a white stallion from the president of Mexico. The writer sent a clip of it from a newspaper that bore a caption straight from biblical prophecies: "Behold! A pale horse!" I passed it along to Hunter, since I found it hard to disagree with the assessment of Reagan on principle alone, and the voodoo seemed persuasive.

Hunter got lots of letters from women, ones in prison, ones he met at speeches, ones from *Playboy,* women he'd known for a while, women who wanted him to call or move in or just stop by with some drugs. One commercial greeting card from Hollywood reads "I Fucked My Way To The Bottom" inside and bears the note, "Hunter— You always say it was you that made me what I am today. Here is just a little example of what you've taught me. Thanks + Good Luck! Love you! Elaine."

Another, typewritten from a woman in Palatine, Illinois, begins with "Dear Dr. Thompson:" and closes with "I craved F&L in Las Vegas! It attaches to a loose, but vital, wire in my fuse board. I see you as a sort of Central Office; one who transmits for the A.T.&T. of 60's consciousness. This is not a fuck offer or request necessarily, BUT I would like to talk with you. So, if you're ever in the Chicago area give me a call, because I can honestly say you wouldn't get a bad connection. At any rate, you are appreciated. Peace and Love, Ann, P.S. I'll supply the awe, you supply the drugs."

An example of the kind of card any writer would viscerally fear a parent might find came to him from Bellingham, Washington, inside of a "Donna Louise Beats the Blahs" card: "Dear Mr. Thompson, I just finished Fear and Loathing in Las Vegas and it is undoubtedly the funniest, driest, book I have ever read. I have since decided to quit school and attempt to recreate the entire novel with a friend. Drug users are in your debt." It was signed by a young woman in what she called "Boringham" Washington.

Eventually, and it didn't take long, I quit reading every piece and stopped asking if I could keep the weirdest ones. About the only thing that kept me interested for the year or so I helped with his mail was the prospect of coming across something good from someone he actually knew and liked, such as a postcard from Ralph Steadman, in Greece, telling him that the BBC in London wanted to do a film of Hunter and Ralph. Ralph had suggested that BBC pay for their passage on the *QE2* to China and make a movie of that, an idea he thought they were "wild" about. "One of my better ones!" he noted.

Always better than reading the things others wrote to Hunter, however, was reading what he wrote. While many people, including most of his friends and relatives, received at least occasional angry and even threatening notes, the ones most of us (except for the lawyers and bill collectors and Garry Trudeau) remember were the funny and thoughtful ones. He didn't often have occasion to send something long and letter-ish to me, but the best came typed on four different kinds of stationery when I was in Kansas for a while in 1989, and it meant a lot.

Jay

Big rain here today. Thunder & lightning; flash floods; the ditch blew out above Stanley's & washed his house all the way down to here, still intact. I can see it sitting down there in the creek almost directly across from me. . . . Looters have been scrambling in & out of it all day. I fired the 300 Weatherby over their heads a few times, but they only cursed me & kept on looting—and then one of the bastards emptied a clip at my back door, on their way out. (see enc. photo)

I called Braudis, but he said he couldn't help me. "Those are the racetrack people," he said. "They work for Hadid. We can't touch them."

Apparently Hadid brought in about 200 vicious outlaw bikers from Oklahoma to come here & work on his new hotel & also to handle "security." Then he bought the racetrack & moved all these brutes and their women into a huge tent city that he built up there & called "employee housing." You can imagine what the tavern is like at cocktail hour these days. Constant violence & people fucking openly on motorcycle seats in the parking lot.

It goes on day & night. The first time Gaylord tried to close the place at midnight, they stomped him into a coma and now George keeps three bartenders there, 24 hours a day, to serve the bastards whatever they want out the back door (& even inside), or they'll swarm in & take it.

Shep has been totally intimidated & even lets some of them run tabs. Life in the trailer court has been like living in the middle of a prison riot, and most of the families have moved out. But every time a For Sale sign appears on a trailer, it gets instantly looted & vandalized & then taken over by armed squatters with no fear at all of the law.

"Downtown" Woody Creek has become like the original set of The Wild Ones, with constant rapes & beatings & burglaries 7 Bonfires all night at the racetrack that light up the sky like the auroura borealis (sp?).

I carry a .357 magnum in a non-concealed shoulder holster when I go for the mail, & I keep a loaded shotgun on nails above every door.

Our only hope now is a huge fire. Hadid has turned into a monster. He plans to level the whole Meadows/Institute complex & build a replica of the Taj Mahal that he says will be a "family hotel" with 300 luxurious units & armed guards.

He has also forged an alliance with Floyd Watkins—that greedhead psychopath up the road near Lenado—to house about 50 of his biker/thugs up there, so there are Harleys rumbling back & forth in front of my house at all hours. . . . My main fear is that the bastards know I have gasoline (that 300 gallon red ranch tank in the yard) and sooner or later I know one of them (or maybe three, or six) will run out of gas at 3:00 a.m. on a moonless night & decide to come after my gas tank, And then I will have to shoot it. Put a tracer into the bugger & blow it up—

Very dangerous. But what choice do I have? They will chop through the gate with bolt-cutters & kick down my doors to get cold beer. The Sheriff says to not even call him, if that happens, because he won't risk the lives of his deputies by sending them out to intervene in what he calls "some drunken midnight quarrel between lawless outlaw factions." And, yes—one of those factions is me. And his only advice is to kill them all at once, or give them what they want & stop whining.

It's horrible, Jay, horrible. I never thought he would go belly up like this, the first time I really needed help. We had him wrong from the start. I wouldn't be surprised if he was the one who tried to put you in Latuna (sp?).

Anyway, that's the report from the Home Front: Abandon All Hope, Ye Who Enter Here. Watkins & Hadid are now in charge, and I think that guy Braun who bought Vagneur's ranch is in with them—along with Stranahan, who now wants to triple the size of the Tavern and move the WC post office up to a new "shopping mall" that Hadid & Jaffee are building in Tent City on the race-track.

And Prince Bandar, the Saudi Ambassador, is building another "private hotel"—(43,000 sq. ft./slightly larger than the White House)—that looks down on all of this madness & has 26 bathrooms.

Yeah. . . . and how are things with you? Can you call out? Ring me collect any time.

Are you able to type or write?

Let me know if you need anything
in the way of special equipment
for professional/writing work.

Or paddle-tennis gear, for yr. new job as athletic director???

Or books? (here's one of mine, for purely instructional purposes—to put some snap in yr. prose. . . .)

Okay. I have to go now. It's 3:37, & I have to finish a column before dawn. At`e logo. Send word. Yr. friend, Hunter (HST).

8

Lawyers, Guns, and Money

I'm hiding in Honduras,
I'm a desperate man.
Send lawyers, guns and money,
the shit has hit the fan.

—Warren Zevon

Lawyers

Hunter needed lawyers the way a farmer needs rain, and I believe in some parallel universe he might have actually become a lawyer himself. He saw practicing law as very well-paid performance art that could make a real difference in people's lives. He admired attorneys and had many as friends, even though he regularly told the crowds at his speeches, "Lawyers are the true criminals of our society. They have double joints in every direction." Still, he dedicated a considerable portion of his income over the years to legal counseling, in the manner of people who believe that it's a sign of power to lawyer-up every time something happens they don't like.

Hunter dabbled in the criminal life at a young age and had the FBI on him by the time he was eight for blowing up a mailbox. Before long, having renounced crime in favor of another treacherous career, writing, his style also naturally put him at odds with a lot of people whom he offended or possibly even wronged, if a court should so decide. The magazines he wrote for and the publishers who produced his books all had legal staffs, or at least an attorney on retainer, to deal with writers such as Hunter. But on a number of occasions, Hunter felt *he* was the wronged party and tried to pursue legal action against others.

Given his lifestyle, Hunter found himself in more or less constant and legitimate need of counsel. "Hunter is a lightning rod," summed up his good friend and attorney Gerry Goldstein, one of the leading First Amendment lawyers in America, when his client was still alive. What with Hunter's wanton lawlessness and constant public currying of that outlaw image, it's astounding he wasn't locked up permanently. As it was, the cops came after him fairly often. When you have a person writing things that shape public opinion on sensitive political matters in ways that irritate the powers that be, also proclaiming that he never leaves home without holding, usually in felony weight, you have someone with a target on his back. This resulted in what he referred to as "political busts" that he actually used to relish for a time. It kept attention focused on him, but it also brought a lot of pressure with it, ratcheting up his already substantial natural paranoia levels and turning even ordinary outings into potentially ugly criminal confrontations.

Lawyers were often fascinated by Hunter. He was in many ways the perfect legal crash test dummy, the guy who would expose himself to prosecution for things he didn't believe should be criminalized, and then let the lawyers run with it. But beyond his ready availability as a customer, Hunter's attorney friends liked him for the same reasons the rest of us did: he was bright, engaged, funny, and interested in them. Most of all, he was someone they could talk to about their world and his and enjoy it and come away feeling as if it meant something.

"Indeed, some of my best friends are lawyers," Hunter wrote in *Kingdom of Fear.* "I have other good friends who are law enforcement professionals, but not many. It is not wise, in my business, to count too many cops among your good friends, no more than it is wise to be constantly in the company of lawyers—unless, of course, you are about to be put on trial in a Criminal Court, and even then you want to be very careful."

When they were working for or with Hunter, the lawyers often loved it, whether the cases always made sense or not. They were getting all of his attention and wisdom and he was getting theirs. Hunter's mind loved the intricacies and infinite permutations of the legal business and he could come up with enough disaster scenarios, what-ifs, and variables to keep rooms of attorneys occupied indefinitely. They liked talking to someone as devious and labyrinthine as themselves about such matters, especially when the conversations constituted billable hours. And if they had trouble getting paid, at least they'd had some stimulating conversation. Or that's the way Hunter often looked at it, and the way many attorneys finally had to as well.

Hunter also had a tendency to take up for others in legal trouble, from hippies busted for vagrancy in Aspen in the late 1960s on through to the celebrated case of accused cop-killer/conspirator Lisl Auman in Denver he became involved with in 2001. He never shrank from putting himself publicly on the line for his causes, whether in the protests at the Chicago Democratic National Convention in 1968, by running for sheriff in 1970, opposing bad land use decisions in Pitkin County, or forming fast alliances with some of the prominent members of the National Organization for the Reform of Marijuana Laws (NORML), well before such relationships were fashionable.

The cases he became interested in that didn't involve him directly were like sporting events for him: he always had a rooting interest and sometimes for much larger reasons than winning a bet. Often the motivations were protecting civil liberties—specifically, the First Amendment—and guarding against power run amok. The Lisl Auman case was a prime example, where a young woman companion of a robber who killed a cop had been convicted as an accessory to murder, even though she hadn't even been with the alleged murderer when the crime was committed. Auman was finally pardoned and granted a new trial after Hunter died.

Legal proceedings always offered the prospect of good stories, he felt, and even more so when they happened to him. Sometimes you had to wonder if he wasn't creating problems just to supply material. He could, and did, write about everything from his drunk driving arrests in Aspen to fender benders in San Francisco, but that writing was rarely good or actually made money by the time you subtracted the legal costs. One of his most famous cases in Aspen, sometimes referred to as "The Case of the Twisted Nipple" (keep reading), cost him into six figures and certainly never made that much back. Still, he viewed anything to do with lawyers as action that didn't require a lot for him to instigate and saved him from having to run around trying to drum up another story.

Conferring with lawyers was also another good diversion from his real writing. He was able to keep his hand in with lots of memos and notes but could suspend all the other tedious chores of reality—returning phone calls, talking to editors, paying bills, meeting deadlines, simple civility—and get himself really wound up, chemically and naturally, bringing all of his energy to bear on the enemy. Whether he was rallying forces to fight an expanded local airport or the way they were installing new phone lines to Lenado; dealing with his personal concerns in the forms of divorces, problems over being defamed in print, battles with publishers over the libelous potential of most of his books, or just issues with the size of his tab at the Woody Creek Tavern, Hunter loved nothing more than any crisis that could subsume everything else and keep him at the center of the action. Though he abhorred a bunker mentality when it was adopted by Richard Nixon or Ronald Reagan or anyone else in government, going to the mattresses sometimes perfectly suited his own moods and occasional desire to just hunker down and withdraw, while still feeling important and involved.

Going legal didn't hold the same interest for most of the people around him, especially those who knew from experience where it was likely to lead. This included the lawyers who often had to regard Hunter's cases as an ersatz form of pro bono work with the possibility that they might get mentioned in a story somewhere. Prominent attorneys such as Gerry Goldstein, Hal Haddon, and others have noted frequently in print and speeches that they were seldom paid in full, if at all. Says

Hunter's longtime personal assistant, Deborah Fuller, "He had many lawyers as good friends that he could consult about any issues concerning the law in politics and in general for his writing and therefore had them to consult and hire if he came up against a personal legal issue. I always found these lawyers very generous with their time and they often made allowances when finances were tight."

It was never a good sign when the War Room lit up, and cars and cables and faxes came and went as if Owl Farm were a foreign embassy, and the talk turned to nothing but law. To deal with every crisis, real or imagined, Hunter would stay up for days at the beginning, turning quickly belligerent and dour. The agitated, knitted-brow glare would come over him and no one who knew it wanted to be there. You sure as hell didn't want to find it directed at you. You also didn't want to be the one he could accuse later of deserting him when he needed help the most. So it was easier for almost everyone except his current love interest and his assistant to just hover around the edges of the tempest and try to stay available but otherwise out of harm's way. His sense of humor was usually one of the first casualties of such episodes, and when that happened you knew it could be another day or two before he'd wind down enough to be human again.

During some of his most formative years in the late 1960s and early 1970s, most Movement people and recreational drug users learned to be pretty savvy about the law and to have ready access to sympathetic lawyers. Generating publicity for his lawyers in lieu of paying them was a tactic Hunter employed from the beginning when he wrote early and often about attorney Oscar Acosta, as well as about Movement lawyers who didn't work for him directly but might be of service later. By the time he was writing his columns for the *San Francisco Examiner* and later for ESPN, attorneys who were his friends and had been repeatedly helpful to him, such as Gerry Goldstein, Hal Haddon, and Michael Stepanian, got regular mention.

It would have behooved Hunter to always have an attorney with him, but obviously that wasn't practical. I thought he might marry one, just for simplicity's sake. But in spite of all the seeming provocation that his entire life represented—taking drugs constantly and writing about it, calling elected officials and police everywhere he went criminals and sleazebags, giving speeches at colleges where he openly imbibed all kinds of illegal substances—he managed to avoid serious trouble most of the time except when he was driving or being set up.

As someone who fancied fast machines and ass-hauling, late-night cruises along the freeways, the driving thing was a problem and Hunter knew it. He quickly understood that as an increasingly notorious loose cannon on the deck of the 1972 presidential campaign, he was under close scrutiny from various law enforcement agencies everywhere he went as he followed the candidates. This was good for a thrill and keeping his mind and reflexes sharp, but it could wear on a man. As it did in Milwaukee for the Wisconsin primary when his nerves were already on edge. In *Fear and Loathing on the Campaign Trail '72*, he wrote:

> The car was extremely unstable—one of those Detroit classics, apparently assembled by junkies to teach the rest of us a lesson. . . . there was no way to cure the unnerving accelerator delay. It was totally unpredictable. At some stoplights the car would move out normally, but at others it would try to stall, seeming to want more gas—and then suddenly leap ahead like a mule gone amok from a bee sting. This would cause the car to fishtail erratically, making Hunter a nervous wreck.
>
> By the time I got to the Milwaukee Inn I had all three lanes of State Street to myself. Anybody who couldn't get safely ahead of me was lagging safely behind. I wondered if anyone had taken my license number in order to turn me in as a dangerous drunk or a dope addict. It was entirely possible that by the time I got back to the car every cop in Milwaukee would be alerted to grab me on sight.

It didn't happen that time, but it was definitely a fair premonition from a man well aware of his circumstances. It just took ten years for them to catch up to him. When he was charged with drunken driving and failure to stop by a highway patrolman near Aspen in 1981, he had never been arrested in the valley before during fourteen years here, and had only been issued one speeding ticket. Considering the absurdly low speed limits on rural and county roads back then, the latter was something of a miracle. I got two speeding tickets the first six months I had my license.

Hunter's drunk driving charge was thrown out because, according to Deputy District Attorney Blaine Stokes, "There were no blood tests made and no incriminating statements by Thompson were made." Hunter pleaded guilty to running a stop sign at about two in the morning and admitted, "I did jump out of the car and start raving."

He got pissed, he told me, with the state trooper. "A big linebacker, hayseed type, started yelling at me and asking me what I was doing driving around and running stop signs that time of night." When Hunter told him it was none of his goddamn business, that he had very definitely come to a complete stop and bounded out of the car to suggest that the officer, Bradford Bitterman (no less), might need to handcuff him, the cop panicked and called for backup. Hunter knew back then that if there was any contraband in your car, you were wise to get out of the car to remove any probable cause for a search. And a righteous indignation at the officer was his excuse for refusing to take any alcohol tests, a technique he had mastered in California and that still worked then. Today some policemen shoot you dead for leaving your car without permission, and if you refuse a breathalyzer or blood test they automatically suspend your license.

But it all worked out for Hunter. Stokes's summary later for the newspapers was, "We figure he did a Hollywood stop at a stop sign and the officer felt his authority had been challenged and arrested him." The DA's office said that none of it would have happened if both men had kept their tempers. Officer Bitterman later claimed, "Thompson was out of the jail before I was."

In what was typical of the way Hunter often dealt with these things, after the case was resolved he announced he might sue the *Aspen Daily News* for erroneously reporting that he had rolled his car in the parking lot of the old Holiday Inn and been hospitalized. He never actually took the paper to court, but the driving ticket and the prospect of a lawsuit occupied weeks of his time, dithering, ranting, and plotting.

As a puckish Lady Luck would have it, at this very time we'd been discussing his writing a book called *The Art of Driving,* and he envisioned this episode as an entire chapter. He also had an idea he was going to elaborate on in the book, only half facetiously, to deal with the crusades against drunk driving and what he considered the dangerously overzealous advocacy of Mothers Against Drunk Driving. "I think there should be drunk lanes," he told me, arching one eyebrow. "Instead of passing lanes they need to take one entire lane and block it off with Jersey barriers, and make it for drunks only. That way they can't hurt anyone else and they only have each other to deal with. You know when you take that lane what you're in for."

Hunter had long maintained, as do most heavy drinkers of my experience, that blood alcohol levels were, up to a point, irrelevant. The question was, could you still be as much in command of your faculties and still drive better than most of the other half-wits on the highway? Hunter never doubted his abilities in that regard, unless he was so deep into a binge that even he realized that if he could barely walk, driving was out. That's usually a call very few serious drinkers are capable of making. It's also not a trait, along with being a better driver smashed than most people are cold sober, that you want to rely on too often, especially as you get older.

On May 16, 1985, he was once again arrested by highway patrol officers in the wee hours for drunken driving. This time it was in San Francisco when he rear-ended a car with three people in it near Highway 101. He was spending a lot of time in San Francisco and Oakland at that point, putatively researching a book that became just a story called "The Night Manager" about his experiences with the Mitchell Brothers and their O'Farrell Theatre, an infamous strip joint and porn palace.

This time the cops were pros, the evidence substantial, and Hunter was found guilty in court two months after the arrest and sentenced to three years of probation, fined eight hundred dollars, and ordered to pay restitution to the people in the other car, none of whom were seriously injured. Having been soundly thumped, this wasn't a case he wrote much about except in vague, tangential references. "I was arrested seven times in six weeks—or at least charged, or accused or somehow involved with police and courts and lawmakers so constantly that it began to seem like my life," he wrote in "The Night Manager."

In his last really famous DUI bust he suspected, with some cause, that he'd been set up following a rally in Aspen opposing the proposed expansion of the local airport.

"It was a flat-out political bust," he told the newspapers. "He really wanted me. The other cops, all the rest of them, were embarrassed."

An Aspen city cop whom Hunter claimed had old grudges against him made the stop at about 2:30 a.m. on November 7, 1995. Officer Dan Glidden was the son of well-known Western author Luke Short, whose real name was Fred Glidden. Fred was a longtime Aspen resident and had strongly opposed Hunter when he ran for sheriff, taking out ads calling him a communist. Hunter maintained that the younger Glidden still bore him malice from those days, and many close to the situation told me that was the case. But Dan denied it and there was no proof either way.

When they breathalyzed Hunter at the scene, according to one officer Hunter spat repeatedly into the machines and only blew .053, still legal. Later, at the Pitkin County jail he blew .080 and was charged with "driving while ability impaired," or DWAI. Throughout his career, Hunter developed and relied on innovative methods to protect himself in court, with spitting as the latest manifestation. Saliva was said to water down, so to speak, the alcohol content of one's breath, and it obviously worked. Sort of.

Anyone who knew Hunter knew that any time he was driving, he almost certainly had a blood alcohol level over the permissible limit, most likely well past "impaired" and deep into "under the influence" territory. That said, most of us also knew for many years that he really did seem to metabolize alcohol like some kind of freak and could function capably after many more drinks than most people. As evidence of our faith, some of us repeatedly trusted our lives to him when he was driving. Eventually, as he got older and less capable of holding his liquor, I began to insist on chauffeuring, though that often had more to do with wanting my own escape pod if he decided to spend all night somewhere.

Back in the day, the certainty that Hunter would be legally drunk and probably in possession of controlled substances almost every time he got in his car was never considered sufficient cause to pull him, or anyone else, over. You had to be committing a traffic violation, something Hunter prided himself in being very careful about not doing. "They tailgated me all the way to the Slaughterhouse Bridge," he said about the incident with Officer Glidden. "I could see them, I knew there was a cop behind me. I was giving a clinic in driving skills."

Not according to Glidden, whose story changed but who insisted Hunter crossed a yellow line by about six inches for a distance of about forty feet. This apparently didn't sound as feeble to the DA's office as it did to many observers, and they let the DWAI charges stand.

By then, Hunter had taken to hiring what the newspapers referred to as "teams" and "entourages" and "legions" of lawyers. For this case the staff included Gerry Goldstein, the former president of the National Association of Defense Lawyers; Abe Hutt, a big-time Denver DUI lawyer; and local counsel John Van Ness.

"Hunter was so open and obvious it made him bulletproof," noted Goldstein, speaking at an Aspen symposium about Hunter after his death. "The pitfall for me was he was a pain in the ass as a client. He got a lot of money from a thing with *Rolling Stone* over using his image without his permission. But Michael Stepanian and I never saw any of it," he chuckled affectionately.

Much against Hunter's better judgment he agreed to waive his right to a speedy trial in the drunk driving case by delivering himself of a statement to the Pitkin County Court:

> It is with solemn heart and a weary soul that I come here today for the melancholy purpose of WAIVING MY CONSTITUTIONAL RIGHT to a fair and speedy trial—but I have come to understand that ancient Chinese axiom often attributed in error to Chief Justice Oliver Wendell Holmes (though actually coined by that famous jurist Friedrich von Logau): "For the Wheels of Justice to Grind Exceeding Fine, they Must Also Grind Slow."

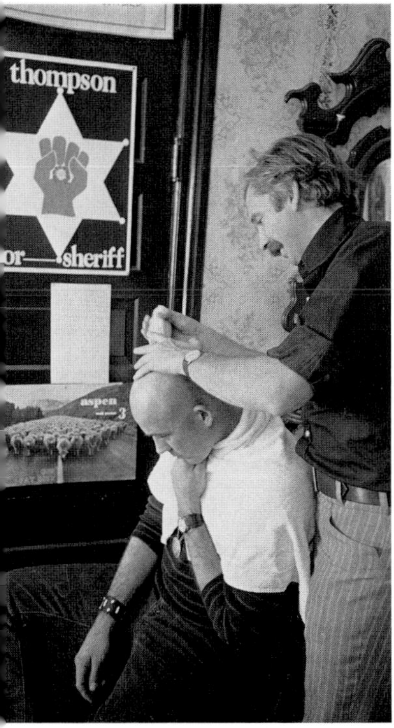

While running for Pitkin County Sheriff in Aspen in 1970, Hunter Thompson had his head shaved by friend Bill Noonan, the candidate for county coroner on Thompson's Freak Power ticket. The poster on the wall was designed and printed by his close friend, the artist Tom Benton.

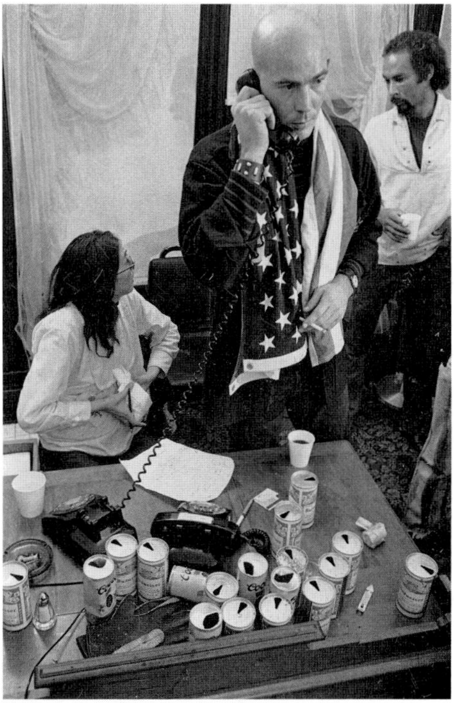

Hunter Thompson at the Thompson for Sheriff campaign headquarters in the Hotel Jerome in Aspen in 1970.

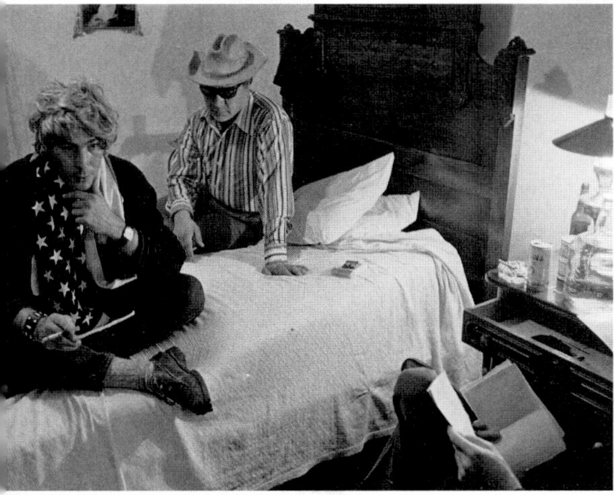

Hunter Thompson wearing a wig and wrapped in an American flag, sitting on a bed in campaign headquarters in the Hotel Jerome during his run for sheriff in 1970. Oscar Acosta, activist Chicano attorney and Thompson's good friend, confidante, and role model for the Samoan Lawyer figure companion in *Fear and Loathing in Las Vegas,* is seated behind him. **Photos on this page by Bob Krueger**

Juan Thompson received early instruction in how to use a gun at Owl Farm in the 1970s. **Photo by Bob Krueger**

In 1981, Hunter Thompson took a turn at the helm of the Haere Maru charter fishing boat off the Kona Coast of the Big Island of Hawaii, during research for his book *The Curse of Lono*. **Photo by Jay Cowan**

The red Jeep Wagoneer parked at Owl Farm that Hunter famously used for explosives testing and target practice. **Photo by Jay Cowan**

Hunter and close friends Tom Benton and George Stranahan preparing to blow something up on the grounds of Owl Farm. **Alan Becker Photography Inc.**

The Dunhill cigarette and Venturi Tar Gard holder were a trademark of Hunter's and were featured prominently in many photos. **Alan Becker Photography Inc.**

Despite his love for firearms, Hunter Thompson wasn't an excellent marksman, even shooting with an Olympic grade target pistol. **Alan Becker Photography Inc.**

Hunter Thompson and author Jay Cowan at the Cowan's 1978 wedding at Owl Farm. **Photo by Jay Cowan**

On-the-set pins, from Jay Cowan's collection, created by Hunter Thompson and Ralph Steadman for cast and crew of the film *Where the Buffalo Roam*. **Photo by Jay Cowan**

Yellowstone National Park flyer warning of dangers of wild buffalo. A similar flyer was given by Jay Cowan to Hunter Thompson and formed the basis for Thompson's debut column for the *San Francisco Examiner* in 1985. **Photo by Jay Cowan**

WARNING
NEARLY A DOZEN VISITORS HAVE BEEN GORED BY BUFFALO THIS SUMMER.
Bison can weigh 2000 pounds and can sprint at 30 mph, three times faster than you can run.
All animals in the park are wild, unpredictable and dangerous.
Stay in or near your car and do not approach wildlife.

Hunter had a weakness for guns and explosions. Here he's blowing up a keg full of gasoline with gunfire on the grounds of Owl Farm. **Alan Becker Photography Inc.**

Never one to shy away from a chance to self-promote, Hunter posed with a golf club on the hood of his famous red Wagoneer for a 1988 magazine cover. **Alan Becker Photography Inc.**

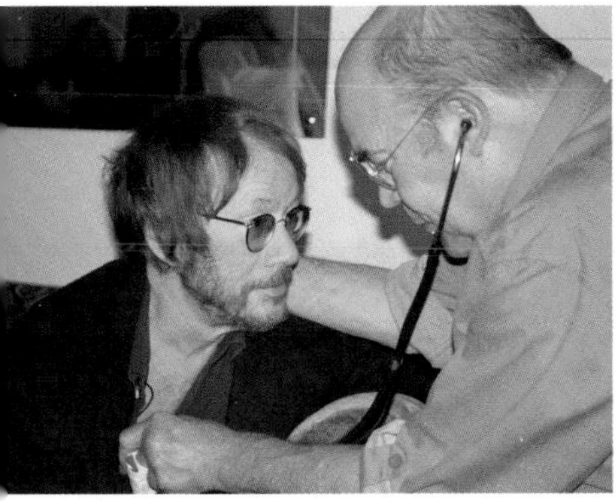

r Thompson and friend Warren Zevon after had been diagnosed with fatal mesothe- ancer. **Photo property of Crystal Zevon**

The Woody Creek Tavern was one of Hunter Thompson's famous haunts. The buffalo head behind him was a gift from Thompson to the Tavern. The poster on the wall is by his friend Tom Benton. **Photo by Bob Krueger**

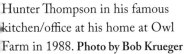

Hunter Thompson in his famous kitchen/office at his home at Owl Farm in 1988. **Photo by Bob Krueger**

The double-thumbed peyote fist cannon on the grounds of Owl Farm just prior to the second memorial service for Hunter Thompson—wherein his ashes were shot from the cannon—the creation of which was commissioned by actor Johnny Depp for the occasion. **Photo by Don Birnkrant**

Well-known artist Paul Pascarella, who designed the double-thumbed peyote fist Gonzo insignia for Hunter Thompson in the early 1970s, created this painting as an homage in the week following Thompson's death. **Photo property of Paul Pascarella**

> This wisdom applies equally to the struggle of putting together a FOURTH AMENDMENT CHALLENGE to one of the most menacing and insidious threats to the PERSONAL PRIVACY RIGHTS of every American or even Swede or Wetback who drives a car today on any public road between New York and Seattle or points south—THE ROGUE COP, the Foul Ball, the bigoted, half-bright bully—LIKE MARK FUHRMAN—who give all HONEST Law Enforcement Officers a BAD NAME.

Eighteen months later, to no one's immense surprise, a deal was struck whereby Hunter received a deferred prosecution as long as he didn't commit any major crimes for two years. (Instead he almost immediately went out and got into trouble in Boulder for what he claimed was accidentally spraying a man in the face with a fire extinguisher. That was quickly lowered to a petty offense and he pleaded no contest.) Back in Aspen he was also required to complete a level-one alcohol education class. At home. In his house. That determination produced a surprised collective guffaw in the courtroom, to which the DA basically shrugged. Hunter didn't withdraw his charges of prejudice on the part of Glidden nor constitutional violations in the conduct of the officers involved. The police continued to insist that no conspiracy against Hunter or illegal conduct was involved.

As part of the plea deal, Hunter issued the following statement and what he called The Sharp Necklace Agreement, signed by him and the district attorney, H. Lawson Wills:

> I despise drunk drivers just as much as I hate crooked cops. I fear anybody on the road who is out of control for any reason—and that would have to include, by universal agreement, public servants who use their badge and authority to settle personal grudges or enforce their political beliefs. This agreement we're executing today will serve as a Sharp Necklace to crooked cops as well as dangerous drunkards.

The agreement itself was as elaborately crafted as the Vietnam peace accords and consisted of six tit for tats. Aspen police Chief Tom Stephenson, a friend of Hunter's, was just glad, he said, "that Dr. Thompson's circus is over with. He needs to get on with what he does best—which absolutely doesn't include driving."

You could search long and hard and never come up with a more convoluted or unique conclusion to a drunk driving case in this country. I have no idea what Hunter spent on lawyers to achieve it, but if they had all billed him as they would have billed you or me, and we had paid, it would have been a hefty five figures.

When it came to matters other than driving, Hunter's legal issues ran the gamut. Gerry Goldstein remembers, "He was always on me about suing Garry Trudeau." Other examples included his disquiet over Sally Quinn's imputation about the amount of fiction in his political writings; a guilty plea to a misdemeanor possession bust in Florida in 1978; book, magazine, and film company payments and expenses contracts; frantic efforts to retain his credit cards when editors had—he insisted—failed to reimburse him for huge expense accounts; ruthless damages to rental cars, boats, hotels, and apartments; disturbing the peace by discharging a shotgun on the Aspen municipal golf course while playing a round with his friend CBS newsman Ed Bradley in 1987; setting off smoke bombs in the Woody Creek Tavern; allegedly attempting to intimidate a neighbor by shooting at his house in 1989; and writing to ask a judge for leniency in the case of a twenty-three-year-old woman who faced possible jail time for punching a jailer after her arrest for drunk driving in Pitkin County in 1990.

Many of the situations worked out without resorting to actual courtrooms or even formally employing a lawyer. Several of his attorney friends were usually willing to send notes or requests on his behalf on their firm's letterheads when they thought it appropriate, and often that was all it took. But his to-do lists were constantly populated with the names and numbers of lawyers for him to contact, usually underlined to reflect their urgency.

One of the other things that I suspect Hunter liked about lawyers was that they were worthy adversaries when the occasion demanded it and could give as good as they got. And when they couldn't, "It's always entertaining to watch them squirm," he said. He heard from attorneys frequently in adversarial situations ranging from editorial demands that he often equated with censorship to being notified of liens or attempts to collect debts he owed. One such letter, from one of the senior partners in a prestigious Los Angeles firm, arrived in January 1979, and he gave it to me with a thin smile, followed the next day by a note to pay something to the man. Obviously the letter had an impact as it calmly suggested the attorney found Hunter not just rude but somewhat pathetic and included lines to the effect of "Whatever it matters, your money does not make or break this office, and the attitude 'I really don't give a fuck' certainly arouses no sympathy from my end. Our office is not one to sue but rather to express compassion."

One of the most daunting legal messes Hunter faced was a case that he harped on for so long and often in print it hardly needs recounting. The gist was that on February 18, 1990, he was arrested for alleged third-degree sexual assault of porn film actress Gail Palmer-Slater, who had come to his house to interview him. He supposedly twisted her left breast trying to get her into his hot tub.

Milt Blakey, the district attorney, soon thereafter was dismissed and charged with perjury, unrelated to Hunter's case. Meanwhile, he used Palmer-Slater's allegations that she had seen Hunter plunge his face into a pile of white powder alleged to be cocaine or PCP and snort deeply while she was there to authorize an extensive search of his home that only yielded relatively small amounts of drugs: less than a tenth of a gram of coke, thirty-nine hits of LSD, four and a half ounces of pot, and four Valiums. Hunter suggested that the headline should be: "Lifestyle Police Raid Home Of 'Crazed' Gonzo Journalist; Eleven-Hour Search By Six Trained Investigators Yields Nothing But Crumbs."

Friends of Hunter's thought it indicated that his mind was still pretty sharp if he'd been able, as they suspected, to clean up most of his other contraband prior to a search that he seemed to know would happen. Given the amount and variety of drugs to have passed through his home in nearly thirty years at that point, many found it remarkable he could locate all the forgotten stashes and spilled excess. And almost everyone agreed there was no way that the amounts uncovered would have been so small had Hunter not tidied up the premises.

Complicating matters were four sticks of dynamite and three blasting caps that were also uncovered, along with a triple-beam scale and a .22 caliber machine gun. The result was three felony drug possession charges, one misdemeanor drug charge, one felony explosives possession charge, and a misdemeanor sexual assault charge. A felony drug use charge was dropped when Palmer-Slater couldn't positively identify the drugs she claimed she saw Hunter snort.

Hunter regarded this barrage with typical gravity at the beginning, ranting and fuming that he was set up and might go to prison because of a crooked DA and a bimbo porn star. I heard from very reliable sources that federal agents were actively seeking Hunter's arrest at the time. Soon enough, though, he turned the whole thing into the kind of theater that best suited his purposes. He arrived in a blond pig-tailed wig at the courthouse riding in a red convertible with the top down, elaborately pantomiming for the cameras as fans paraded in support of him. While it's unlikely this actually helped his case or pleased his well-known Denver lawyer Hal Haddon, whom Hunter called "The Wolf" after Harvey Keitel's character in the movie *Pulp Fiction,* all the charges were dismissed soon after court proceedings began, due to "discrepancies between sworn testimony and previous statements to investigators."

Greg Ditrinco wrote on the front page of the *Aspen Daily News,* "Most of Aspen seemed to stand up and cheer Wednesday afternoon when word ripped through town that sex and drug charges will be dropped against local anti-hero and writer Hunter S. Thompson."

Hunter was obviously exultant, hailing the outcome, naturally, as a victory for all Americans. But in spite of having previously conceded that he "wasn't born to be in court rooms. You have to get up too early," he also pronounced himself disappointed. "We had the ammunition, we would have had fun. I was really looking forward to going to court next time. I'm a warrior."

This was the pose, however difficult it was becoming to maintain, that endeared him to fans and lawyers everywhere. The latter rewarded him in their usual fashion when Gerry Goldstein later wrote to Hunter:

"What you did was important. Thank you for letting me be a small part of it. As J. Frank Dobie said: 'You'll do to ride the river with.'"

Hunter's reward to his lawyers was to employ them to threaten to sue the DA's office. On May 30, Haddon and Goldstein filed notice of intent to bring a twenty-two-million-dollar civil lawsuit against the district attorney's office for "malicious prosecution, gross negligence and criminal malfeasance." By August 22 that was amended to a warning from Haddon that Hunter would seek to recover an estimated one hundred twenty thousand dollars in legal costs ("Goldstein's jet fuel is already at sixteen thousand dollars," Hunter told the newspapers) and other unspecified damages. That suit was never formally filed.

Regardless of Hunter's long symbiotic relationships with lawyers, he often remained publicly scornful of them, to the extent that even a good friend such as Gerry Goldstein wondered if Hunter really ever liked him or not. I think one of the published references of Hunter's that sums up his feelings best came from his story about the Roxanne Pulitzer divorce trial in 1983, later anthologized in *Songs of the Doomed.*

> Bestiality is the key to it, I think. I have always loved animals. They are different from us and their brains are not complex, but their hearts are pure and there is usually no fat on their bodies and they will never call the police on you or take you in front of a judge or run off and hide with your money. . . . Animals don't hire lawyers.

Guns ("I Feel Lucky and I Have Plenty of Ammunition")

"I own property and I frequently shoot sporting guns, just for the practice. Practice is absolutely necessary for the expert shootist," wrote Hunter in his "Hey Rube" column in 2004. When I heard that he had shot himself, just over a year later, I thought it must have been a mishap. First because I agreed with our friend Sheriff Bob Braudis who later told me, "I never thought he'd cap himself." Second, Hunter was a little . . . accident prone. When you spend as much time as he did shooting guns in less than top mental shape, something bad can easily happen. Third, he was a lousy shot. For Hunter, I think biting the barrel might have been a practical decision, though others around him at the time talk of it being "military style." Whatever the case, it ensured the job got done.

That may sound cruel. But when you set out to shoot yourself, accuracy is important. And no one was going to say of Hunter what he had written about Ernest Hemingway in the *National Observer* in 1964: "He was a fine shot, even toward the end, when he was sick." Hunter was quoting Hemingway's friend Chuck Atkinson talking about the man who, even so, chose to kill himself with a shotgun.

It always struck me as odd that someone so unskilled with guns as Hunter should be so enamored of them. He was a good athlete and his eye-hand coordination always seemed up to other challenges. But in all the years that I shot guns with him and watched him do it, I never saw him hit much, especially at any distance.

He also wasn't an actual hunter in spite of his name. There were episodes with magpies, which he disliked for their fearless consumption of his peacocks' food. And I believe almost anyone could hit a magpie on the ground at ten paces with a twelve gauge. But he never went out to put meat on the table or trophies on his walls when I knew him. There are stories about him hunting in California and allusions in his own writing to hunting trips in Colorado when he was young. Still in all, he was never a very good shot.

This didn't stop him from doing it all the time and exaggerating about it under various guises, including his Raoul Duke persona in the opening paragraph of a 1970 piece for *Scanlan's*:

> Weapons are my business. You name it and I know it: guns, bombs, gas, fire, knives and everything else. Damn few people in the world know more about weaponry than I do.

What he loved most was the notion of him as a weapons freak and authority. Actual expertise wasn't the issue. He was always more interested in certain aspects of guns that were exhibited by the gift he received from his friends the Mitchell Brothers, who presented him with a Feinwerkbau Olympic championship air pistol, personally engraved with "For The Business We Have Chosen." As it happened, this was not long before one of the Mitchells shot and killed the other. But Hunter loved that gun for all that it represented: the edgework of their lives, true fraternity, and scary accuracy.

As early as 1962 Hunter was writing to his editor at the *National Observer* from Lima, Peru, about his belief in firepower. "Some S1/2&??& has been throwing rocks at my window all night and if I hadn't sold my pistol I'd whip up the blinds and crank off a few rounds at his feet."

Shooting was used by Hunter for many things. To get outdoors. To get the adrenaline pumping. To let off steam and create some mayhem. He also famously employed shooting as art, riddling posters of people such as J. Edgar Hoover, Michael Eisne, and himself, then splattering some paint on them in a frankly Steadmanesque manner and selling them for the "huge sums" he long envied his artist friends for receiving.

Gunplay as a backdrop for interviews, either print or video and with the likes of late-night talk show host Conan O'Brien and other notables, was a way of entertaining the interviewers and their ultimate audience, and also of hazing his guest. "Let's see how they react to this." Then you take them outside and blast away with Mac-9s at an old, blown-up Jeep Wagoneer in the field.

Being seen constantly shooting guns was a good layer on his militant Gene Skinner attitude, and also fun. He didn't have to leave his compound to do it and he genuinely loved it. Why not? With lots of whiskey, incendiary charges, tracer rounds, bootleg fireworks, and exotic herbs and stimulants, any afternoon and night could turn into the kind of party that was big hoots for everyone except the neighbors.

"I did, after all, have weapons," he wrote in the *Vegas* book. "And I liked to shoot them—especially at night, when the great blue flame would leap out, along with all that noise. . . . and, yes, the bullets, too. We couldn't ignore that. Big balls of lead alloy flying around the valley at speeds up to 3700 feet per second. . . . But I always fired into the nearest hill or, failing that, into blackness. I meant no harm; I just liked the explosions."

The grounds of Owl Farm always had the look of a psychotic sculpture garden, with perforated hot water heaters, signs, cans, wood, and other mostly inanimate objects strung around. Presiding over the ever-mutating shooting range was Hunter's old red Wagoneer, left by some woman or guilty of some failure (the stories changed) and set out to pasture in spectacular fashion. Even though it took some fifty-five hours to stage, "It was over in 22 seconds," wrote Hunter in "Orgy of the Dead," for one of his *San Francisco Examiner* columns, later included in his book *Generation of Swine*. "Nobody was injured and no animals were killed, despite the ominous presence of Russell Chatham, the famous meat-eating artist from Montana." The vehicle, wrote Hunter, "had been packed full of dynamite, soaked down with gasoline and then blasted at point-blank range for two hours . . ."

However, it ultimately required the services of Hunter's friend, George Stranahan, to finish the work. Stranahan later wrote in *The Woody Creeker* magazine, "There's some discrimination required when mixing whiskey and dynamite." They blew parts for hundreds of yards in every direction. The Wagoneer's shockingly substantial remnants then became ever more aerated from various weapons and ammunition over the years, ranging from black powder rifles and atlatls to .45 caliber hollow points and 30.06 rounds at close range.

"I've been on three networks this year, grinning and shooting . . . well, call them assault weapons," Hunter told me for a story in 1988. "It's crazy." Once was during an interview on ESPN that was spliced into the middle of the Aspen World Cup ski races. "They had me on right after Zurbriggen's run," he chuckled, naming the best ski racer in the world at the time. "The sponsors were enraged. They couldn't believe Beattie would feature me, talking about killing rich people and shooting guns, in the middle of a ski show. I never even mentioned the race."

Hunter's longtime neighbor, Bob Beattie, was a former U.S. Ski Team coach who became an ABC ski racing announcer and the owner of a successful television sports production company. He still lives just across the road from Hunter's place several hundred yards away and quite a bit lower, nestled down along Woody Creek. Lots of trees and shrubbery surround Beattie's house today that have grown up over the years, providing not just privacy but a shield from the noise of Hunter's shooting sprees and even the occasional stray bullet, which at one time or another plagued most of Hunter's neighbors.

Once again, even though Hunter often felt he was unfairly persecuted, he also recognized when he certainly could have gotten in a lot more trouble, such as over the matter of these errant shots. They were part of the package and I used to insist that you couldn't really call yourself a friend of Hunter's if he hadn't fired a gun at you. He famously, accidentally wounded his longtime personal assistant, Deborah Fuller, with buckshot while chasing a bear off the farm. It was at enough of a distance that it wasn't lethal or permanently disfiguring. Just a little Cheneyesque miscue, many years before the vice president's own.

He awakened Deborah, who for a time lived in my old cabin after I moved out, early one morning around 6:00 a.m. with frantic messages saying, "Deborah, there's a bear right outside your window," she recalls. "So I got up, half awake, played the messages back, and got worried. So I looked out at the dumpster at Hunter's and there was a black thing next to it that looked like the bear. I opened the door and saw Hunter standing on his porch. I opened the door with my right hand just as Hunter shot a shotgun into the dirt behind the bear. But at the same time the pellets ricocheted toward my door. Like a fool I opened the door at the same time," she says with a laugh. "And my right arm and leg got hit with pellets. I screamed 'You son of a bitch, you shot me.' And poor Hunter. I don't think I had ever seen him run so fast. He felt horrible." Later when the sheriff's deputy said that he understood the shooting was an accident, Fuller said, "Of course, I'm the last person he'd want to shoot. I'm his personal assistant and best friend."

The stories of Hunter shooting at trespassers and invited guests alike are legion. And the notion of a lunatic roaming the grounds at all hours firing randomly at anything that moved helped keep Owl Farm relatively free of intruders. It did, however, have its downside. I once arranged, while I was leaving town, for friends to pick up a decommissioned BMW of mine from Owl Farm and take it to Montana on a trailer. Hunter and I discussed this at length, and I called him again when my friends, some of whom he knew, were on their way to his place. Nevertheless, he greeted them with a shotgun and rained buckshot on them all the way out of the driveway. I suggested later that he might have just been firing over their heads, to get their attention. To a person all four insisted he was aiming straight at them. Today they think it's a great story, but they were incensed about it at the time.

There were also occasions when Hunter sent a round or two my way, just across his driveway. It was always very late, or very early, after multi-day binges and when women were involved. But the closest he came to actually doing me harm was all in the name of education. Before I ever moved out to Owl Farm he came by frequently to visit at my apartment in Aspen, set in a quiet grove alongside the Roaring Fork River. One time I had the music on, it was getting into the shank of the evening, and I brought out a new .45 caliber semiautomatic pistol to show him. But I made the mistake of handing it to him loaded, and he proceeded to give me a primer on proper gun handling.

Yes, I know how insane that sounds. But I was young then, and it seemed that if anyone could enlighten me in the etiquette of large handguns and mixed company, it would be Hunter, though technically, and just for the record, I hadn't really asked for his advice. He just commenced it by muttering, "Always clear the chamber before you give it to someone," which he did, ejecting a bullet, "and pop the clip," which he also did. "Then you're not handing some crazy fucker a loaded gun." He grinned knowingly.

As well he might have. One of the first stories Hunter ever told me about himself and guns was when he met his first mother-in-law. Not knowing she was coming, he had eaten acid, and Sandy was otherwise occupied when the phone rang announcing that mom was at the Aspen airport.

"It was horrible," he said. "I had to go pick her up, so I called Michael Solheim to drive me and wrapped my head in bandages, like a mummy, so no one would recognize me and try to talk to me, and she couldn't see how weird I was." He gave one of his lopsided grins at the thought. "When we got home I saw some magpies eating the peacock's food and went in and got my double-barreled shotgun and was hurrying back out when I almost physically ran into my mother-in-law. I was so startled I pulled both triggers and emptied the gun into the wood floor. There was this deafening goddamned roar and a bunch of smoke and splinters. It had to scare the shit out of her, but I just pushed on past and outside and shot some rounds at the birds, like that's the way we do it out here, and she never said a word."

Hunter, I believe, related this to me as a kind of parable of weapons safety, because when that gun discharged it was pointing at the floor, instead of, say, Mom, thus rendering the incident relatively harmless. It had just been instinctive for him to have a weapon aimed someplace safe while not using it, as on that night when he pointed the pistol in my apartment away from anything living and pulled the trigger to get the hammer uncocked.

This is just a reflex move once you've got an empty chamber. The only problem was that the chamber wasn't empty. The proper sequence, as Hunter knew but had been too distracted to remember, is to eject the clip *first,* then clear the chamber. Doing it the other way around only replaces one bullet with another. With a loud thunder in the late night, that bullet went straight into the volume control of my stereo's Marantz amplifier. After we stopped staring at each other in giddy shock, we found the slug, flattened like it had hit stone, under the amplifier that was still pumping out the Allman Brothers.

While I quickly straightened up the room, clearing tables of various legally tenuous sundries in case neighbors came to see if anyone was dead, Hunter remarked, "They've done studies that show it takes more than one shot for people to even be aware there's been gunfire, let alone know where it came from." He was right, of course. So instead of fending off curious cops, or anyone else, we were soon calling friends of his in the music industry to see if we could interest anyone in an idea for an amplifier ad. And thanks to his wise tutelage, I have never handed anyone a loaded weapon again.

There is no doubt that Hunter became more drawn to weapons as a political and personal statement when the peace-and-drugs culture of the 1960s gave way to the massacres of the late sixties and early seventies (including unarmed college kids at Kent State University and Jackson State and the Black Panthers in their beds) and a dark host of new political realities.

At times, as with everything for a man who was first and foremost a writer, Hunter's gun love also took on poetic overtones. Some of the shooting art, and even the videos and still pictures of it, achieve an odd grace and power. And his writing on the topic could flirt with verse. "A full moon tonight, and a cold bright sky above the long pool behind the Jerome Hotel," he wrote in 1976 in notes later published in *The Great Shark Hunt*. "The Milky Way looking down from so close that it looks like a madman with good reflexes could shoot the stars out of the sky, one by one, with something like a .264 Magnum or maybe a .220 Swift."

The most serious side to Hunter's view of guns that I ever saw was when I was visiting Tom Benton in his studio one night and Hunter showed up with an unusual-looking group of people in tow. There were three or four men and women, well-dressed, very straight, and grim. This was in 1981, not long after Ronald Reagan had been shot, and it turned out they were family and friends of Reagan's press secretary Jim Brady, who had been badly wounded in the shooting and was still in critical condition.

While Hunter was friends with Ron Reagan Jr., he obviously had no great fondness for his father. But like virtually everyone who knew Jim Brady, Hunter liked and respected him. I can't remember now who was there that night, but I feel like one of them was Brady's daughter or sister, and possibly her husband. They were still very upset and talking about the shooting and about gun laws. Hunter was subdued and sympathetic, to the point of even appearing shaken, which didn't happen often. And he was agreeing with his guests that we needed some kind of stronger gun laws in the country.

I'd been having these conversations about gun control with Hunter for a while. When guns are so widely available, who gets to say where personal protection leaves off and aggression begins? How can the police feel safe to do their jobs when every person they encounter may be armed? And how do you keep weapons away from the gangsters, murderers, and wack jobs like John Hinckley and Mark David Chapman?

In the end, we had concluded that these consequences were ones that had to be endured in order to ensure the rights of reasonable, ahem, farming and ranching folks such as Hunter and myself to have guns. It wasn't an entirely comfortable stance for a variety of reasons. Still, we felt it was imperative to uphold people's right to own weapons.

That notion was at odds with some of the other things Hunter believed, but there it was. Gun ownership and frequent gunplay as sport embodied the militancy in his political views, the man's-man credo that he tried to embody, the style of writing and reporting that he embraced and enlarged, the sense of security that he felt only he could provide in the weird world he had created for himself, and an activity that gave him great pleasure without too much cost or consequences (unlike drugs and women).

Now here he was, backsliding on all that in what seemed to me a less than honest way to appease these distraught victims. At first I figured he was just being polite and empathetic. But on that night he seemed particularly dark and mournful and angry at a world that would shoot someone like Brady. After he had harped for a while on gun legislation that would keep things like this from happening and Tom and I had kept our peace, I finally called him on it.

"As tragic as this is, which we all agree," I pointed out, "is it only time for new laws when it happens to someone you know? This goes on a hundred times a day all across the country, but we don't want to do anything about it until it happens to someone important?"

"Maybe it shouldn't be going on a hundred times a day," he snapped back, glaring at me. Benton shrewdly went back to work on some of his screen paintings, and Hunter's friends looked aggrieved. I knew I was out of line, but that rarely shuts me up.

"No, maybe it shouldn't. We've talked about it," I reminded him. "I'm just not sure how much sympathy I can work up for someone who puts himself in the line of fire like that."

The room got very quiet. I couldn't take it back. "I have friends who have been shot, too," I babbled lamely. "I still don't think we should start banning handguns because of it."

Hunter looked at me like I was drunk. Sloppy drunk. I wasn't, I was just trying to hold him to the standard he held everyone else to. Obviously this was not the appropriate occasion for that. I felt like an ass, but it was easy to get crosswise with him when he was in that mood. And so was I.

He and his friends left in a huff, and Tom and I talked about it and decided he was just posing. His gun use and advocacy did nothing but pick up pace after that, so I guess we were right. Ultimately, we all agreed that the Brady Bill that finally made it through Congress wasn't a terrible thing, probably because it had been watered down from what was being talked about that night in Tom's studio.

By the new century, Hunter was more convinced than ever that good people were under siege and might have no other recourse than to defend themselves to the death. "The other shoe is about to drop, and it may be extremely heavy. The time has come to be strong. The fat is in the fire. Who knows what will happen now?" he asked in "When War Drums Roll," for an ESPN column just one week after September 11, 2001. "Not me, buster. That's why I live out here in the mountains with a flag on my porch and loud Wagner blaring out of my speakers. I feel lucky and I have plenty of ammunition. That is God's will, they say, and that is also why I shoot into the darkness at anything that moves. Sooner or later I will hit something Evil, and feel no Guilt. It might be Osama Bin Laden. Who knows?"

He thought it more likely it would be his own government coming after him yet again. Eventually what he did hit, shooting into one of his darkest moments of all, was himself. And I'd have given even odds on him missing that one too. It would somehow be more palatable to me, albeit less romantic, if it had been just a stupid accident.

Money

One of the reasons Hunter was attracted to writing was because, in theory, it meant he could work for himself. Many of us have been seduced by that lie. It only becomes true at a rarified level that most writers never achieve. When you can truly be writing only *what* you want, *when* you want, and still supporting yourself in the manner you would like, then you have succeeded as a writer on the business side. And that is very uncommon.

Certainly Hunter reached the point in his profession where he had the right to expect that he should be rewarded with a nice living. And he was. Why he never really thought that was the case is open to discussion. Anyone who spent as much time with him as I did, or made a thorough examination of his correspondence, his relationships with lawyers and agents and his life in general, knows that one of his searing preoccupations in life was with money. Welcome to the club. It's just that lots of the people in that club haven't generated Hunter's amount of income during their lives.

"It was always that way when I was around him," says Deborah Fuller. "There never seemed to be enough money for all of his responsibilities, not to mention his generosity toward others. He would always, as a lot of authors do, live beyond his means. He'd get a new contract and that was great and he'd catch up on outstanding commitments and spend the rest completing the next assignment. And he was, as I say, generous to a fault. It was important to him to have a full frig of beer and food and everything else when people came over. Gifts for family and friends. That's just who he was."

We talked about money a lot, and he always insisted he wasn't that ambitious in terms of glory or achievement and just wanted to make money in the easiest and fastest possible way. The disturbing implication was that it's quite possible that if he had succeeded more lavishly on the financial side with anything else, he might never have written a word.

However, the evidence of his life suggests just the opposite, since he wrote almost compulsively for much of his waking life. But he also jumped at a lot of schemes and business plans on a regular basis because he could see people all around him making money like they were printing it themselves, and he wanted in on it. His friend Jimmy Buffett turned a devoted musical following into a very successful cottage industry of Parrothead products, concert tours, and best-selling books. Jack Nicholson, whom Hunter respected immensely, makes many millions on every movie. Norman Mailer, Tom Wolfe, and Kurt Vonnegut never seemed to have financial worries. The list, in Hunter's mind, was endless. Jim Harrison sold his novellas to the movies for a small fortune. Tom McGuane took his book and movie money and bought ranches in

Montana. Russell Chatham sold his paintings for princely sums, drove big cars, indulged in elaborate gourmet meals, and "generally comported himself like Samuel Coleridge," wrote Hunter.

When I first met him, you could not have persuaded me that Hunter wasn't one of these gilded artists, famous and flush on every front; in part, because I was so young everyone else looked rich to me. But also because Hunter just seemed like he *should* be doing well, given all his writing successes. And he played the part of a moneyed artiste like a natural. He seemed to own his own house outright, bought drinks for everyone, was generous with his drugs, drove a nice car, and was famous. He reminded me of what I always heard about Dan Jenkins, the great sports and golf writer. Jenkins would stay out drinking with the golfers and socializing into the wee hours, after all the other writers had already left to file their pieces, then retreat to his room and spend all night writing another award-winning story. He got lots of good anecdotes in those bars, then worked long and hard but never let anyone see it. It just seemed to come effortlessly, which is the gift of great writing. That's how Hunter used to strike me, and I assumed the money poured in as easily as the stories seemed to pour out. Clearly this was the naïveté of someone who was not yet a professional.

Why wasn't Hunter ever as rich as he thought he should be, and maybe deserved? The reasons are legion. First, how many people are as successful as they think they should be? But beyond that, writing, except for a small handful, isn't especially enriching. Even for scribes on Hunter's level, it isn't fuck-you money—it's not blockbuster movie money, island-owning drug dealer money, major athlete money, or famous painter money, unless you're Stephen King, J. K. Rowling, Dan Brown, or the latest self-help guru. Hunter never sold in those realms and did not reasonably expect to.

On the other hand, during forty-plus years he did produce a dozen books, dispensing millions of them to the world in multiple languages. *Fear and Loathing in Las Vegas* was still selling sixty thousand to seventy thousand copies a year while he was alive. Not all of his books sold as well, of course, but he was reasonably prolific. After a while his works were mostly collections. *The Curse of Lono,* one of his last wholly original books, didn't sell well and was never reprinted until 2005 when it came out in a giant coffee-table-book format in England. *Screw-jack,* which was at first issued as a private printing for friends and acquaintances then as a public offering, is so tiny (fifty-eight very small pages with very large type) and almost offensively priced at fifteen dollars and so warped it repelled many potential readers, and was also not a big seller. It was left to ten books to do most of the heavy lifting in terms of making a living for Hunter. If his contracts for some of those weren't always the best (he complained that he got very little for *Hell's Angels* and that it was never promoted or reprinted as it should have been), he still made a lot of money throughout his career. So what happened to it?

Obviously his lifestyle was that of someone with substantial disposable income, even though that wasn't his actual situation. Like a trust funder who's always spending three months ahead of his stipend checks, Hunter's money rarely arrived in sufficient quantities to compensate for the outgo. He had a son, several ex-wives, and a mother and brothers he sent money to when he could. There were note payments on the cars, plus the cost of ammunition and imported cigarettes, fine whiskey, and girlfriends. Hunter also liked to travel, and not in steerage. He stayed at nice hotels, rented flashy rides, ate well, and liked his toys. Not all of that could be put on an expense account, no matter how hard he tried, as illustrated in one of many notes to me: "Call L'Ermitage Hotel in L.A. to get the amount of my recent bill plus rental of 450 SL Mercedes for 5 days—all this is on AmExp, + should be billed to Paramount inre: Cg. Key."

Hunter's impulse-laden expenditures were burdened by two other significant habits I've already discussed. Good drugs and good lawyers are rarely cheap and never get comped forever. Those are bills you either have to pay or find new connections and new lawyers, a tiresome and time-consuming process that always involves a degree of trust in circumstances where that doesn't come easily. Along with that two-million-dollar lifetime coke tab I cited earlier, he probably ran up another million on legal assistance, never mind that he neglected to pay at least half of it. It was no wonder, in the end, that he always seemed broke.

Most writers have a tendency to work their positions for as many freebies as possible, often as much on principle as anything else. If a twenty-five-thousand-dollar goodie bag will lure actors who make twenty million a movie to be presenters at the Oscars, then free merchandise, food, and trips will certainly chum less-well-funded writers into almost any project. Hunter was no exception.

Hunter, like many writers, was also acutely conscious of bringing attention to the places and people he wrote about. Just as he felt that mentioning his lawyers in his stories was a form of advertising they would never get otherwise, he believed that doing the same about the places where he ate and drank and vacationed should be rewarded. It wasn't just that he wanted to be accurate when mentioning Duke Zeibert's in Washington, D.C. He wanted to go there himself, gather material, be treated well, and not made to pay much, if anything, beyond what his expense account would cover.

The same held true around Aspen, whether he was at the Jerome Bar or the Woody Creek Tavern. He knew when he mentioned those hangouts in his work it brought them business, people wanting to be where Hunter and the other stars were. So Hunter ran tabs anywhere they'd let him and then put off paying them as long as he could. His reasoning was that a certain amount, if not all, of what he owed would eventually be forgotten in return for the publicity he provided. This was true, up to a point. But eventually no one could justify endless days of hundred-dollar-plus tabs without some remuneration. A dozen Wild Turkeys for himself and perhaps equal numbers of drinks for friends, along with an extended lunch, multiple times a week, added up quickly and equaled more than any reasonable manager or owner could think would be covered by an occasional mention in one of Hunter's stories.

The result was that Hunter spent most of his life being dunned. In some cases it was good humored enough, in some cases not. He was never actually refused service at the Jerome or the Tavern, for instance. And he developed his own way of dealing with many of these situations. Very early on, when all he had was a Carte Blanche credit card and his privileges kept being suspended when he was way overdue, he told me how he handled it. "When I have the money to settle my account," he explained with a happy grin, "I tell them I'll send them a check immediately, but only on the condition that they give me back my card. And that's what their business is, letting people run up big tabs and then sticking them with all that interest. So they always give me back the card. And if they don't, they don't get paid."

It was a technique he applied to other accounts as well, such as in a note from 1978 he wrote me about getting in touch with an officer at the local bank. "I must call Harvey Hoff in/re: getting another loan if I pay this one off now." This approach had its roots in several aspects of the way Hunter did business. First, he never had enough money, so he had to figure out how to stretch it. Second, along with others of his and my generation, he had grave misgivings about how ethical it was for banks and credit card companies to be charging usurious interest rates while their chief executives made millions and their customers faced ruin just trying to survive.

This attitude was often adopted by those who couldn't pay their bills anyway and were looking for good excuses not to. It also had some legitimacy, however, as was illustrated every time one of these companies took him up on his offer to only pay a part of what he owed, or to pay everything as long as his line of credit was kept open. He was just ahead of his time. Today, such strategies have been formalized for years by agencies whose sole function is to negotiate settlements with banks, credit card companies, and others that people have become hopelessly indebted to beyond their ability to ever pay.

Of course there are problems with living like this. Hunter spent too much of his time haggling over bills, working himself into a daily lather over the unfairness of their demands and his inadequate income. It colored his moods as often as it does those of anyone facing that constant stress. It shamed and embarrassed him, and that quickly turned to rage. And while he stomped around and whined, he was always plotting how to free up what little cash he ever had available to meet his most pressing obligations.

"Hunter always cried poor," says George Stranahan, who along with Bob Craig first leased Hunter what became Owl Farm. "It was for about half of the going rate, and I got a check sometimes, or a little note from Hunter to compensate. Finally they quit coming at all and we had the Frank Discussion. And Hunter said something like, 'I'd feel a lot better about this if it was a lease/purchase arrangement.' So I said OK, and still no checks. He told me, 'It hurts me more to have to write you those checks, than it hurts you if you don't get them. So in terms of the overall collective hurt, me not paying you hurts less.' And I understood him," laughs George. "So finally I just pretty much gave him the property, but I kept the right of first refusal of any legitimate offer on it, for 50 percent of that offer."

Even that wasn't the end of things, however. A few years later, "The fucker wound up with an eighty-thousand-dollar tax bill he couldn't pay, and his lawyer came to me and said 'We have to keep him out of jail, we'll sell you the back sixty acres at half of whatever they're worth,'" relates George. "And Sandy was leaving and wanted a trade for her interest in Hunter's property for some other property I had. So I made her the same deal, with first buy-back rights, but she couldn't sell it for five years. Eighteen months later I had to buy it back and at one point I ended up sending fifteen hundred dollars a month to both her and Hunter for property I gave them."

Beyond the obvious distraction that constantly haggling over money with your friends introduces into your daily life, it makes things hard on people it shouldn't. The waitresses at the Woody Creek Tavern, most of whom adored Hunter, also frequently complained that they never made much in tips from him. He was always generous about writing in a tip at the end of any visit, but he so rarely paid those tabs that by the time he did they had been reduced to the point where he wasn't even covering what he had consumed, let alone the services of those who provided it. That wasn't his intention and he'd rail about the businesses themselves screwing the staff, then try to make it right by buying presents for the waitresses. The simplest way to have handled things would have been to put everything on his tab except the tips and to pay those in cash on the spot. But he rarely did.

For a man who prided himself on taking care of his friends and the working people around him, this bothered him. But it was easier to invent some labyrinthine justification for it than to do the right thing. This was a pattern throughout his life. After creating some bad problem, he'd devote his considerable intellect to making it someone else's fault, then spend still more time letting everyone know why it wasn't his responsibility, and whose he thought it was.

On the other hand, one of the things Hunter valued in other people was when they paid their debts, especially gambling ones. When he got to know the legendary yippie, writer, and politico Abbie Hoffman years after his brief flurry of fame, Hunter spoke well of him to me and capped it by saying, "He lost a hundred-dollar football bet to me and he paid it. That says a lot."

Such things were matters of honor and they meant something to him. So he tried to be good about paying the bills that he thought were important to him and the people he owed. I know it pained him to always be scrambling to cover his action. It pissed him off and put him in turmoil, and he developed ways of coping with that. Often it was simply to believe that the person or companies he owed didn't really need or deserve to be paid or had done something malicious and rotten to him anyway, so fuck them. At least for the moment. That way he could turn it into a little joke, some repartee, and a drawn-out stall until he could get square or at least make a payment. The amount of energy and time this required was ridiculous after a while, but he looked at it as making him money every time he was able to pare down or completely eliminate some debt. Which was true, but the havoc it inflicted rarely seemed worth it.

Hunter was usually fair with me. Although it could be like pulling teeth to get him to make necessary repairs and improvements to the cabin, that isn't rare among landlords and they eventually got done. He didn't often owe me money for long because we were friends and he knew I never took advantage of him. The fact that he died owing me money was something I wrote off to bad timing and not malice. Even though he'd owed it to me for seventeen years.

When I moved out of Owl Farm for the last time, he bought my old 2800 BMW, a very fast but unlucky car that I prized. Before he finished paying for it he drove it into a ditch, messed it up, and lost affection for it. This was the car I tried to have some friends pick up and take to Montana for me, and he shot at them and called them thugs. After that he pulled it around behind his house where he kept it undriven and semihidden and refused to ever discuss it with me again. I half expected it to turn up in my driveway someday, resurrected as a gift, and I like to think that his suicide just preempted that plan.

As much effort as Hunter put into avoiding paying some of his bills, he also devoted his time to other enterprises he hoped would produce an income. Many of them were literary in nature or connected to his writing. There were almost constant requests for him to write or be interviewed for all kinds of outlets, from *Quote* to the United Kingdom's *Telegraph Sunday Magazine* to the local Grass Roots television channel, not to mention talk show hosts Charlie Rose, Conan O'Brien, and so on.

In 1977 there was talk of Warner Brothers' putting out a recording consisting of selections from some of Hunter's speaking engagements in the United States and Australia. That got Hunter very excited, even though the concept may have originated with someone who had never actually heard him speak, an art that was not, as I've noted before, his strength. In the end something about the plan didn't pay off.

Over the years, we worked on some promising projects that Hunter could do while never leaving the Farm. One was *The Gonzo Book of Etiquette,* a radical updating of Emily Post that would instruct modern people on such niceties as how to tell your parents that your significant other is a drug dealer; how to cope with partiers or guests who won't leave when the festivities are over; how to respond, legally and shrewdly, to various forms of police interrogation (the "What Marijuana?" chapter as we called it); what to wear to a wedding between a rock star and a stripper; how to explain what a Deering grinder full of coke is to your mother-in-law; how to get the car keys away from a drunk without being stranded; using gun safety around drug abusers, and so on. I don't know why he was never able to sell that concept.

Some deals, such as with the *Omnibus* television program in England that Ralph Steadman helped set up in 1978, worked out well. Hunter was paid several thousand dollars plus expenses to let himself be filmed at Owl Farm and in Las Vegas for a couple of weeks. Ralph sent him a postcard with a pitch, then followed it with a telegram: "HUNTER STOP NIGEL FINCH TO MAKE PENULTIMATE FILM OF YOU FOR BBC STOP FLIES OUT NEXT MONDAY TO SEE YOU STOP MEET HIM OFF PLANE ASPEN STOP RING ME FOR DETAILS STOP RALPH STOP GOD BLESS." Obviously Ralph's idea of the show's paying for a voyage on the *QE2* hadn't panned out, but the project still put some money in Hunter's bank account with minimal effort on his part.

The best financial bumps of all came when he'd get a contract for foreign book sales, TV, movie, stage rights, or some other sale of work he'd already completed and didn't have to adapt or rework. They weren't always huge checks, but it was like collecting residuals. He told me, "Imagine if you were a big weed dealer and you sold someone a ton of pot for a quarter of a million dollars, and then every once in a while someone else came along and paid you another ten or twenty grand for the same load. I love it."

The stage version of *Vegas* opened after protracted negotiations on May 11, 1982, in London. The U.S. premiere was in Chicago in 1991, with John Cusack directing and Ralph Steadman doing the sets. Both were mildly successful but also included the inevitable squabbles with Hunter over money.

His books were translated into a variety of languages. The Spanish version of Hell's Angels is *Los Ángeles del Infierno: Una Extraña y Terrible Saga,* with a really ghastly biker illustration on the cover. It was first published in 1980, and Hunter gave me a copy with the inscription "Jay, Happy Birthday . . . + how's <u>this</u> for weird? It reads better in the Spanish, I think—especially the part where they all eat shit + die. Okay. Be careful. And for Christ's sake, get rich. Yr. Friend, Hunter (HST)"

Getting rich was a goal a lot of us shared, and it always seemed possible. I wrote, taught skiing, and was a consultant for various people and organizations around the world. They were exciting times and everyone Hunter and I knew seemed poised on the verge of making it big. Just like him. I sometimes think that the prospect of making it, together with our friends, was more important than the money itself, but I doubt Hunter ever felt like that.

Along with trying to keep his writing train on track, Hunter was always open to other business possibilities. Sometimes that took the form of outright loans from anyone and everyone he thought had lots of money and liked or owed him. He had several steady patrons, and his to-do notes were sometimes little more than lists of whom to ask for money.

To be fair, for all his "lazy hillbilly" protestations, Hunter did put in the time and work to try something different from writing and wheedling. His ideas were frequently unproductive or patently unreal, but they were always entertaining. In 1983 he and Tom Benton announced plans to publish a Celebrity Map of Aspen, listing "at least fifteen super-stars" along with their addresses, post office box numbers, unlisted phone numbers, sexual preferences, drug habits, and where their stashes were hidden. "This is the clean industry we have been looking for," said Tom. "Celebrity tours are a year round attraction that will lift Fat City out of its current slump as well as strengthen our competitive position in the marketplace."

"This will be a memorable event in the life of a Fat City tourist," added Hunter. "It is a unique, quality resort experience well worth its modest cost and the proceeds will go to worthwhile charities." Use of the map, written in invisible ink, would have required special codes, plus pissing on them and then holding them over a flame in order to read. Alas, in the end it was all just an April Fool's joke in the *Aspen Daily News*.

On a more practical note there was Hunter's merchandizing, for which he was really something of a pioneer in his profession. The first gonzo T-shirts hit the market in Aspen in 1978, sporting his soon-to-be trademarked insignia, designed by his friend, artist Paul Pascarella: a dagger with a two-thumbed, peyote-button fist for a handle and the word "Gonzo" as the haft. They were quality T-shirts, the printing was good for the time, and soon everyone in the valley who wanted one had one. Nevertheless, Hunter lost money on the deal and spent years trying to refine the methods of peddling accessories in the days before e-commerce Web sites were at everyone's fingertips. In a long memo to one of his assistants at the time he wrote a few telling lines: "Call Patty about her plan to sell Gonzo Tee-Shirts—But this involves getting all the books, money, stock from Barry + Elaine—somebody owes me at least a receipt for about a $6000 loss on this gig."

Merchandizing, especially with Hunter at the helm, wasn't easy, and I took it as evidence of how seriously he needed money for him to keep at it with such diligence, however jangled. In an era when even moderately aggressive self-promotion was considered selling out, long before Dylan and Beatles and Rolling Stones songs were serving as advertising jingles, this risked—and indeed drew—serious criticism. It was hard to imagine Ken Kesey hawking T-shirts or Tom Wolfe or Norman Mailer making buttons with their famous quotes on them. By the same token, they weren't writers who came packaged like rock stars either. And rock stars were making extremely successful ancillary careers out of T-shirts, ball caps, posters, and anything else their fans would pay a decent price for. Part of Hunter's justification for peddling his persona was that others were selling unlicensed Gonzo products and making money, so why not him? It seemed the only way to fight it, and his speaking events created built-in marketing opportunities.

Ten years later he was still wrestling with the whole endeavor, never really getting ahead on it but never losing enough to totally discourage him, when he hired Greg Ditrinco. "Hunter was a buddy of Jimmy Buffett's," recalls Dintrinco. "And Buffett has a Midas touch. He was telling Hunter to start a newsletter to sell the accessories and clean up. They had crazy huge markups on the products. And either Hunter was jealous of Buffett or Buffett prodded him into it, I don't know how that worked. But he decided to do a newsletter. He already had the products, nice stuff, Gonzo insignias on coats, T-shirts, and so on, he just needed a vehicle to sell them. And Buffett told him that a newsletter was how he did it, it was much better than a straight-out catalog. I was one of a long line of short-lived editors for the newsletter and lasted two or three months. There was no newsletter actually published that I can remember."

The problem, as usual, wasn't with the concept so much as the execution. One of Hunter's favorite quotes was, "Between the idea and the reality . . . falls the shadow," by T. S. Eliot. Never did that seem truer than on most of his elaborately conceived business deals.

"Hunter or one of his assistants would throw me three thousand words for an eight-hundred-word hole in this newsletter," says Ditrinco, explaining the mechanics of the business and why they rarely worked. "He was a freaking word processor, there was never any shortage of copy. And he clearly embraced the fax machine. I'd get all this copy from one of his handlers, I'd try to make it fit and then fax it back or make a live drop somewhere. He'd mumble at me over the phone or scrawl something back without ever reading it. Then at three in the morning I'd hear my fax kick on, then something on a CIA or White House letterhead would come out, 'I'm gonna chase you across the frozen tundra like the rat you are—Don't touch my copy!' It would be terrible," chuckles Greg, "these terrible remarks, and his handlers would try to appease me with some money or posters or something."

Other opportunities, of sorts, would come Hunter's way that he found equally hard to make work. Adventure Travel tried for several years to get him on a complimentary raft trip on the Zambezi, one of those luxe expeditions that cost everyone else ten grand even back then, and all he had to do was write a blurb about it in their catalog. Any other story he got out of it was his, plus the free trip. It never happened because he could never get it together, blaming scheduling conflicts between his itineraries and the rainy seasons in Africa.

He did eventually manage to craft a deal with the J. Peterman catalog company to write a very good, very short piece about their Waxed Cotton Portmanteau Jacket.

> It was around midnight. The rumpled brown jacket lay on the pool table. I grabbed it and stuffed the pockets with bundles of cash, then streaked up Van Ness Avenue to the City Cafe.
>
> Skinner was in a corner booth. He ceremoniously removed his Super Bowl ring, slid it across the table toward me, and sighed. "Got a flight to Costa Rica in three hours. Take the ring, give me the jacket and all the cash you have on you."
>
> Skinner never asks for favors. He makes trades.
>
> I took off the coat and handed it to him. "Don't hock the ring," he said, sliding out of the booth toward a waiting limousine.
>
> "As long as I get the jacket back," I said.

It made for a great page in the catalog and I always hoped he got more than just a free $179 coat out of it. But I wouldn't be surprised if he took whatever else he might have had coming in merchandise.

By the early 1990s Hunter had turned his prodigious energies to art. In the same way that Buffett's successes had inspired Hunter's merchandizing, and Jim Harrison's novella sales to Hollywood had driven him to film, so too his longtime envy over the successes of his artist friends such as Tom Benton and Russell Chatham led him into art. Plus it was something he could do with guns.

His initial efforts consisted of simply setting up various objects or images and shooting them. When I pointed out that this was difficult to distinguish from simple target practice, he muttered for a while and then began to elaborate. Specific posters were chosen, paint was applied and the results were framed in innovative ways. The first piece he ever had shown for sale in 1991, titled *The Director*, was of J. Edgar Hoover, riddled with bullet holes, splashed with paint in a stylistic cross between Jackson Pollock and Ralph Steadman, and mounted on a mirror and some barn wood. Aspen Art Gallery owner Mary Grasso, who displayed the piece, earnestly described it as, "very artistic. He uses paints and a variety of guns and explosives." These were techniques most other artists had either overlooked or not admitted.

Another portrait, of right-wing Republican senator Barry Goldwater, Grasso described as "the most gruesome thing you've ever seen. He shot out the eyes and mouth. It's violent. It's scary." Always cutting edge (whether intentionally or not), Hunter was just doing what he had done for years, but it happened to fit in well with the nihilist, slacker/punk mood of the moment, not to mention the celebrity-art trend in general, proving he usually knew his market well.

Stunningly, to me, Hunter's work immediately fetched up to ten thousand dollars from fans. "People are obsessed with him," said Grasso, "and anything he does visually is a collector's item." Prices quickly escalated to twenty thousand dollars, claimed Grasso, while Hunter merely smirked and brandished one of his guns. His mediums soon involved three-dimensional sculptural forms, but the market for his work inevitably began to shrink.

I actually liked what he did. It had a modern art patina and appealed to my anarchic tastes in general. I would have bought something if they hadn't been so pricey. Or I hadn't burned all his IOUs. Mainly I wished I'd saved the old hot water tank he tied to my bumper when I got married and had him shoot it a few more times and sign it.

After the Aspen Art Gallery closed, Hunter was next represented by David Floria, soon-to-be curator of the Aspen Art Museum, who had a gallery and frame shop in Woody Creek next door to the Tavern. He regularly had Hunter's work, which was in very limited supply, in stock. In 1994 David hosted a seminal show featuring Hunter along with William Burroughs who was also using guns in some of his creations.

"I went to Liberty, Kansas, to meet Burroughs, and it was a real pilgrimage point, on the circuit of those kinds of places," recalls Floria. "Kurt Cobain and Ornette Coleman and Alan Ginsburg had all just been there, separately, but recently. There was art everywhere, and Burroughs had already had a couple of shows in New York, and some of his things had gunshot holes in them. So he was into it. He was a trip, in fairly good shape, smoking pot, and drinking whiskey and who knows what else. Kind of the Hunter regimen. And we had some of his work shipped to Woody Creek." The show was a big hit and CNN sent someone out who interviewed Floria and Hunter and followed Hunter through his process at Owl Farm. The result was an eight-minute clip on the news, a big chunk of time for television.

"Hunter sold quite a few pieces, and some of them definitely for twenty thousand dollars," confirms Floria, who did all the mounting and framing. "We sold more of Tom Benton's 'Hunter Thompson for Sheriff' posters for five hundred dollars. If he shot them or wrote on them they went up to two grand. But the bigger pieces weren't an easy sell," he notes. "I heard that one of the Tysons, from the chicken family in Arkansas, bought one for twenty thousand. I think it was mostly people like that, rich Hunter Thompson cultists who had the money."

While there is no evidence that even Hunter put his art in a context other than just financial ("Art should be more fun," he often said. "Artists take themselves too seriously."), it can be done. "I see connections with performance art, abstract expressionism, even folk art, and of course political art," says Floria with amusement. "His pieces always had messages. And they were like the ultimate action paintings."

As usual, this wasn't a traditional genre. It might not have originated with Hunter, as his style of writing did, but it wasn't widely practiced and he did make good money at it for a while without much work. I've always felt that the most emblematic and ongoing piece of his art was the blown-up Wagoneer that was regularly used for target practice by all kinds of friends and famous visitors. Properly presented it could turn from just more hillbilly lawn trash into his most enduring sculpture, worth who knows how much, and guaranteed to attract the attention of any homeowner's association wherever you tried to display it.

By the mid-1990s Hunter had less time for creating art, which jibed well with the falling demand for it. He moved on to other projects, including on-the-bottle copy for George Stranahan's Broadway Brewing. George decided to combine the artwork of Ralph Steadman with Hunter's words to create provocative presentations on beers such as Road Dog Ale. I think once again Hunter took his payment in product.

Even getting their initial offering of Doggie Style beer accepted as a national brand, because of its name, was a feat, said George. Then Road Dog came along with Hunter's endorsement: "Good beer, no shit. Good people drink good beer. Just look around you in any public barroom, and you will quickly see: Bad people drink bad beer. Think about it." George didn't even bother to apply to the Bureau of Alcohol, Tobacco, and Firearms for approval to ship it interstate since he was sure they wouldn't grant it for reasons relating to obscenity laws. At first they changed the words to "Good Beer, No Censorship." Eventually the American Civil Liberties Union took their case and won. So the beer, with its "No Shit" label is today shipped wherever they want it, another landmark case in Hunter's long campaign for free speech.

The one most obvious way to make money that surrounded Hunter on a constant basis was what we informally referred to as "The Business." Everything about drug dealing fascinated him. Not in a groupie kind of way, but in terms of kindred spirits, good material for his writing, and the sense of "that could be me" that seemed to always pervade his attitude. In the same way that many people, rightly or wrongly, are pretty sure they could be great writers if they wanted to be—regardless of whether they've ever written much of anything in their lives—Hunter was convinced that he could have been a big-time drug dealer. He was, however, even more convinced that he didn't want to run those kinds of risks. As far as I know, he never participated in The Business on any kind of meaningful level.

This is in spite of the fact that many people tried to get him involved, for whatever reasons. Some of them undoubtedly were cops. Hunter was considered a priority target by the Drug Enforcement Agency. Some people thought he'd like to be on the inside of a good story. He got letters often, phrased as obviously as, "hoping to get your interest in a gardening possibility, wink, wink." Others thought he'd like to finance some deals and make some easy money. "Yeah, we do it every week, regular as clockwork," I'd hear someone pitching him at the bar. At the bar, no less. And if he wanted to kick in ten or twenty grand they'd double it for him and more, just because they dug him. Right. Most of the dealers who wanted to meet him figured that regaling him with tales of the trade was a good way to endear themselves and keep him current with a world he admired and wrote about. If he chose to ask to become directly involved, then so be it. But he never did.

I think this was the biggest temptation in life Hunter didn't succumb to. But it was hard. He was very attracted to the juice, the thrill, and the adrenaline, as well as the glamorous and profitable lifestyle of drug dealing. Not that his own lifestyle wasn't plenty glamorous, but it seemed to him to have more obligations, more people telling him what to do, and less money. Also less excitement. When he wrote about the dope business he was often in south Florida, and he did it as though he was a player and Gene Skinner or someone similar was his contact. In addition to stories in *Rolling Stone* and columns for the *Examiner,* two unfinished novels/film treatments were dedicated to the trade, *Cigarette Key* and *The Silk Road.*

Hunter was constantly surrounded by a tribe of wild boys and beautiful women who lived the life, always had drugs and guns and parties, stories they could only share with each other, and a general disdain for any rules that weren't their own. Many of them played it up big for Hunter and he bought it. "Fucking so-and-so made a million dollars last year," he told me one night at a party in the late 1970s. I was impressed. "On three loads. I couldn't write three books in a year if I tried." He knew there was more to it than that, but he still needed someone to envy. And given his own fame and good fortune, there weren't that many other occupations or people that he thought had it better than he did.

As with other people I've known and read about, Hunter liked to pretend he was involved in the kinds of worlds he never fully comprehended. In Vietnam he was intrigued by the notion that the Viet Cong leaders thought he was CIA. In "Whooping It Up with the War Junkies," anthologized in *Songs of the Doomed,* he describes a press briefing he attended in Vietnam in 1975 conducted by the Viet Cong shortly before they seized control of Saigon. The presiding Vietnamese colonel says that of the press corps, only "the many American military personnel posing as journalists" had anything to worry about. "He had used this phrase three or four times," wrote Hunter, "and each time I noticed that he was looking directly at me, which was not especially surprising, to me or anyone else, because if there was anybody among the hundred or so journalists . . . who looked like every career VC colonel's perfect image of an ex-Green Beret major trying to pass for a journalist, it was me."

Here was a man who virulently detested almost every aspect of the CIA yet didn't mind looking and acting like a spook or being misconstrued as one if it made him seem more mysterious and interesting. After all, a number of journalists worked at least occasionally for various intelligence services around the world, so it wasn't that improbable. And if it was sometimes in the cause of clearly fascist and wrong policies, at least they led exciting lives, performed significant work in the middle of some of the biggest action going, got to wear aviator shades and carry guns and cash, and be on the inside of things that most people would never even know happened.

The same was true, more or less, of the drug business, which was an easy enough masquerade since it was never necessary to go into very complicated detail about your work and in fact much more believable if you were tight lipped. The less you said and the more you denied, the more likely it was you were a player. Simple stuff.

During one of Hunter's extended stays in Florida and Key West, he ran into a wealthy friend of mine from Montana who also had trouble distinguishing between reality and fantasy. His name was Ford Bovey and he came from serious money on both sides of his family and had, as a result, developed many nasty habits at an early age. He variously thought of himself as everything from a modern-day pirate to a mountain man to a major businessman to a movie producer to a serious dope dealer. He was a big, charismatic, and very bright guy who had crippled himself in a mountain climbing accident when he was barely twenty-one and died eventually of what was either an accidental or murderous drug overdose. With long dark hair, a full beard, gleaming eyes, a closet full of expensive leather biker clothes, and flamboyant tattoos everywhere, plus the money to lend credence to anything he said, Ford cut a noticeable figure wherever he went.

He was so determined to make himself into a Falstaffian figure, and so immune to the truth as to actually believe most of his own bullshit, that he was, in the end, one of the biggest characters I've ever known. He always wanted to meet Hunter, but I'd never had a chance to introduce the two of them because Ford rarely came to Aspen. People like them, however, tend to move in the same small circles, and one night at a well-known doper bar in the Keys, Ford found himself there at the same time as Hunter and went over and introduced himself. It was a match made in some kind of bad Bizzarro World and they immediately took to each other and believed all of each other's lies.

I think Hunter, as often happened with such encounters, did most of the listening while Ford fantasized. It was a few days after he'd been home at the Farm before Hunter mentioned to me, very casually, that he'd met a friend of mine in Florida. At that point, this could have been any one of a number of people and it made me instantly nervous because he referred to the person as "one of your partners." It was only after several devious smiles and secretive mumblings that he produced a name and closely watched my reaction. Which probably wasn't what he expected, because I laughed. Loudly. Maybe too loudly.

I was never partners with Ford in anything, let alone whatever Ford had implied and Hunter was thinking. Ford was crazy in a lovable but altogether undependable way, and even getting him to meet you for dinner within a week of when you scheduled it was tough. He also couldn't keep his mouth shut under any circumstances, let alone when he was really loaded, which was most of the time. The notion of anyone who wasn't completely out of their mind being a partner with Ford in anything was truly laughable. Except to Hunter. He interpreted my disclaimers as a cover and simply nodded at me with that thin smile of his, muttering, "Of course, of course, I understand. You don't have to tell me. No big deal. We're all friends here. I'm not like the others," until I wanted to slap him and shout, "No, you don't understand. Listen to me!"

Instead I finally just gave up. Here, I realized, was a perfect storm of bullshit, one of those uncontestable confluences where two crazy people met, spun yarns about things they would never know, and walked away believing more lies than the people who voted for George W. Bush. In business, as in the rest of his life, it was often easier to get Hunter to listen to a total crock than the truth.

9

Road Work

Being on the road became, for better or worse, as big a part of Hunter's life as it is for most rock and rollers. In part this was because of the college speaking tours. Considering that he was generally a terrible speaker whose low, full-tilt mumble frequently lapsed into complete incoherence, this was quite a feat. But he managed to pull it off for a long time, deriving enough money to keep afloat in the lean years and to provide decent pocket change even when times were good. It also pumped up his book sales where they were always strong, on the college campuses of the country. These were his people, and the speaking tours did for his books what concert tours do for musician's record sales. Besides that, the tours were a chance to party and have some fun.

Or at least that's how he tried to view them, even if his wives, girlfriends, assistants, handlers, and even audiences at times didn't agree. Traveling with Hunter was no picnic. His speaking appearances frequently turned into serious binges replete with nightmares of miscommunications, missed flights, late arrivals, slurred and incomprehensible performances, frequent escapades with the female journalism students sent to help him, and a general bacchanal the entire time he was away from Owl Farm.

Many of the schools where he spoke were good about absorbing expenses, some of which were contractual anyway, and Hunter would sometimes make up for extremely late appearances or no-shows by rescheduling. In other cases he figured fuck 'em, they'd still have a story to tell because their school had to kick him out for being a drunk, insulting the audience, or throwing whiskey on them. For as many catastrophes as there were, however, there were more successes, where Hunter was crisp and engaging, the students were knowledgeable, and those who were there remember those nights well, and some of them still tell me about them.

Hunter was always very ambiguous about the whole thing. He knew public speaking wasn't his thing even though he was called on for it fairly often in the form of paid events, television interviews, and rallies for various causes. He usually refused to just deliver a talk, preferring to take questions from the audience instead. Sometimes, if he was especially late and the crowd especially sullen, that didn't go well. And he wasn't sure how much he wanted to trade on being a "character," with goofy kids throwing joints, pills, and booze onstage, and Hunter stomping around to their beat and expectations, too often living down to them.

As a result of these anxieties and his general discomfort with being considered a public entertainer, he frequently left for the speeches, or any kind of road trip, in a simmering huff, snappish about everything. It was no one's favorite time to be around him. "Hunter often agreed to speaking dates that were months away, but as the time to travel arrived he would get very nervous. Every detail had to be perfect. And I mean every detail," says Deborah Fuller. "Traveling companion, airlines, huge bags filled, hotel room with flowers, fruit, liquor, typewriter, contacts, transportation, that the stage and sound system were all checked. And of course he just basically hated leaving his daily routine and whatever he was working on at the time. Transitions were not his idea of fun. The nightmares of travel, new people, performing and all that it entailed."

What's more, he usually insisted on hauling more crap with him than the queen of England. This included various bags and satchels, leather valises and large duffels stuffed with bulky jackets, ten pairs of shorts, a backup pair of sneakers, several bottles of booze, random cans of Mace, handcuffs, blowup dolls, cartons of cigarettes, honorary police badges, spare baseball caps, stacks of manuscript pages, books, tape recorders and portable stereos, numerous vials of pills, potions and powders, a can of tennis balls, a putter, tropical shirts, logo sports shirts, and a second sport coat as a backup to the one he was usually wearing when he flew. If he could wedge in a portable fax machine, a case of grapefruit, a bowling ball, and some tanks of nitrous oxide, so much the better.

Even pre-9/11 this wasn't the guy you wanted to be behind going through security or clearing customs, and traveling with or anywhere near him could be like a curse. In some cases it was actually better for him to travel completely alone so there was no one he felt familiar enough with to shriek, bellow, and go theatric on. I ran into him by happenstance more than once on flights where he was by himself and behaving like a normal human.

Probably the last time he really traveled with any economy of belongings and style was on the campaign trail of 1972, when he first started complaining about attracting too much attention to do his job properly. After that, airports became like stage sets for his forced appearances, and he often dealt with the prospect badly, though not unpredictably, by getting royally wasted and short-tempered.

I don't think Hunter was that different from lots of veteran travelers who love the road and have sought it out over their lives but who still feel conflicted every time they have to leave home. Even without getting really trashed and trying to drag everything you own with you, any substantial travel can be a pain in the ass. For Hunter it could be an ordeal just to go into town from the Farm.

The speaking tours were always logistical scrambles from beginning to end, owing to weather and Hunter's condition and needs on any given day, and school contact people determined to prove they were at least as crazy as he and could get just as fucked up. The latter was one more manifestation of what he had to deal with all the time, involving people who seemed determined to perform their bad impersonation of him for him. It was flattering, and he knew it, but he got tired of seeing himself through other people's eyes, especially when the view wasn't so great.

Hunter learned after a while that he could set things up so he could also see his agents and get other business done when he was on a speaking tour, and in theory all of that was good. Actually pulling it off was another matter, but it happened often enough to keep the ball rolling for many years.

In 1976 Hunter was presented in Sydney and Melbourne in Australia as "The Dean of Gonzo Journalism," promoted with huge posters with an image of him that he used for years afterward. The trip was a hit and helped further his reputation as a lively, if not always prompt or friendly, performer.

We got occasional glimpses of what he did on tour at home in Aspen when he'd appear here for rare events. One of them happened in typical fashion in 1977 when he hosted a benefit for George Stranahan's Community School. Hunter put an announcement on the local radio station that musicians Glenn Frey, Jimmy Buffett, and Steve Weisberg would be joining him, but he never told Buffett who happened to hear the ad. "I was glad I found out about it. I think he doesn't like to lay an egg by himself and would rather take his friends with him," Jimmy told the crowd.

The show began with one of Hunter's many self-recorded cassette tapes being played at high volume, this one of indeterminate screeching and discordant chanting of the word "mantra." Hunter eventually made himself comfortable with a bottle of Wild Turkey at a table and chair that he compulsively rearranged as the musicians took over. Included in their set was an impromptu rendition of "We're Gonna Have a Hunter Thompson Weekend," all about a cabin in the woods, a woman, and lots of drugs and liquor. This was followed by a screening of a BBC documentary on Hunter's 1970 run for sheriff, and finally after he'd smoked a joint on stage he fielded a few questions from the audience. In Aspen people were never quite as ardent to publicly quiz him as were audiences on the road, so he wisely kept that part of this show to a minimum.

That same year Hunter did an eastern swing at the Harvard Law Forum, Vassar College, Brandeis University, and Orlando, extending his stay in Florida for a couple of weeks with his son. Organizing the whole thing took way longer than the trip and drove everyone around him mad. And the speeches didn't go that swimmingly. At Harvard observers said he was in such bad shape that the organizers had to pull a phony fire drill and lead him by hand off the stage.

The next year he made another big swing through the country. In March he appeared at Boston University on the thirteenth, Brandeis on the fourteenth, and WBCN on the fifteenth, selling out all of them and moving on to a West Coast leg in April. When he had bright, articulate kids in the crowd, Hunter rarely failed to impress. At Boston University, the crowd "exploded in wild applause when he came onstage" according to *The Daily Free Press*. He spent two hours there, and "His quips and allusions to drugs met with very favorable reactions from the crowd."

Hunter typically answered a wide range of queries. About Muhammad Ali: "He's a wizard. He's a very strange bastard. He can do anything he wants to do. Ali is one of the few I've ever met who is as fast and as weird in his verbal exchanges as I like to think I am." About Garry Trudeau: "If he makes a mistake legally, I'll have him trimming trees in my garden. I resent it enough to sue him." About why he wasn't in jail: "I felt guilty when I was young and I learned. I found out about jail at a very early age so I've stayed out of it." About his worst drug experience: "A few months ago this guy gave me two lines of what I thought was cocaine when it was actually PCP [also known as elephant tranquilizer]. I was sitting in a restaurant just nailed to my seat; I couldn't move my feet or hands from their positions. It was like being shot out of one of those huge missiles that circle the earth. They shut the restaurant down and let me ride it out." About his responsibility for helping elect Jimmy Carter: "I'm afraid I might have had something to do with it. Keep in mind, though, the other options at that point were Humphrey or Ford. Given those options, I'd do it again." And about how he could justify taking money for his performance: "A more pertinent question is why are you here?" replied Hunter, who had been asked the same thing before.

A writer for *The Justice*, an independent student weekly at Brandeis, summed up the sentiments of those who weren't sure what to make of him: "Whether you think he's a self-centered put-on or whether you think his pioneering style of Gonzo Journalism will revolutionize

American media, you have to take him in stride. He's a jester, not a professor."

Like a standup comic, Hunter was road-testing material throughout his speeches that would show up in his writing. In 1985 he was still dealing with controversies surrounding his requiring a bottle of good whiskey to be provided for his consumption during his show at places such as the University of Montana in Missoula. It turned out he had a problem in Missoula because of a specific ban by the State Board of Regents on speakers' drinking alcohol following his visit in 1976. In a profile and interview in *High Times* magazine he was quoted still riffing on many of the same questions he had been for a decade. About his experiences in Saigon: "In Vietnam, we were the Nazis being run off, the orphans at the end of an empire." About Reagan: "The State is being invaded by a Yahoo-ism parading around in jackboots. This gibberish can't go on. These profiteers, these free-enterprise princes want to break down government until it doesn't exist anymore, while elderly people get thrown out in the streets like bags of meat." About Garry Trudeau: "I feel ashamed for him, ashamed for his family. They saved and saved for their son to have the opportunity for a good education at Yale, and he ends up making his living stealing from other people."

The gigs never got any easier for him, however, and not everyone saw the Hunter they thought they knew and respected. In New York in 1988 he was booked on election night into a twelve-hundred-seat venue to talk about the presidential race. One observer was quoted as saying, "They wanted some political insight. What they got was a drunk old man." He reportedly imbibed heavily and slurred all evening and got panned by *People* magazine and the *New York Post,* which described it as a "full-fledged fiasco." He was two and a half hours late, responded to complaints about how he could justify charging twenty dollars a ticket by saying, "I do it all the time," and virtually emptied the house when he pulled out a rifle onstage.

By the early nineties Hunter had rallied and was making more sense more consistently, but his days of traveling to speak were drawing to a close because of health and injury issues. He delivered a strong speech at Denver's Paramount Theater in 1990 in the midst of his sex, drugs, and dynamite troubles in Aspen. "We've got a berserk situation. People had better realize that nobody's safe when the police have the right to come in and search anybody's house for any reason. While democracy is gaining ground in communist countries, America is moving the other way into a repressive, rules-oriented, money-crazed age of fear." It was a good rehearsal for his forthcoming book, *Songs of the Doomed*. He still made public appearances after this, most notably on behalf of Lisl Auman, for whom he spoke out passionately in 2001 at a rally he organized that included Warren Zevon.

Hunter's travels in Florida were frequently textbook cases of running amok, whether he was stalking the Roxanne Pulitzer case, trying to muscle in on the Mariel boatlift, running fast Scarabs through the Keys at night with no lights, or wrecking expensive runabouts at Boog Powell's marina. Life on the road was lived to the full rock-and-roll ethic of being as crazed as you could contrive to be as often as possible.

One of Hunter's main contacts in Florida was a native son named Montgomery Chitty who was a mutual friend of ours with his primary residence near Aspen. "Hunter joined me in Florida just about every year from March through early June from 1975 through 1990 to escape the cold weather and mingle with smugglers, commercial fishermen, customs agents, and Santeria practitioners," Monty recalls now. "South Florida and the Keys were where the action, and the drugs, were during the seventies and eighties."

It was always a big deal for Hunter to head south, or anywhere else, and it required months of setting up. In 1979 I got a frantic phone call one day in June because he needed to talk to his insurance agent. "My goddamned boat went crazy on me and did some damage at Boog Powell's marina down here," he grumbled. He'd been alone in a boat he was thinking about buying, coming back into Angler's Marina, when he dropped a bottle of whiskey over the side. When he lunged for it, he followed it into the water himself. In the process he cranked the wheel sideways and the empty boat circled back on him. "It tried to fucking kill me and then roared up onto a dock and over a parked boat and came back at me again until it finally crashed into another dock. They're all over me about the damages and I need to see what my insurance company says. I think the damned boat was defective." The haggling with the marina and Hunter's insurance company lasted for a long time and I don't know who finally got stuck for the tab.

Hunter's travel, even when it was ostensibly on assignment, was often about getting out of Aspen in the winter. It was a big reason he first took on the mission for *Running* magazine to cover the 1980 Honolulu Marathon. It looked like a great excuse for a tropical holiday.

By the time he had determined to make a book out of Hawaii and was plotting a return trip, I already had plans to visit Kauai and extended them to meet him and Laila and Ralph Steadman on the Big Island. The idea of participating in and even winning the Kona Gold Jackpot fishing tournament, a big deal in sportfishing circles, had come up when Steve Kaiser, whom Hunter had met in Hawaii, came to Aspen to visit him and went skiing with me. Steve owned a fishing boat on the Big Island and mentioned that there was this big tournament in Kona in May he wanted to tell Hunter about. It sounded good to me and Hunter liked it immediately. He had been on a trip with Steve before where they spent a night out on the water on hallucinogens, which Hunter vividly recounts in *Lono*. The fishing tournament seemed like the meat for good adventure and a logical rounding out of the book.

By the time I got there, Hunter was already deep in the throes of strategizing for the tournament where they would be fishing for giant marlin and ahi, something he had zero experience with. It made him nervous, but he had already purchased a big, carved and inlaid Samoan war club, persuading himself that he would need it to brain any marlin he might get to the boat. Mostly he just liked the club, and he often bought something similar to it on his road trips. He did end up using it, as he describes in the book, though he wouldn't have had to. All the other fishermen let their crews handle the gaffing and actual slaying of the marlin.

Ralph arrived a day or so after we did, having traveled, unhappily, halfway around the world in one go. He was billeted at the King Kamehameha Hotel, had no idea what day it was, seemed very wobbly, and right away changed into what turned out to be his typical tropical island wear: khaki shorts with lots of pockets worn over bright floral boxer underwear that was longer than his outer shorts. This isn't uncommon with English tourists I've encountered, but it was odd to see it on Ralph. Laila and Hunter eventually talked him into making some adjustments. "Jesus, Ralph, you look like a shameless old pervert," Hunter told him as soon as he saw him. "Didn't anyone ever teach you how to dress?"

Hunter returned to Ralph's room at three thirty the first morning he was there, depressed about the boat they were supposed to be using in the tournament that was being completely torn apart by mechanics. He finally passed out on the balcony of Ralph's oceanfront room just as the cannon sounded in Kailua Harbor, sending an armada of 199 frenzied fishing boats churning white foam out toward the open ocean to begin the tournament. There should have been two hundred boats, but Captain Steve's *Haere Maru* wasn't running. In a misguided effort to get it in top shape for Hunter's arrival, Steve was having the engine completely rebuilt, but it was still in pieces.

Following Hunter's awakening and an inspired balcony harangue where he wielded his club and jabbered to people below in what he thought might pass for local pidgin, Hunter did eventually persuade Captain Steve to rally and get a backup boat out on the water and competing for a few hours that day. Ralph had meanwhile spoken to Steve about his own deep gloom and distress at traveling twelve thousand miles only to find a boat with many wires and things mechanical strewn about, numbers of "greasy people" scrambling around on it and cursing lustily, and an air of abject failure hanging heavy in the harbor.

The effect of this rant on a person in Steve's condition—bereft of sleep for days, recently out of coke, without an intelligible voice, many dollars down to a mechanic who had thrown up his arms and left in despair at 6:00 a.m., and in short hosed in every way possible and now being held accountable for the long and arduous travels of a famous Welsh illustrator—was horrible to behold.

On the second day of the tournament someone on Captain Steve's boat hooked up a good-sized ahi, a competitive fish I was assured, but the gaffer missed, and according to Hunter a horrible silence ensued. Missing an important gaffe in competition means almost certain dishonor, and a kind of doom settled over the boat. Most of the crew mutinied that night and one of the sports, a United Airlines pilot named Mitch, had to leave early and gave Ralph his seat on the boat. Ralph, in his mind, went instantly from being the man who would never set foot on a fishing boat again (after a catastrophic previous experience in Hawaii) to the man who would catch a two-thousand-pound white marlin and win the tournament. Meanwhile, Captain Steve had flown in an expensive chrome prop from Oahu to act as a lure for the big marlin.

On the final day of the tournament the team was penalized an hour for missing its start and fined for switching crews. Since one hundred and ninety boats had already headed north, Steve decided to follow the remaining handful south. Way south. The hope was that a couple of big marlin had been pushed in that direction by all the action up north, but no one near them hooked up. And when there was only one boat left, Hunter suggested they head back to the harbor while there was still someone else nearby, just in case. He was worried about a mechanical breakdown, not running out of gas, which was what they promptly did. Steve had only taken on two-thirds of a tank of fuel because they were running late, and he hadn't originally planned to go as far south as they did. So now it was getting late, there was a storm brewing, and they were dead in the water and out in the channel. If missing a gaffe is a sin, running out of gas, especially in a tournament, was far worse and completely unheard of by professionals.

That one boat they'd been staying ahead of proved to be their salvation, and eventually, after more travail, towed them into the harbor, the worst humiliation imaginable for a charter boat. Hunter called it "The Shame of the Human Race." When they reached the gas docks, Hunter and Ralph abandoned the ship, divorcing themselves from the whole enterprise. As a parting gesture Hunter threw his *Haere Maru* team shirt into the waters, maligning the captain publicly. "You've never even caught a fish in your life, you lying swine!" Onlookers had already heaped the crew with abuse as they were dragged in. It was the final ignominy of an ill-fated tournament, and the trouncing was so complete that by the time we reached the Kona Inn, it had become funnier rather than more depressing. Later, Hunter did finally manage to catch a three-hundred pound Marlin aboard a boat called the *Humdinger,* even though the tournament was long over by then. But the debacle of it all left Hunter and Ralph concerned about what to build a story around now, and Ralph headed home a couple of days later. In the final cut of the book, the fishing tournament barely received a mention.

Now Hunter began to take a heightened interest in everything else about the Big Island, since one of his main hooks for the book had lost some luster. Finally he began to have some intimations of his true reason for being there, the whole nature of his attraction to Hawaii in the first place. The story was not, as he originally suspected, about him as a champion sportfisherman. It lay in his being the second coming of Lono, the great Hawaiian god for whom Captain Cook had once been mistaken. Truth comes in many forms, as does inspiration and a theme for a book. Lono, not being dependent on the outcome of a botched fishing tournament and having somewhat larger implications in general, definitely seemed to be a better angle. As this realization came over him, Hunter's mood lightened and he began to enjoy himself more.

We went out with Captain Steve one day to do some proper diving after Hunter started thinking he'd like to find some black coral that Steve had been talking about. Steve took us down to a bay called Captain Cook that had a monument where Cook had been killed and the kind of difficult access by land back then that made it very quiet. It was well sheltered from most surf, making it an excellent diving and snorkeling spot. Hunter got more nervous and grumpier as the scuba dive neared because he hadn't done one for a while. But he finally got in the water and returned half an hour later with some good black coral that Steve said doesn't grow above depths of about ninety feet. So it's a macho coral, which Hunter liked, and he later had it carved into his signature peyote fist and hung from a gold baht chain from Thailand I sold him. I got to do some beautiful snorkeling and took photos on the way back to the harbor when Steve let Hunter pilot the boat.

It had been such an unusually nice and mellow day that we had to offset it by having a typically gonzo round of golf the next day at the Keahou Resort, now known as the Kona Country Club. Hunter hadn't slept, Laila was pissed off at him, and he and I were late for our tee time. There was no real problem except that the starter kept trying to impress on us that a Japanese men's club group was teeing off soon, and they liked to play fast. If we let one of them play through we'd have to let all thirty of them go.

I tried to hurry us along and that just made Hunter slower. He had to go back to the clubhouse after the second hole to re-up on balls after errantly firing two sleeves straight out into the lava before getting zeroed in. He rarely kept score when he played golf but had a very good swing for someone who never played much. It came from caddying as a kid in Kentucky, he said. He had no qualms about hitting multiple balls on every shot, which always annoyed people behind us and had repercussions on his ability to keep enough ammunition on hand to finish a round. By the fourth hole he got nervous that we were running out of booze and roared back to the clubhouse, leaving me to practice and await the inevitable arrival of the Japanese men's club.

Fifteen minutes went by, I smoked a joint and watched the ocean and Hunter barely got back to me before the Japanese did. He said there had been some difficulties along the way, and I suspected he'd rankled some of the other golfers by roaring heedlessly through them in his cart. I also figured he'd stopped for a bump or two. "And I had to piss, and they get weird around here about indecent exposure," he mumbled, then blasted a three-hundred-yard drive straight down the fairway.

Even so, within a hole the Japanese had caught us, and within minutes of that, after watching Hunter repeatedly hit a handful of balls on every shot, they started yelling and raining balls down on us. Hunter had just written his story for *Running* magazine about the annual Honolulu Marathon that took place on December 7, the anniversary of the attack on Pearl Harbor, and had a huge mob of participants including many Japanese.

> There's no sane reason at all for these runners. Only a fool would try to explain why four thousand Japanese ran at top speed past the USS *Arizona* sunken memorial in the middle of Pearl Harbor, along with another four or five thousand certified American liberals cranked up on beer and spaghetti and all taking the whole thing so seriously that only one in

> two thousand could even smile at the idea of a 26-mile race featuring four thousand Japanese that begins and ends within a stone's throw of Pearl Harbor on the morning of December 7, 1980. . . . Thirty-nine years later. What are these people celebrating? And why on this bloodstained anniversary?

His story had dwelt on this odd circumstance, and now here he was, literally being bombed by Japanese himself, and rightfully so. We ducked out of the way, waving the first group through while continuing to look for our lost balls. After that we waved many more through, but found enough balls to keep playing. By the time we wrapped up our nearly *six-hour* round, it was almost dark and we were the last ones on the course. There wasn't even anyone still working when we turned in the cart.

Hunter had quickly nicknamed the Kona Bali Kai "Thug Central" because lots of young surf rats hung out in our parking lot. Laila's moped was vandalized on the second night they were there and semi-regular civilian and cop patrols toured our parking lot at night. One cop told Laila that this was a rough neighborhood, for things like burglary and vandalism. But I never had any trouble and Laila and Hunter came to think of it as home too. This in spite of the fact that Hawaii was acquiring an ugly reputation at that time for violence, coming on the heels of the apparently random, separate murders of three Canadians by locals angry at the tourism industry. There had also been some nasty incidents on the Big Island where people had been tortured and killed, sometimes over drugs, sometimes over nothing, cut up to bleed and left in the ocean to wait for the sharks.

Hunter was always interested in violence, as long as he wasn't on the receiving end, and played on this theme later throughout *The Curse of Lono*. He began to take on the persona of the rough-living professional fishermen who frequented the local bars. "I can drink with the fishermen now. The big boys. We gather at Huggo's around sundown, to trade lies and drink slammers and sing wild songs about Scurvey. I am one of them now," he wrote in *Lono*. It was all silliness, of course, but how long you could attempt to be a dabbler in that scene and survive was open to speculation, and it began to obsess him near the end of his visit. So much so that he felt obliged to kick the owner of the Kona Inn restaurant, Bob Mardian, in the nuts the night before Hunter and Laila thought they were leaving.

"For no reason at all," he later told me, other than a need to vent. When I pressed him about it he said, "I don't know. It just seemed like a good idea. His wife kept saying, 'He's the fastest man in his karate class,' and there he was in a comatose crouch on that lava rock wall in his own bar for an hour and a half." In fact, Hunter suspected Mardian was part of a local cabal of realtors and developers who were spreading ugly rumors about him, or perhaps the truth. This turned out to be bullshit, of course, and Hunter ordered a dozen roses sent to the Inn. "I've never sent flowers to a man before," he chuckled. "At least not a living one."

The *Lono* book that came out of all of this was a major task. It was Hunter's first piece of new material, rendered in one cohesive story, since *Campaign Trail.* In form and content, it was the only time he attempted what might be considered a sequel to *Vegas,* even though he never called it that. Because of a vast number of lavish illustrations by Ralph Steadman, the book had special problems right from the start. The only way to do justice to Ralph's vivid color pieces was to publish a full, four-color book. This was generally only being done in big coffee-table formats at the time, and there were active debates on the publishing end over whether this work qualified as a coffee-table book. It certainly wasn't one in the traditional sense.

Additionally, Hunter was filing reams of writing that would have required such a thick book, if combined with all of Ralph's drawings, that it would have been almost prohibitively expensive. Or at least that was the contention of Bantam Books, which eventually issued a glossy, full-color, one-hundred-sixty-page creation about the size of a big hardcover novel, only much more slender and in a slick, heavyweight, soft cover. It came out in November 1983, sold modestly, and was never reissued in any form until 2005. Then it was produced in coffee-table size and was forty pages longer but with the same content as the original—the art was just given more room to breathe.

Hunter had labored mightily to find some larger themes for *Lono*. The whole concept of the City of Refuge had great appeal to him, and he loved his epiphany that he, in fact, was the god Lono. The last time there'd been a mistake about the return of Lono to the islands, Captain Cook paid for it with his life. And it still didn't save paradise from being invaded and proselytized.

Attempting to tie all of this in with big-time sportfishing, real estate developers, the Honolulu Marathon, and some fast times on the Big Island was difficult. Hunter ranted and raved and despaired and finally decided to give it more of a *Letters from Hawaii* flavor, à la Mark Twain than an impossible-to-re-create air of *Vegas. Lono* would have to be his travel book, for which there is a more than honorable tradition and for which he had great material. The writing, because it had been pared back substantially, was funny and rollicking and even years later still feels fresh and alive. Describing the property they were renting on the Kona Coast after it had been assaulted by major storms, high waves, and then barrages of Chinese firecrackers he kept setting off, he was at his poetic best, with the killer closer that brings us back to the point:

> There was also the problem of Mr. Heem, the realtor, who wanted the rent for the compound—at least two thousand in cash, and questions would certainly be raised about the crust of red scum on the property. Once it hardened, only an industrial sandblaster could get it off. I liked the color myself. It brought back oriental memories. There was a strange red glow on the whole property in the afternoon hours. I drove past it a few times and noticed that even the grass on the lawn seemed to glitter. The swimming pool appeared to be full of blood, on some days, and the dense green foliage on the lemon trees seemed about to burst into flame. The place had a different look now, an air of mystery and magic. Strange and powerful things had happened here. And perhaps they would happen again. There was a certain beauty to it, but the effect was very unsettling and I could see where Heem might have trouble renting it to decent people.

Still in all, Hunter felt let down by the *Lono* project. Ralph had created some remarkable art for it, but the story wasn't the homerun that Hunter, the critics, or the average book buyer wanted. Overall, the book may have been a little obscure for most readers and just didn't resonate. There's some outstanding writing in it (Ralph even took the title of his own book about Hunter—*The Joke's Over*—from it) that I think has been underappreciated. Hunter lost some faith in it, but it quickly became a cult favorite and collector's item because it was never republished. And by the time he got around to reexamining it in light of Ralph's efforts to get it brought out in the larger format originally envisioned, he was a little surprised to find how good he thought it was.

There is a reason why Laila is listed in the front as the book's producer. This isn't usual in the industry, but because Hunter and Ralph ended up being cocreators, working mostly from opposite sides of the Atlantic, and because the whole project turned so vastly complicated and put Hunter in such a hateful mood toward the publishers, Laila's services were desperately needed, or the book may have never been finished.

It's probably never good to make your fans wait so long for something. Word filters out that it's going to be sheer genius, then that it's a terrible flop, then that there is no new book at all and may never be. Ego gets tangled up with expectations and in the end no one is happy. Or at least that was the lesson of *Lono,* which deserved better. Hunter was never thrilled about having to share billing with his illustrator on the book, even though everyone agreed that Ralph's contributions constituted a full half of the final material.

Everything combined to leave a bad taste in his mouth over a work that may have looked too much like some of his other recent, largely aimless magazine ramblings because it included reprinted versions of his letters to Ralph and extracts of background history on the islands that overresembled actual travel guide material, presented periodical style in highlighted sidebars and boxes that sometimes read like filler.

On his last trip to Hawaii in 2003, on the twentieth anniversary of the publication of *Lono,* Hunter broke his leg in Honolulu, an injury that really may have been the beginning of the end for him. He finally had to be flown home in Sean Penn's private jet, and I don't think he left this world with any great affection for Hawaii.

Wherever Hunter ended up traveling, from colleges to Key West to Kona, his destinations were always made more vivid by his presence. He always needed to liven up his own life, and that meant he had to take everyone around with him on the ride. It was fun for a while for almost anyone, and he traded on that. Learning when your regular friends have had enough, and how far you could push things in new surroundings with people who didn't know you as well was a critical skill to develop if you were Hunter. Knowing when to leave is one of the most important intuitions in many fields of endeavor. That much became acutely apparent to Hunter with the Hell's Angels, and he tried not to miss any really obvious signals after that. Frequent road work helped keep his instincts sharp. It also gave him enough time away so that his friends back home were usually happy to see him again.

10

My Name's Thompson, I'm in Show Business

From the time he first started making speeches for money, saw himself turned into a cartoon character, and began to feel like he was too well known to continue to do his job as a journalist, Hunter had a line he liked to trot out: "Hi. My name's Thompson. I'm in show business." The comment was a sarcastic joke, an acknowledgment of some reality, and a fond wish all rolled into one.

For Hunter, the desire to be a part of show business was mostly about the money, but he also admired the lifestyle. Fame could be a pain in the ass, but it had plenty of perks. People in show business are often very famous, he reasoned, and appeared to live more or less as they pleased no matter how degenerate that might be. Of course, that all traced to the money, and there seemed to be boatloads of it floating around Hollywood. They were paying more just to option a piece for the movies than Hunter was being paid to write many of his stories to begin with. Plus, the studios threw expense money around like it was something they were trying to get rid of as fast as possible without having to literally set fire to it. This seemed like paradise to Hunter, and why not?

The trick, of course, was to either have the studios want to make films of things he'd already written or for him to write something expressly for them. Hunter had lots of wild ideas and those are, for a while at least, good currency in Hollywood. Especially when you know the right people. With the help of his agents and friends in the business and the contacts made during the production of *Where the Buffalo Roam,* Hunter was primed to invade the movies in full force for a three- or four-year period at the end of the seventies and in the early eighties.

The whole notion of generating ideas, treatments, and screenplays had a beautiful allure to it. Being able to turn any of those things into large amounts of money was your basic golden California dream and legitimized all kinds of craziness under the pretext of doing whatever it took to get inspired. Everyone had ideas, especially when the drugs were flowing. If for less effort than writing a quasi-journalistic piece and without having to leave your home you could come up with things that attracted the interest of the movie people, then life would truly be perfect.

I helped Hunter with an elaborate thing called *The Mole,* which he was discussing with Tom Mount at Universal. I'd written a spy novel that Bantam had passed on, and Hunter saw in it a germ of an idea for a CIA movie that he thought stood a chance of actually being topical and newsworthy. He liked the concept of being able to break a story as a movie instead of straight journalism. But really, he was willing to go right across the spectrum in search of traction.

I also did voluminous research and worked up a very topical treatment of *The Day the Blood Ran Out,* with lots of references to the ongoing illegal organ and blood trade all over the world. But we both kept wanting to push the story to the really bizarre science-fiction side, which included a lot of Hunter's general weirdness that seemed to bog everything down at a certain point.

We actually tried to turn the *Gonzo Book of Etiquette* into a romantic comedy, something I think could have been more easily accomplished than it sounds. But we lacked the motivation to proceed with something no one had yet expressed an interest in. And we had no real grasp of how to structure a form fairly alien to us. Hunter's humor, we began to fear, might not always translate well to the screen, especially as anything light or even semisilly.

Instead, Hunter decided to focus on things he already had in hand, insisting on playing his deranged tape about *Guts Ball* to anyone even vaguely connected to Hollywood who would listen. It involved Secret Service people and some of the Watergate felons, such as Haldeman, Erlichman, Kleindeinst, and others, all flying across the country on a big DC-10 commercial flight. In order to relieve their stress they start this kind of a rugby game that turns really violent and they force regular passengers to play and start flogging them if they refuse or screw up. He thought it was the most hysterical thing he'd ever conceived. I never did see people do anything but shake their head over it and change the subject. I don't think it advanced his cause in general, let alone as a project itself.

About this time, in the late 1970s, Monty Chitty and Hunter rented a house on Ramrod Key, about twenty miles from Key West. "Tom McGuane finds me one afternoon while I'm fly-fishing, asking if Hunter was staying with me," relates Monty. "He invited us down for a Chinese dinner Jim Harrison had been preparing for three days. . . . the four of us, plus Russell Chatham and Guy de la Valdène. Hunter lights up like a roman candle. . . . of course we'll come."

This wasn't long after Jack Nicholson had sold Harrison's three novellas for film rights. "Jim had just returned to the Keys after two months in Hollywood, gleaning instructions from studio bigwigs on how to rewrite the novellas into scripts," says Monty. Hunter was eager to learn all he could and this was the perfect opportunity. "Around 4:00 a.m., Harrison pulls me to the side and begs help with removing Hunter back to Ramrod. Jim needs sleep. Hunter has shamelessly badgered Harrison and McGuane for the past nine hours on the structure and style of treatments and scripts to satisfy Hollywood tastes and reap the big bucks. But of course they enjoyed every moment. For the next three months on Ramrod, Hunter pieced together *Cigarette Key* and *Silk Road*."

Cigarette Key was going to be his ultimate work about drug smuggling and was part of a three-picture deal Jann Wenner had with Paramount. Hunter was telling everyone that his other projects dealt with the beginnings of the hippie movement and contemporary high school life. But the drug smuggling movie was the top priority. Bits relating to that kept surfacing in his treatments for the *Buffalo* movie, and he liked the idea of following them further. This gave him a legitimate reason to bone up on his drug smuggling knowledge, hit the locals in Florida for info and samples, and include some decent sex scenes.

One version of the story began with a long tracking shot zeroing in on a skiff rocking back and forth in the shallows and gradually the audience would see a man's white ass rising and falling until the camera zoomed close enough to show him making love to a beautiful Latino woman on the floor of the boat.

He hoped for a while to cannibalize some of *Rum Diary* for the screenplay, because he saw similar stories in it. But ultimately he felt a little protective of the fact that *Rum* was an already finished project, for better or worse. And he wasn't sure how well its more realistic and character-based plot would mesh with a *Cigarette Key* story line that variously involved everything from smugglers with submarines to Cuban gangsters chopping up cops.

Another idea that we followed together was so totally up his alley I was surprised it never worked out. While we were talking about *The Day the Blood Ran Out,* Hunter kept veering off on tangents, of course. He loved folktales about the brain-sucking jungle monsters in Central America; the mysterious black helicopters being used to mutilate cattle in the American West; heroin being traded for guns in the Bekaa Valley of Lebanon; the rumors that Robert Vesco had financed, and lost in a plane crash, a huge load of Chinese gold to pay for arms left over when the United States fled from Vietnam; and the persistent stories about the Drug Enforcement Agency creating a new drug that would eventually kill or render crazy everyone who used it.

Some people thought the latter was all about crack. But Hunter wanted to fictionally invent his own drug, a type of LSD called BZ that would be used by the CIA to destabilize unfriendly governments and citizenries. We developed some lengthy notes on the idea. But in the end there were just too many different pitches floating around to follow up on all of them. Too many, like this one, would start off solid and then descend into raving and gibberish with no character development or cohesive plot, let alone a real denouement, because Hunter would come down, lose interest, get distracted, become obsessive on one theme, foresee too much work ahead, or just move on to another project.

One of our last drafts of *The Magician,* his tentative title for the BZ movie, was handwritten by Hunter and included scene notes such as: "—assignment-vague-off to Africa with BZ (headlines "Africa Is Burning"); —enter Perry White, boyhood friend, with more acid + new plans (violence) recall first acid in Cozumel/HST (Moss meets CIA); —Great Fear sets in—Moss pleads with White for Escape—scenes of BZ madness in Imperial Palace-firing Soviet anti tank guns at night, orgies/Russians/Cubans/French—White/CIA panics—but Moss can't stop it—he writes letters/cables to Senators, The President + pleads with his old friend White—who sneaks into Ngola's court + locks Moss in a tank with 20k mikes of acid." You get the idea. Lots of drugs and madness. Who'd have thought?

By 1978 and 1979, Hunter was popping out new script ideas constantly in what might have seemed a frantic effort, except for the fact that he had these kinds of flights of fancy pretty regularly anyway and just wasn't sure what the prevailing tastes were in Hollywood. But he knew he had good contacts for the moment and that he shouldn't waste them. He was also determined to stick with his plan of "retiring" from journalism and felt that film was the only way he could do that. The issue, as with so many things, was whether film would cooperate with Hunter's plans any better than most other venues did. The volume and tenor of his notes relating to needing money was so far unaffected. All that had changed was where he was trying to get it. Now his lists were populated with such things as, "I must call film/agent Bob Bookman at once—inre: $7500, and Paramount owes me $12,500 for services, and Call Tom Mount at Universal—THE MOLE, and I must call Jack Nicholson + arrange a business talk this week, and Call Linson inre: The Mole."

Meanwhile, the parts of showbiz that seemed to be serving him best were his connections at *Saturday Night Live*. From the beginning various people expressed interest in making *Vegas* into a movie, and Hunter wanted to cast Dan Aykroyd and John Belushi in the leads. For him, as for many people, one of the fun parts of making movies was getting to talk about who you wanted in them.

The harder part was developing workable screenplays. Working on *Where the Buffalo Roam* quickly led him to believe that no matter how well he wrote, he wasn't going to get the screenplay credit or money. Whether this was just the curse of Hollywood many writers eventually allude to, an insider's network that's hard to crack, or his struggles with maintaining a viable narrative arc, Hunter began to feel his talents were better deployed on ideas and treatments. I think he was assisted in those realizations by his agents and others connected to the industry. And also by the sense that it was easier to come up with a quick couple of pages outlining the story, and perhaps just as profitable on an hourly basis as grinding out long and much-revised screenplays.

While he toiled away on the set of *Buffalo* attempting to generate scenes he received payment for but no ultimate screen credit, some good material was produced, including Bill Murray's speech for the final scene:

> It's sad but what's really sad is it never got weird enough for me. I moved to the country when the boat got too crowded. Then I heard President Nixon had been eaten by white cannibals on an island in Tijuana. You hear a lot of strange and unnatural things about people these days. Lazlo and Nixon are both gone now, but I don't think I can believe that until I can gnaw on both of their skulls with my very own teeth. If they're out there, I'll find them. And I'll gnaw on their skulls.

Most of the time, however, it seemed like he was running up his expense account and trying to stay amused with the Hollywood way of life. He and Ralph Steadman and Laila designed a series of political-style pins used to identify the insiders on the *Buffalo* production. The first was white, featuring a buffalo head that looked like Hunter, with gleaming red eyes and chomping on a cigarette holder, and the words

"Gonzo Guilt" on it. They made these just for friends, but, "Pretty soon everyone had one of the damned things, including people we didn't even know," complained Hunter.

So a second one was forthcoming, in dark blue with white lettering in Steadman's hand reading, "**I AM A REAL FRIEND** of Dr. Hunter S. Thompson." Before long, this too was everywhere, and they were becoming wiser to the insidious ways of movie sets where everyone maneuvered constantly to buddy-up with whomever seemed most important and to appear to be among those who were in the know about what was really going on.

The result was the last button in the series, a very limited edition that almost no one received. It was red with a warped, taloned, ratlike drawing on it spewing out of an open mouth in white lettering: "I AM NOT LIKE THE OTHERS." This, Laila assured me, was the rarest of the pins, and they brought me back an entire set to Owl Farm.

As long as Laila was around, the movie dreams seemed to stay alive. But Hunter still had the same problem completing things, whether it was a treatment, a story, a book, or a column. And ultimately it wasn't any easier for him to pry money loose from the studios than it was from publishers or magazines. When *Buffalo* was a commercial flop, his other ideas immediately lost some currency, and he began to think it might be better if he just optioned his existing works from time to time rather than wasting energy pursuing new screenplay ideas that never went anywhere.

In return for all of Laila's help, Hunter gave her the right to produce any film version of *Fear and Loathing in Las Vegas,* which she had believed for years could make a great movie. Hunter had seen so many passes made at it without fruition that he was happy to have her committed to working on it. Even after they broke up, she retained the rights and his full cooperation.

At one point early on, Jack Nicholson had agreed to play Hunter, who was extremely flattered that he would consider it. We all thought Jack would make the movie important and funny, as well as a big hit. It could be in the same continuum as *One Flew Over the Cuckoo's Nest.* When timing problems developed for Nicholson, Marlon Brando was approached and found to be interested. As time passed, Belushi and Aykroyd came on board and then were ruled out after Belushi's death. Next, John Malkovich was considered, followed by John Cusack, before Johnny Depp as Raoul Duke and Benicio del Toro as Dr. Gonzo were selected.

A similarly august list of directors attempted to get the film off the ground before moving on, including Oliver Stone, Martin Scorsese, and animator Ralph Bakshi, who couldn't persuade Laila to let it be made into "a cartoon." Hunter was adamant, having long ago soured on *Doonesbury* and not caring how much different Bakshi's work might be.

A coherent screenplay was one of the two big problems everyone had with doing *Vegas* as a film. Absent much of a movie-friendly story line or plot in the book, or one that might have been supplied later by Hunter (but wasn't), there were big challenges. In the end, as with many movies, multiple names were listed in the screenplay credits—Terry Gilliam and Tony Grisoni, Alex Cox and Tod Davies—and it took a threatened lawsuit to arrive at that listing. Hunter contributed several scenes directly to the film, and it was so faithful to his book that both he and Gilliam pronounced themselves pleased, and frankly shocked, at the lack of interference from Universal.

Nevertheless, the film makes poor use of one of the great screen artists of our time by giving Depp very little to work with in developing his character beyond two dimensions of wackiness. Depp's response was to overdo a relatively small bag of Hunter's most arch mannerisms, intentionally exaggerating his walk, hand movements, and the way he shifted the cigarette holder in his mouth until Hunter appears as some horrible cross between Groucho Marx and the Penguin from *Batman.* The film even deprived Depp of the voice-over narrative.

Hunter had managed to provide Raoul Duke with some actual substance in the book in several places and wondered aloud why those scenes, such as The Wave soliloquy, which he considered some of his finest writing ever, hadn't been emphasized more. The badly slapstick drug scenes were dragged out until they became the entire film. The real meat and brilliance of the writing, on the other hand, was reduced to bare sound bites. Gilliam showed very good instincts in believing as strongly as he did in the diner scene, revealing the main characters in a seriously flawed light. With a couple more of those really human aspects of the book thrown in and extended, it might have had a lot more reach.

The other main issue about making *Vegas* a movie always centered on how to handle the psychedelia, the hallucinations, and wild outbursts of fantasy—how to render them on screen in all the glory of their finely crafted written descriptions and with the lush insanity of Steadman's illustrations. This was predigital and before animation had achieved the respectability it has since. But this kind of thing was one of Terry Gilliam's specialties, and many critics, including those who hated the film, commended his handling of the special effects.

Gilliam has always said that he was never a big druggie in spite of the assumption that all the members of Monty Python were. "We weren't," he insists. "We were really very buttoned down in many ways." In spite of my affection for Gilliam's body of work, and the critical praise he got for the technical end of this movie, I think even that aspect was weak in ways that undermined everything else. And I wonder, in spite of earning Hunter's endorsement, if the movie didn't suffer because Gilliam had never taken acid. I wonder the same about the critics who lauded the imagery. "The closest sensory approximation of an acid trip ever achieved by a mainstream movie and the latest example of Gilliam's visual bravura," wrote Stephen Holden in an otherwise tepid *New York Times* review. The sequences were technically well done, seamless, and striking, but just so over the top that they combined with the exaggerated rest to feel like a bad and stupid dream.

Hunter had such respect for Gilliam, Depp, del Toro, and everyone involved that I think even though his feelings about the result were decidedly mixed, he always gave the movie his full support. Depp had been quoted repeatedly in the press saying that the only thing that really mattered to him was what Hunter thought of his performance and the film. And Hunter was gracious enough to take the point.

In a long letter to *Vanity Fair* in 2004, Ben Affleck quoted Hunter calling Hollywood a "cruel and shallow money trench, a long plastic hallway where thieves and pimps run free and good men die like dogs."

But some of Hunter's brainstorming did pay off in various ways over the years, and might still do so for his estate. In the mid-1990s, a movie idea of his was adapted by CBS television and his neighbor Don Johnson and turned into the long-running Nash Bridges series.

For all of its seeming made-to-order nature for Hunter, he has yet to succeed in feature films. I believe it could still be done, and will be. There is room for a reasonably broad-appeal, avant-garde project like the *I'm Not There* Bob Dylan film, or even *Being John Malkovich*. A biographical look at Hunter's life in the manner of *Leaving Las Vegas,* only employing one of his own stories for a framework, could be very workable. There is also hope for a good, literate, dark comedy on the order of *Hospital* or *Broadcast News* in material such as *The Curse of Lono* and other Hunter stories and unpublished movie ideas. Posthumous success in Hollywood would be the final irony in Hunter's tortured relationship with show business.

Documentaries about Hunter have enjoyed better fates than films based on his works. The BBC produced several over the years, as has filmmaker Wayne Ewing. The documentary on the filming of *Fear and Loathing in Las Vegas* is better than the movie itself. A collection of Charlie Rose shows with Hunter, released right after his death, has proven very popular. And the theatrical-release documentary *Gonzo,* which debuted at Sundance in the spring of 2008 and was directed by Academy Award–winner Alex Gibney, has met with some critical and commercial success. Several of Hunter's closest friends, including Bob Braudis and Laila Nabulsi, have pronounced themselves less than dazzled by it. The narrow focus on the era of the late sixties and early seventies and the broad assumption the movie seems to endorse that Hunter produced no good work after that, have been taken to task. Still, the fact that people continue to be attracted to Hunter's story is an indication that there could also be a market for movies made *of* his works, rather than just about them, if someone put the whole package together, starting with a viable script.

11

The Sporting Life

Just a Nice Guy and an Athlete

Though there are many views of Hunter, and while he may cast a long and mutant shadow, I like to think of him as he liked to think of himself: "Just a nice guy and an athlete," he used to say, smiling wickedly.

People were frequently surprised when they met Hunter and found that he was taller and bigger than they anticipated. He blamed this on the *Doonesbury* factor because people would actually say, "You look smaller in the comic strip." In addition to his size, in his prime and even on into his early sixties, Hunter had the look of an athlete. Perhaps one gone slightly to seed after his retirement, but many pro athletes look like that.

First, there was the way he dressed, which always featured tennis shoes unless there was two feet of snow outside. For many years they were just old-fashioned Converses that he bought four pairs at a time. After hooking up with *Running* magazine he became a Nike guy. Shorts of one description or another were his stock wardrobe, often even when there *was* two feet of snow. He usually wore a Sun Devils or some other team T-shirt from one of the colleges where he spoke, and in the winter he'd slip into one of a series of shiny parkas with sponsor patches on them that looked like he might have stolen them from a pro snowmobiler. For the most part, Hunter dressed like a sporting man on his way to a casual paddletennis match, the golf course, or maybe a pickup basketball game down the street.

Sometimes that was actually the case, when he could finally be pried loose from his home. He was occasionally dragged out to the golf course, sometimes by me, sometimes by Ed Bradley, or for a benefit tournament. We managed to get in some fairly bloodthirsty, high-stakes badminton in his front yard when the wind wasn't blowing. And Hunter loved his paddle ball outings because he could play just up the road at Stranahan's, in comfort and privacy and whenever he managed to show up, as George tried to be flexible about that.

This was because if he had slept (which was always desirable), Hunter would not likely get up until midafternoon. Then he would eat, limber up, medicate, check his lists, load an Igloo cooler full of beverages and picnic supplies, spend half an hour searching for things like his new motion-sensor siren to demonstrate for George, and take longer gathering all his supplies: Dunhills, lighters, ice, a bottle of tequila and one of whiskey, several forms of stimulants and muscle relaxants, a couple of rackets and some balls, maybe a camera, and a gun of some kind. By then it was probably after five, so if it was the middle of summer we had a shot at getting in a couple of hours before George had to turn on the lights.

"The hardest part for me is getting me up and getting me out," he explained needlessly for a magazine story I did on him. "But once I'm there I've never pulled a 'Sorry, I'm just not up to it.'"

This will all sound a little tame, but behind it there really was an athlete. I hadn't considered that possibility when I first got to know Hunter until we were lobbing a football around his yard one day and he kept feathering off perfect thirty- and forty-yard spirals. When I asked where he'd picked up that talent he said that his first big choice in life had actually been between crime and sports when he was in high school.

He talked about playing football and doing robberies in the bright green summers of his youth in Louisville, Kentucky, home to many a sports hero, including Muhammad Ali, who grew up only a few blocks away from him. Hunter was a good quarterback, he allowed (and I believed him), and even played Little League baseball. "One game I had to pitch in front of a full crowd, under the lights at night, and I walked twenty-two straight," he told me, with a faraway wince in his eyes.

Crime seemed like a better way to make money for a while, but once he was cured of that he turned to writing. And for several years it was sports writing. That influence can be seen throughout his adjective-laden prose and exaggerated metaphors. Not even a stint as a bowling writer in Puerto Rico discouraged him. "Bowling promoters are among the most wretched people on earth," he used to say.

Sports were simply in his blood, sometimes if only as a tool for betting. But not all sports, of course. He never did cotton to skiing, for example, even though he lived around it for forty years. The bad impression made by the Killy story didn't help. Nor did the idea that he'd have to gear up pretty significantly if he wanted to pursue the game. Unbeknownst to most, however, he actually did ski. It was only once, as far as I'm aware, and a friend of mine, an Aspen ski instructor, got him out.

Ken Oakes had known Hunter for a while and one night at the Hotel Jerome offered to take him skiing. "And he actually showed up," smiles Kenny. "He made the date and came on out. I think it was around noon and we skied the rest of the day. This was probably in 1976 or so and he did great. He wanted to go right to the top and do it. We made two or three runs on Home Road," says Ken, referring to one of Buttermilk Mountain's legendary long learning trails. "He had a beer each time to steady his nerves, and he was pretty high to begin with. We had to be sure we put the bar down on the chair to keep him from jumping," he laughs. "He had a good time."

I think once he had satisfied himself that he could actually do it, he wasn't sure he liked being outdoors in the winter well enough to pursue it. And even though he liked Kenny and me and other skiers he knew, he really wasn't convinced we were representative of the sport's population at large, with whom he seriously doubted he had much in common. Not enough, at least, to make him endure long, cold lift rides in their company.

Lots of skiers liked *him,* however. And not just people who skied but serious, competitive racers. Especially some of the craziest ones. The Canadian men's ski team in the 1980s, for example, who were called the Crazy Canucks and featured some of the best ski racers in the world, came to Aspen every year for the Roch Cup downhill, also known as the Aspen Winternational.

In 1982 they showed up in force with one of their troops leading in the race for the overall World Cup in the downhill event. No North American had ever won that particular cup, and the Canucks had been pounding on the door for a few years. Canadian Steve Podborski won the race in Aspen and wrapped up the cup as I watched and cheered from courseside. Afterward I got a call from Hunter.

"Some Canadians want to come over to meet me," he growled. "Some silly name. Crazy Canucks. They're apparently fans. Their coach just called me. Who are they? You know how I feel about ski racers."

I was floored. "Did he say if Steve Podborski was one of them?"

"Yeah, I guess. Did he just win some cup?"

"Yes, he did . . ."

"Well, he's coming out, so are some others, along with this coach who seems to know something about my work. What are you doing?"

I cleaned up, ate, and went over to find Jann Wenner, who is a skier, trying to fill Hunter in on the Canadian downhill team. We both assured him that these guys were good, probably certifiably insane, used to making their living going eighty miles an hour down ice-covered mountainsides and spending a lot of time painfully rehabbing major injuries when things went wrong. That didn't do much to convince him of their intelligence, which was what he most doubted about all ski racers.

But once everyone arrived things went fine. Their coach was a true fan of Hunter's and so was Podborski. I'd been told by my friend Andy Mill, who raced against Pod and knew him well, that he was a great guy who really deserved the title. So here he was, with one of the biggest achievements in the history of North American ski racing less than a few hours old, trading stories with Hunter and Jann and me in Hunter's kitchen.

Most of the rest of the Crazy Canucks were there as well, including Jim Hunter, Dave Murray, and Dave Irwin. I mentioned to Hunter that all of these guys were famous for their injuries as well as for winning races in the go-for-broke style of the team at that time. So they spent half an hour swapping tales of battle wounds while some of them would occasionally slip into the back bathroom for a discreet bump, courtesy of the house.

I asked about some of the stories I'd heard of the biggest and baddest of the European downhills, and Hunter listened with genuine fascination. They talked about how nuts some of the races are—the Hahnenkamm in Austria, the superfast downhill in Germany, the Criterion in France—and illustrated their points with their own worst wrecks on them. Hunter compared it to the fun of riding motorcycles fast in the dark, and they all agreed.

"Well, of course I think all of you are ignorant fucking white trash for doing stuff like this anyway," he grinned, "but what the hell. It's a living, right? And probably better than mine."

They hooted and everyone drank and the talk turned to other things than just going fast and getting hurt. Gradually Hunter seemed to relax and so did they. Jann got everyone talking about some of the wild parties on the World Cup circuit and the places they traveled. They stayed for a couple of hours, even though they were due at various other major parties in Aspen to celebrate Podborski's big win. When they did finally leave, Hunter pronounced himself persuaded that not all ski racers were humorless drones.

Even though there were sports such as skiing and bowling he had scant affection for, he could become a convert, or at least temporary viewer, as long as they had potential for betting. Sports provided endless entertainment for Hunter and were also the inspiration for some of his best work. He loved and wrote frequently about boxing and basketball, football and fishing, and even made money from skiing and bowling. *The Curse of Lono* grew out of his coverage of marathon running. Writing about the Kentucky Derby launched his whole career. And going to Las Vegas for an off-road race was the genesis of what is widely viewed as his greatest book and one of the landmarks of American literature.

That ESPN recognized this about him and hired him to write his "Hey Rube" column online for them when he was over sixty was a testament not just to their understanding of him but to his knowledge of sports, and his ability to give it greater reach and readability. It also allowed him to take advantage of what he did anyway, which was watch TV constantly and not feel like he had to be out doing the research firsthand or participating directly in the story himself. He could call up coaches and athletes he knew to cover that aspect of the piece and also indulge his fantasy/fiction riffs where he chose. In short, it was a good arrangement for both sides, allowing him to do what he knew and loved.

The Campaign Trials

Another thing Hunter knew and loved was politics. And what is politics after all if not just a weirder, meaner sport than most? And it was the sport that his interest always reverted to. I know people who thought that was true even to the detriment of his writing, while I felt just the opposite. As a politically engaged human, my tastes would be unreliable on this matter. But I have always felt that when he was focusing on politics Hunter's writing was unforced, free flowing, and at its most expressive. I honestly think his best book is *Fear and Loathing on the Campaign Trail '72*. Almost no one else agrees with me, and some of Hunter's biggest fans who are not political by nature found *Campaign Trail* nearly unreadable. I understand that. But I believe that in his heart of hearts Hunter was a profoundly political being who was more energized and fascinated by politics than anything else, including drugs, sex (thus his book about politics called *Better Than Sex*), guns, and even making money. And I think that he was at his best when he was writing about politics in one form or another, as in this excerpt about the 1972 Republican convention in *Fear and Loathing on the Campaign Trail*:

> For the first and only time during the whole convention, the cops were clearly off balance. The vets could have closed all six lanes of Collins Avenue if they'd wanted to, and nobody would have argued. I have been covering anti-war demonstrations

> with depressing regularity since the winter of 1964, in cities all over the country, and I have never seen cops so intimidated by demonstrators as they were in front of the Fountainbleau Hotel on that hot Tuesday afternoon in Miami Beach.
>
> There was an awful tension in that silence. Not even that pack of rich sybarites out there on the foredeck of the Wild Rose of Houston could stay in their seats for this show. They were standing up at the rail, looking worried, getting very bad vibrations from whatever was happening out there in the street. Was something wrong with their gladiators? Were they spooked? And why was there no noise?

Hunter took politics very personally, as we all should, because it is being done to each of us and is, in his oft repeated words, "the art of controlling your environment." And it wasn't just that he was a control freak; that's what we all need to be when it comes to people creating laws and legislation that will directly affect everyone. People who don't take a personal interest in politics are leaving their fate in the hands of gods who are blind, or at least supremely indifferent, to their existence.

Of course, most people simply don't have the time to deal with politics or the resources to know how. We would like to trust our fellow citizens and our government. Failing that, we would like to think that they will, even by accident, at least get it right some of the time. If nothing else we would like to believe that our interests might occasionally be coincident with those of the people running things. However reasonable that may sound, there is nothing in history to suggest that it is reality.

For such reasons Hunter was very big on controlling his own environment, especially after the first time he got a whiff of the possibility that it could actually be done, during local political races in Aspen. When he almost succeeded in getting a mayor elected here, it opened his eyes to a whole new realm of possibilities. When he almost got himself elected as sheriff, it turned him into at least a temporary believer. And as he used to say, there is nothing more dangerous than believers. Usually to themselves.

Coming out of his near-miss for sheriff, Hunter was swept up in the feeling that many of us had then, a sense that it was our time, we were riding a mighty tide that would lift all boats and carry them to greatness, or at least to goodness, rather than just to crash on the rocks. Hunter was afflicted with the notion that it wasn't just possible for a Freak Power ticket to prevail in a tiny, anomalous enclave such as Aspen but worldwide. Or at least nationally. We had, after all, brought an end to an insane and immoral war and driven Richard Nixon from office.

The forces of justice seemed to be on a roll and there was actually evidence of a sort that they could prevail. It was all self-deluding bullshit, of course, but hearts swollen with faith are famously easy to mislead. Unfortunately, the beginning of the end of this great wave was already upon us. The opening shots, quite literally, had been fired in 1968, but we would only fully understand that in retrospect and not for four or five years at that.

The truth is that for those who are truly addicted to politics, some kind of faith, however warped, still remains at the core of what they do. It may be a faith that right will triumph or it may just be the hubris of thinking they can influence events, but they have an implicit belief that they can make a difference. Such was always the case for Hunter. As he wrote in his 1994 book, *Better Than Sex,* "I got into politics a long time ago and I still believe, on some days, that it can be an honorable trade. . . . That is not an easy belief to hang on to after wallowing for 30 years in the belly of a beast that has beaten and broken more good men and women than crack and junk bonds combined."

That belief, however, was not what made him famous and respected in political circles. What caused that was his remarkable ability to know who to talk to and who to believe and to translate that into pronouncements of unusual prescience and endorsements of unusual significance.

Considering Hunter's background and reputation, this was astounding. It was the peacock factor all over again. The rest of the flock, recognizing the severe impediments Hunter had handicapped himself with—the outrageous behavior, the ongoing illegalities—couldn't help but be impressed that he was still able to exert the influence he did. That had to require genuine brilliance on his part. If you were a lifelong political operative devoted heart and soul to your work, and you suddenly encountered this wild, criminal beast coming out of deep left field with no visible qualifications, no background, and nothing to suggest that his ideas should even be countenanced, let alone heeded, indeed everything to suggest that he should be locked up and forgotten, and yet here he was, being quoted, sought out, and listened to—well, it made Hunter a genetic gold mine, an obvious champion among mortals, some kind of serious evolutionary leap to whom attention must be paid.

When Senator John Kerry came to Aspen during his doomed presidential campaign of 2004, the first person he met with was Hunter. Aspen has long been a good stop for progressive Democrats seeking the nation's highest office, and indeed during 2007 most of the major contenders from both parties visited town. A lot of big money is available in this small valley and it's a chance for politicians to raise substantial funds without having to strain themselves. Though considered a last bastion of liberalism, our community contains both sides of the political fence, including the Sam Wyly family, the principal funders of the Swift Boat Veterans for Truth group, which wreaked so much sleazy havoc with Kerry's campaign.

Kerry had not come specifically to see Hunter, but Hunter made it a point to meet him at the airport when he first arrived. For a man such as Kerry, who proved so circumspect in so many regards, meeting with Hunter publicly as his first official act upon arrival in one of America's best-known party towns made a statement that surprisingly few people noticed. One might have thought that as a politician seeking always to portray himself with as few potentially negative associations as possible, even being caught in the same room with an outspoken advocate of every kind of illegal drug use known to man would be considered undesirable.

But Hunter's surprisingly welcome support of candidates began as early as 1968 with Eugene McCarthy and George McGovern in 1972. Their acknowledged radicalism almost mandated that they invite him to the table. By so doing they established that he was not toxic but in fact shrewd and effective on their behalf. That paved the way for his unexpected endorsement of the much more mainstream Jimmy Carter and, reluctantly, Bill Clinton. In both cases there were indications that Hunter's, and *Rolling Stone*'s, backing helped get them elected. The only candidate he favored who didn't win his party's nomination was Gary Hart, and that could hardly be blamed on Hunter.

In *Better Than Sex,* he ventured an explanation about why he wasn't a persona non grata on the campaign trails in spite of his reputation.

> Most people will deny their addictions—but not me. I have an addictive personality, and medical experts agree that I can't be cured—which used to worry people running for President of the United States when I showed up with no warning at their homes late at night for random confrontations on issues of national security or regressive taxation or rumors of ugly personal scandals in the family. . . . No candidate will risk being linked with a "suspected" addict—but a registered, admitted addict is a whole different thing. As long as I'd confessed, I was okay. . . . As long as they knew that I knew I was sick and guilty, I was safe. They were only trying to help me.

This theory had its limitations, and Hunter tested them early on. He felt comfortable with Jimmy Carter and the people surrounding him because they seemed to understand him and value his contributions to their campaign and subsequent presidency. He also told me when he was first being courted by Carter that several of his aides were regular pot smokers and occasional cocaine users, a fact that pleased us. That people actually making the policies for the country were active drug users was encouraging when compared to the grimly virulent anti-drug stances of other administrations. Finally it seemed that some of the counterculture dreams about inheriting a more tolerant world were coming true.

After Carter took office, Hunter continued to be close to some of his chief aides. In the fashion of significant contributors to any successful presidential campaign, Hunter was soon invited to the White

House. Being Hunter, he didn't arrive until late in the day and was shown around after hours. After he returned to Owl Farm he was coy about what had transpired but flashed that conspiratorial smile and touched his nose and mumbled about spending some quality time in the Oval Office.

Not long after that he was featured on the cover of the September 1977 issue of *High Times* magazine and in a long interview inside. When he received the galleys of the interview at Owl Farm all hell broke loose, and he summoned me over to help with what he cryptically told me over the phone was "a crisis that could bring down the president."

Hunter had demanded final-cut approval on the interview and was threatening *High Times* with pulling the entire piece when I arrived. He had, it turned out, spoken more freely during the interview than he should have, with the understanding that certain things wouldn't be included. But in the first draft he received he was quoted as saying that he had, in effect, snorted coke with prominent members of the president's staff in the Oval Office.

I thought it was funny, but Hunter had been up for days, was cranked to the gills, and in no good humor about anything. "I can see why they'd want to run the quotes," I told him. "It's pretty dramatic stuff."

"It's fucking nitroglycerine!" he shouted at me. "If this runs they'll lynch Carter on the front steps of the White House, and that'll be after his people have me killed or thrown in some unlisted dungeon somewhere."

"What do you want to do?" I asked.

"Sue them blind, then slit their throats and watch them bleed. I told them they couldn't use any of this. They're a bunch of addled freaks who have no idea what they're screwing with here. It won't just burn Carter and us, but the whole damned country, including *High Times*. Do they think that ugly little magazine will last more than twenty-four hours after something like this comes out? It'll be burned to the ground with all of them in it. They won't even bury them. They'll just cover it with concrete, like Nixon did the White House swimming pool, and turn it into a maximum security prison that'll always smell like bone ash and bong water." He was stomping around his house, slamming stuff around, glaring through maddened eyes, and calling lawyers every few minutes. Eventually we retreated to the War Room, where over the next few days an agreement was hammered out with the magazine, which was already past deadline, whereby the drug use references were changed so that they discussed activity on the campaign trail instead of in the White House.

Both Hunter and the magazine were reluctant to simply cut any mention of the Oval Office incident at all because it was the highlight of the interview and it indicated Hunter's powerful connections and participation in the kind of things most people never even thought of. It was still the "sucking on sleeves in the men's room" that he had talked about back in San Francisco almost twenty years earlier. The mention of doing drugs with key political aides was one of his few overt public admissions about how he came up with so much of his good material during the campaigns. But he wasn't willing to go any further with it.

As a result of their protracted negotiations, Hunter allowed himself to be quoted about a phrase he had coined, "tapping the glass": "That means chopping up rocks of cocaine on a glass coffee table or some mirror we had jerked off the wall for that purpose—but not necessarily with one of Carter's people. The whole point of this wretched confession is that there were so many people tapping the glass in the '76 campaign that you never knew who might turn up at one of these midnight sessions."

When pressed about whether this meant that he had done coke with some people who were now in the White House, he replied, "Well . . . some of them, yes. But let's get a grip on ourselves here. We don't want to cause a national panic by saying that a gang of closet coke freaks are running the country—although that would probably be the case, no matter who had won the election."

Finally, the *High Times* interviewer says, "The inner circle of Carter's people are serious drug users?" And Hunter replies, "Wait a minute. I didn't say that. For one thing, a term like *serious* users has a very weird and menacing connotation; and, for another, we were talking about a *few people* from almost *everybody's* staff. Across the board . . . Not junkies or freaks, but people who were just as comfortable with drugs like weed, booze or coke as we are—and we're not weird, are we? Hell no, we're just overworked professionals who need to relax now and then, have a bit of the whoop and the giggle, right?"

It was important to Hunter to maintain his truthfulness but not ruin people who trusted him and in ways that could be bad for all of us. As he had already been careful to explain, "Carter would put me in jail in an instant if he saw me snorting coke in front of him. He would not, however, follow me into the bathroom and try to catch me snorting."

Of course, any direct revelation about actual cocaine usage by staff in the White House would have created chaos for Carter, put Hunter squarely in the crosshairs of who knows how many federal subpoenas and investigations, and destroyed untold numbers of lives forever. Even though that was avoided, the implications of Hunter's comments were obvious, and the fact that Carter's administration was riddled with casual drug users soon became a matter of common gossip. In 1978 Carter's top drug adviser, Dr. Peter Bourne, had to resign after writing a prescription for Quaaludes for a secretary under a fictitious name. In a subsequent interview Bourne said there was a "high incidence" of marijuana use among members of the White House staff as well as "occasional cocaine use by a few" of his former colleagues.

After this kind of dangerous behavior by Hunter and the President's men, it wouldn't have been surprising if Hunter had been shunned forever after by anyone with serious designs on the presidency. But that didn't happen, and the fact that he had the kind of access he obviously did, combined with the important people who had been compromised by their drug use with him and therefore were anxious to keep him happy and on their side, actually increased his reputation as a consummate insider who knew many things no one else could. He laid out the risks in this kind of thing in "The Banshee Screams For Buffalo Meat," in *The Great Shark Hunt*.

—one of the darker skills involved in the kind of journalism I normally get involved with has to do with the ability to

> write the Truth about "criminals" without getting them busted—and, in the eyes of the law, any person committing a crime is criminal: whether it's a Hell's Angel laying an oil slick on a freeway exit to send a pursuing motorcycle cop crashing over the high side, a presidential candidate smoking a joint in his hotel room, or a good friend who happens to be a lawyer, an arsonist and a serious drug abuser.
>
> The line between writing truth and providing evidence is very, very thin—but for a journalist working constantly among highly paranoid criminals, it is also the line between trust and suspicion. And that is the difference between having free access to the truth and being treated like a spy. There is no such thing as "forgiveness" on that level; one fuck-up will send you straight back to sportswriting—if you're lucky.

It was one thing for Hunter to have influence within the Democratic Party, which some already viewed as a hotbed of dopers and communists. But to have the same kind of clout in a general election was another matter entirely. It meant that no matter how much of a monster many people in politics thought he was, they also had to reckon with him—if for no other reason than that he was uncannily accurate in much of what he felt and predicted.

No one was sure whether this was a product of political genius, great inside connections, supernatural intuition, close contact with the prevailing zeitgeist, or just drug relationships with those in a position to know everything he didn't. But no one could afford to take the chance of betting on one or the other of those options and being wrong, so they had to accept, in some form or another, the whole package. Which was only fair, because however Hunter gained the inside info, he was smart enough to know how to interpret and use it.

Hunter being Hunter, naturally let this go to his head. Once he began believing his own press, he got lazier and tended to rely less on well-placed sources and more on his own instincts. When he ultimately began raving at his contacts within the campaign organizations, advising and exhorting them rather than talking and listening to them, they acknowledged his input, no matter how outrageous, because there were occasional truths in it no one else was seeing. But not even he was infallible.

When he saw real promise in a little-known peanut farmer from Georgia in 1976, he was a committee of one in his part of the political spectrum. But he was right and may have even contributed to Carter's victory. The same was possibly also true in 1992 with Bill Clinton. On the other hand, when he decided late in 1992 that Ross Perot was just a stooge for the Bush campaign and began warning Clinton's aides about it, he completely misread the way the vote would go. The statistics actually showed that Perot handed the election to Clinton. Twice. No great handicapper at any sport gains a reputation by publicizing their failures. Instead they focus on their victories and pretend the rest was either bad information or a sinister conspiracy.

For years, one of Hunter's most valuable political contacts was a young lawyer named Bill Dixon, who ultimately ran Gary Hart's campaign for the 1988 presidential election. In spite of all of Hunter's connections and close relationships with past presidential candidates, this was the closest he came to having a true friend and confidante in the White House. Hart was a strong early favorite to win the Democratic nomination and the general election and would have almost certainly appointed Dixon as his chief of staff. They wouldn't have brought Hunter on board in any kind of official capacity, but he would have had the ear of the man closest to the president on a regular basis.

Unfortunately, Hart was also widely known as a womanizer and partier and was being closely watched by a variety of newspeople whom he had directly challenged to prove the rumors that he was running around on his wife. When photos were produced of Hart and actress/model Donna Rice frolicking on a boat called *Monkey Business* in Bimini, as well as meeting at his townhouse in Washington, D.C., the end was brutal and sudden.

"The *New York Times* magazine had just kind of anointed Gary Hart on their cover as virtually a lock to be the next president. And we were on deadline for Hunter's next column when he said, 'Let's call Bill Dixon and do a kind of a celebratory piece on how well Hart is doing,'" remembers David McCumber, Hunter's editor at the *Examiner*. "So we were on a three-way phone conference with Dixon when he got call waiting and then came back and said, 'The *Miami Herald* has Gary trapped in a condo with some bimbo. I've gotta go.'"

When Donna Rice's name surfaced and David told Hunter about it, Hunter said he knew her. "She was Don Henley's girlfriend," he said. "I think I could probably get a picture of her."

"I told him, well, Jesus Christ, that would be great, and so he drove down the road to Henley's place, who was gone, so Hunter broke in and rifled the place and came up with a Polaroid of her that had been tacked to a cabinet door. He air-freighted it to me right away and we beat all the other outlets with the first photo of Donna Rice by a full cycle. It was crazy."

Over the next period of days the story unfolded, and then the news broke about the photos of Hart with Donna Rice partying together on the charted boat. I was in Hunter's kitchen with him and Maria working on the next column for the *Examiner* when Bill Dixon called to say he was on his way to Hunter's, he had just quit Hart's staff and would be arriving soon to talk about what was happening. It sounded like Hart was dropping out and it was a watershed moment in American politics. Bill wanted counsel from one of the men he knew and trusted the most about this sort of thing.

It wasn't the kind of consultation that could wait and we knew that. The problem was that the deadline for the column was just hours away and Hunter was toast. I don't remember how long he'd been up, but he was nearly catatonic. Still, we were sure that if anything would revive him it would be this. The biggest breaking story in the country, perhaps of the entire year, was about to walk in the door of his house. He would not only have all the most intimate details handed to him on a silver platter, but he would have hands-on involvement in its outcome. It was any journalist's wet dream, and even more so for Hunter because he would be a crucial part of it. Nothing would have to be invented or elaborated on or speculated about. It would all be right there at his fingertips and he wouldn't have to leave the house, or even his kitchen, or even his perch on his favorite stool. The only hitch was that he needed to be conscious and coherent and he wasn't, and there was no way to change that.

He was sitting upright in front of his typewriter, he could open his eyes, roll his head around and utter noises, but that was it. By the time Bill arrived, everyone's mutual friend Monty Chitty was with us, and Hunter was still gargling unintelligibly about the unfinished column, trying to read what he'd already written and remember what he'd been thinking when he started it.

Bill would rather have met with Hunter alone and was disturbed to see that there'd be an audience. He was understandably agitated, in a hurry, and not interested in sharing with us. His first move was to ask Hunter if they could talk in private, but when that produced no discernible response he went ahead and tried to explain the situation. It didn't take long before it was obvious, even in Bill's rattled state, that there was something wrong. Hunter would try to focus on him but his eyes rolled and his shoulders sagged. When he was able to say anything it was about the column and his need to finish it.

Bill was stunned. Maria and I tried to talk to Hunter and then explain what was going on to Bill. Like too many other people who didn't spend a lot of time with Hunter, he had never seen him in this condition. He looked angrily around at us and demanded, "What have you done? Why have you let this happen?"

"We haven't let anything happen. This is Hunter. This is what he does. You can't really think we have anything to say about it," I answered. By now I was way too familiar with this version of Hunter and tired of trying to explain it to people who just didn't believe he had this much of a problem. So was Maria.

"Doesn't anyone here understand what the hell is happening? I've just come straight here from the campaign, which is over as of tonight, and he can't even talk to me? Why the fuck am I wasting my time, why didn't anyone warn me?"

The fact was, we hadn't had a chance. And besides, neither of us was in a position to tell someone like Bill that he couldn't come to see Hunter about one of the most important moments in his life. On top of that, too many critical decisions had already been made and acted on. By the time Bill was able to actually communicate with Hunter, the die had been cast. The story and photos had gone public, Dixon's resignation from the campaign had been announced, and Gary Hart had withdrawn from the race.

Hunter would forever insist that if he'd had anything to say about it, he would have told Hart to stonewall and deny everything, claiming he'd been drugged and set up. He would have urged Dixon to stay on the staff at least until the dust had settled and to see how bad the fallout really was. The problem for Bill was much the same as it would be for Al Gore twelve years later. According to Hunter, Bill had talked with Hart about needing to rein in his libido, and Gary had assured him that he would and that there was nothing to worry about. When the Donna Rice story broke, Bill felt completely blindsided. His man had just thrown away the presidency and Dixon's White House office with it.

Using the Hart episode as a lesson, in 1992 Hunter strongly advised Clinton's people that he should deny everything about the festering Gennifer Flowers accusations and get on with his business. It was the "What marijuana?" strategy all over again, and it worked, at least for awhile. By the time the Monica Lewinsky scandal caught up with Clinton several years later, adamant denial was no longer such a slick option, and it was hard not to think that had Clinton simply admitted the blow jobs from the outset and moved on, the outcome would have been very different. At least he couldn't have been found guilty of lying to Congress, and there are many who believe that America, like the rest of the world, was willing to countenance a little hanky-panky from its chief executive and other elected officials if it didn't get in the way of their governing. The idea, as Hunter expressed it, was, "I don't care who he fucks, as long as it isn't the country."

Hunter's advice on all of these sex scandals might have been useful, but it either came too late or not at all. His eventual opinion was that Gary Hart was probably too stupid and perpetually horny to have made a good president anyway, and by the time Clinton was embroiled in Monicagate, Hunter had already decided the president had been set up long ago and written him off as a permanent embarrassment and blot on his own political record.

Hunter continued writing about politics and participating in them locally, as in an address to a peace rally in Aspen in February 2003, where he told fellow protesters, "I've been to a few of these things. I've become almost homesick for the smell of tear gas," and later exhorted them that they could beat city hall and "You can run presidents out of the White House."

Still, the full effect of the national political scene so discouraged and embittered Hunter about the future of politics and the country in general that I think it was very hard on him. Watching Clinton virtually giftwrap and hand the next election to George W. Bush, and then watching Bush have to steal it anyway—and get away with it, twice—was more than he could bear. After his friend John Kerry got whipped on like a dog, Hunter couldn't foresee any end to the madness, or any hope for the world.

In his longtime mortal enemy and worthy adversary, Richard Nixon, Hunter had someone he could fight and beat, a foe who made it fun and worthwhile. The future held none of that and seemed only to promise ruin and apocalypse with no hope of ever winning anything again. If the putative good guys were going to behave like craven swine, and the bad guys were so thoroughly bent and efficiently evil that they couldn't even destroy themselves, then what was the use of fighting it or caring at all? It didn't even make good copy any more.

Add that kind of soul-sucking malaise to a failing body that was apparently determined to deny his doing the sports he loved or being able to write about them with any pleasure or comfort, let alone without constant physical pain, and there was little left to live for. Words seemed to fail him more often than fulfill him. He was actually writing better than he had in a while, but there was nothing he wanted to write about. Sports had become just another cruel hoax. Drugs, which had never provided much in the way of answers, now seemed incapable of providing any fun or diversion either. The last hopes on his list, sex and love, were the only refuge left, and even they looked bleak.

12

Friends and Lovers

Almost everyone has a difficult uncle, an aunt who's a pill, or at least one relative or friend we spend half our time wondering why we put up with. Such individuals are often described, with a slight pause, as "complicated." And if you don't know someone like that, it's usually because you're that person. The degree to which we do put up with those people, or that others put up with us, depends a lot on self-awareness. Most difficult people who are tolerated *know* that they can be impossible, and that's one of their most endearing qualities. There is a sense that they wish they weren't that way, but they often can't help it no matter how much they try, and they genuinely appreciate our indulgence. Hunter, of course, was that person in many people's lives.

I put up with what I did from Hunter (and I think this was true for many) because first of all he put up with a lot from me. He was also one of the most brilliant and funny people I ever met, and he could be a very good friend. He set high standards in everything and expected our best from us. I think most of us took that, most of the time, as a compliment. I know that's the way he meant it. He set the same standards for himself, even if it could be hard to tell at times. But when someone puts the bar that high and then lets you know you've reached it, it makes you feel good. When he shined his light your way—and he was very honest about that, it was rarely phony—there was nothing like it. You put up with a lot to stand in that glow.

Our attraction to such people, I think, comes about because usually they are bright and talented, and by our mere association with them we feel that way ourselves. We must be worthy of their attention when they do give it to us. Plus, they're fun and stimulating. They take us out of ourselves and into worlds we might not otherwise have visited.

Obviously, there is good reason to think that the element of being difficult is part and parcel of being creative, and that we forgive a lot in people who are that way because we recognize this fact. That, in turn, leaves the process open to abuse. There is a very fine line between being allowed to behave in ways that others don't and being a total jerk. Hunter explored those boundaries and walked that line almost daily, like willful children or pets trying to see what the limits really are and how much they are loved.

Insecurity, of course, is another hallmark of creativity. It is a rare artist so confident of what they do that they don't require continual reassurance, whose ego isn't simultaneously so huge but so fragile that they are always mired in a kind of arrogant and demanding doubt. Hunter received sufficiently adulatory feedback on a regular basis to comfort him. Even when those around him were dubious about some of what he was doing, either with his writing or his personal life, he believed in himself enough to persevere, rightly or wrongly. But he was also discerning enough to recognize when people were just kissing ass, or not qualified to be passing judgment to begin with. And this is a continual fear of the famous and successful. When are you being dealt with honestly and sincerely, and when are people simply intimidated, sycophantish, or otherwise incapable of telling you what you really need to know?

Hunter truly valued his friends even if he didn't always demonstrate it, and he had many of them in all walks of life who only wanted a little of his attention in return. This could result in competition to prove who knew him the best and cared about him the most. While he could be very frustrating to deal with because of this fact, and wasn't above playing on it, he also had a pretty keen bullshit detector and paid closer attention than it sometimes seemed to those he cared about the most. He was always conscious of his effect on people and sometimes more tolerant of how they behaved around him than he would have had to be.

For the women in his life, as well as his closest friends, it could be a constant struggle to separate Hunter from the cling-ons and toadies, the groupies and wannabes who can suck up a lot of energy and time. These human black holes are especially common in the celebrity world and are a constant menace because of the vulnerability of such essentially insecure artists. The poor dears. Hunter usually knew when he was being played but wasn't immune to enjoying it. And because he could be so needy, he loved an entourage and he had a tendency to burn through people.

Hunter enjoyed the stimulation of frequent visitors and an ever-changing cast of company. And I think he recognized that those he enjoyed the most also had lives of their own and couldn't just hang out with him all the time. When you really need to have people around more or less constantly, you have to settle for those who have nothing better to do, which isn't always a good indication of their character or stand-alone value.

Drugs were a complicating aspect of Hunter's friendships and associations. He wasn't often willing to tolerate total losers and jerks just so he could maintain his supplies, but making sure he was never left completely in the lurch was definitely a consideration. He always had a couple of people he could count on, especially for his coke, but that wasn't foolproof. Dealers also had lives that occasionally compelled them to be gone when Hunter needed them, and conditions didn't always permit them to have in stock what he required. As with anyone who is fully dependent on anything, Hunter found it necessary to have multiple sources and backups.

In addition to being a habitual consumer he was also a discriminating one who wasn't willing to settle for crap. So Hunter not only needed enough sources to ensure blanket coverage for his drug habits day in and day out, he needed good ones. Because of an almost evolutionary winnowing process in the drug business, suppliers -- especially of The Kind (good, high-quality blow) -- tended for a time to be interesting and reasonably together people who were tolerable as companions as well as connections. They might, however, also be fairly serious abusers of their own product, which could turn them hinky and troublesome, but Hunter was willing to cut them slack under most circumstances.

This was necessary because he didn't want to stock up too extravagantly on coke for a variety of reasons. Often he didn't have the cash available to buy several ounces at a time instead of just eight balls or quarters. He also, justifiably, didn't trust himself to have too much around at any one time for fear he'd just keep binging until it was gone. And drug laws are such that the penalties for possession of larger quantities are much harsher than for lesser amounts.

All of this meant Hunter had to arrange for regular deliveries when he was in town and to have reliable options while he was on the road. In turn, this provided him with an excuse to have people stopping by at all hours of the day and night, often staying for extended periods talking and watching TV, even when his wife or girlfriend would have preferred otherwise.

As a result of his needs, fame, and interests, Hunter had a very wide circle of friends and acquaintances that included dope dealers, artists, politicians, attorneys, stockbrokers, contractors, ranchers, race car drivers, zillionaires, athletes, editors, publishers, writers, strippers, gangsters, musicians, carpenters, tradesmen, crafts people, business people, restaurateurs, bartenders, cab drivers, pilots, kids, models, trust-funders, hustlers, socialites, realtors, doctors, ambassadors, spies, poets, actors, producers, directors, ski instructors, hoteliers, cops, robbers, porn stars, and on and on.

In his last few books he took to the strange conceit of including a so-called Honor Roll page where he would list the names of those he considered to be such loyal and good friends that they deserved, or he owed them, some special mention. This usually focused on names of the moment that other writers tend to put in the form of "Acknowledgments."

From a quasi-objective point of view, it always seemed to me and others who had known him awhile that his best friends were often some of his oldest ones, and I think when Hunter was rational he felt the same way. In the nearly forty years that I knew him well, I never once doubted that his best friend was Tom Benton. They went through some ups and downs, and both had personal problems that would occasionally interfere with their relationship, but Tom was always there for Hunter and vice versa. Tom was smart enough to hold his own, knowledgeable enough to provide Hunter with information and inspiration, wise enough to counsel him and to know when not to, funny and crazy enough to nearly always be good company, and rarely so needy that he competed with Hunter in that regard. He understood Hunter, valued his close friendship and presence, knew when he was out of control and just plain wrong, and knew how to handle that or leave it alone. I never saw him let his own ego get in the way or take personally the petty slights and oversights Hunter was capable of. And with all that, Tom never played second fiddle, never relegated himself to the role of faithful sidekick or pretender. It was an amazingly adroit balancing act that seemed a natural offshoot of their chemistry, and I always admired and respected Tom for it.

Only a handful of others came close to that mark. They were all strong and accomplished individuals who had lives of their own, who loved and endeavored to understand Hunter, usually didn't let his sometimes mercurial temperament get to them, gave as good as they got, and whom he always valued and respected in turn. They included Monty Chitty, Michael Solheim, Semmes Luckett, Bill Dixon, Loren Jenkins, and Doug Carpenter.

At or near the top of anyone's list of Hunter's closest friends would be Deborah Fuller, who started assisting Hunter when Laila Nabulsi left for good. Hunter hired Deborah as his permanent assistant, who then brought others on board as needed. She probably put up with more than any human alive to minister to his personal and business requirements, and no one who knew them believed that she wasn't always in love with him even after their initial romance was over. Regardless of how he sometimes treated her (wounding her with a shotgun, for example), and how things ended (after quitting and being fired many times only to return, she was ultimately sacked by Hunter's last wife, Anita), I know he always regarded her as family.

When I asked her how she hung in all those years, she wrote to me, "Because we became such good friends and family, and even had an affair early on, it was difficult. He fired me and I quit a number of times. It's hard to let go of family. I'm family oriented. I learned to handle things and Hunter better after years of time spent. And I received a great deal from the relationship. I was trusted by Hunter, and that wasn't easy to come by. We developed that early on, probably partly due to what he thought of as my midwestern ethics. 'Goddamnit, I'm gonna teach you to lie and cheat,' he'd tell me. I had a huge responsibility. I liked that and was good at it and got off on that, as well. I became an action junkie once I met Hunter. I received as much as I gave, which was a lot, it was both ways. I had to fight for it and earn it. We had a mutual respect until the day he died. And I will always hold a great respect and love for Hunter."

Though they had ongoing differences over the years, one of Hunter's other great long-term friendships was with George Stranahan, a brilliant physicist by training and rancher by choice, with family money from the Champion Spark Plugs fortune. They only clashed because George was equally strong willed, Hunter often owed him money, they had some disagreements over land-use issues, and because Hunter's gratuitously outrageous conduct could take on an in-your-face aspect when he wanted it to.

"I always told people Hunter was one of my best friends, and certainly my most difficult one," says George. "He had such a fierce loyalty to the people he liked, I just felt obligated to return it. I felt a little guilty I didn't go see him as much as I should have. It was like visiting a hospital, 'I gotta go sit with Hunter.' It was fun when there was a gang there, but not just to babysit. But you know, that's just how Hunter was."

Sheriff Bob Braudis was another who was an intellectual match for Hunter and supported him in nearly every way possible. Braudis has always been politically shrewd and well informed, personally loyal and giving, and was someone Hunter could count on across the board—legally, emotionally, for a good sports bet that he would always honor, as a fair officer of the law, and even for a midnight reference on Latin translations.

In a story I did on Bob in 1988, Hunter gave me a long quote that included the following:

> There may be other cops like Braudis, but I haven't seen many of them. . . . He has to be an expert on a spectrum of crimes and situations that no one else has to consider. I think he's an amazing bastard to have as sheriff. He would be a real treasure to have as a friend, let alone as sheriff. . . . He's one of the original good ones. . . . I wouldn't expect any free passes from Bob. If I'm guilty, he's going to feel bad about it, but he'll do his job. He's told me not to do something to get arrested and expect his help.

In return Bob has always said that he told Hunter early on, "I can be your friend or your sheriff, but I can't be both."

I've known Bob since he moved to Aspen and have always considered him one of the few friends I could really count on period, and Hunter did too. Bob and I have talked about Hunter a lot throughout our lives but especially since he died. "I did have the luxury of more one-on-one time with Hunter than most people because he called me when he wanted that," Bob said for the record one day. "He knew he could trust me. And he also knew that I wasn't a sycophant. I called bullshit on his bullshit."

Sometimes that worked, sometimes it didn't. I once accused Hunter of fomenting crises to avoid other work, and he didn't take it well. But Gerry Goldstein has said the same thing about him, and I mentioned that to Bob. "Yeah, and Gerry felt that he was, more often than he deserved, the object of Hunter's rage and scorn," replied Bob, sensitive to how difficult it was for any of us to deal with Hunter regularly. "And I had to keep reassuring Gerry that their friendship was very solid, and he was the first person Hunter would always call when there was anything remotely related to a legal problem. And their friendship survived an awful lot of 'get the fuck out of here, I never want you back.'"

David McCumber edited two books of Hunter's (*Songs of the Doomed* and *Generation of Swine*), as well as his *Examiner* column for three years. "There were individual times of stress," he allows, "but in general it was pretty much of a delight. Hunter said that writing the column was sort of like learning to play pinochle—there was a trick to it, and once he got it he felt better. The journalism was occasionally mystifying, but usually good and satisfying. The books were even more satisfying, especially *Songs of the Doomed,* because I got exposed to parts of Hunter I'd never known before, and it was fun and wonderful. Having those two books dedicated to me means more than just about anything else I did with him."

It wasn't all hearts and roses of course. "One evening at Owl Farm, working under some personal stress, Hunter took the opportunity to fragment a Selectric with a mallet in the kitchen," recalls David. "I was a little irritable, and when I said 'Are you done?' he came halfway around the counter at me with the mallet. I picked up a beer bottle and after a few seconds we both smiled, and he muttered, 'I think it's time to take a break.'"

Hunter very much prized his friendships with famous and influential people, with whom he often enjoyed a somewhat different and slightly more restrained relationship than he did with the rest of us. Many of them rarely saw him at his worst, when he was quarrelsome, angry, or just so out of it you couldn't talk to him. They not only didn't spend enough time around him in any one sitting to be exposed to some of his less-attractive displays, but he made a real effort not to go condescending or nasty on them.

I hadn't been living next door for long when Hunter called one night and said he had some people coming over and asked if I would like to join them. When I came over he told me that Jack Nicholson and Michael Douglas would be arriving any moment. This was 1976 and they were just coming off a sweep of the big five Oscars for *One Flew Over the Cuckoo's Nest*. I was dumbfounded. The book was one of my favorites, Nicholson was already a legend for *Easy Rider* and *Five Easy Pieces,* and I considered *Cuckoo's Nest* to be one of the best things I'd ever seen. When they got there they had two women with them, one of whom was Anjelica Huston, who was accompanying Jack.

Douglas had been starring on a television cop show and was starting to seem like a much more interesting person once he produced *Cuckoo's Nest*. I was afraid I'd swallow my tongue or otherwise make an ass of myself when they walked in the door, but everyone was very nice and then Tom Benton arrived, which made me more comfortable. We all sat around Hunter's kitchen at first while a plate of coke was passed around. That seemed to make Michael nervous and he muttered to Jack about how this was what he was worried about. Jack just shrugged—he was an old hand with the Aspen scene by then—and launched into a story about how he had this perpetually open sore at the base of his spine that oozed green fluid, and he hoped this wouldn't affect it. I assumed he was joking and grinned at him like a fool, assuring him that I didn't see how it could. With a half smile on his face he continued to insist that it was true and I knew right then why he and Hunter got along.

At one point when Tom and Hunter and I were still in the kitchen and the movie people had relocated to the living room, Hunter went out and insisted on playing the horrible tape of his *Guts Ball* story for them. He walked out of the room just as it started and I got a little worried about what they might think and tried to explain that Hunter thought the thing was hysterical, but that the rest of us just viewed it as deranged. Pretty soon they were all ignoring the tape and singing songs and laughing. I remember wondering if this was how showbiz people regularly passed their time, or if it was just a response to Hunter's strange tape.

Jack also visited Owl Farm fairly often in the company of director Bob Rafelson, with whom he had made *Five Easy Pieces*. Bob was another of Hunter's favorite people. And they were always understanding when Hunter's barbecue dinners didn't even start to get prepared until eleven or twelve o'clock at night, even though they were never tooting and drinking like he was and seemed almost straight by comparison. I began to suspect them of shrewdly eating before they came. Jack and Bob both remained close to Hunter throughout his life. He had enormous respect for them and they in turn regarded him with a level of understanding reserved for kindred spirits.

Jack treated Hunter as protectively as he might a brother with never a bad word to say about him. Like some others, I believe he felt that people who didn't know Hunter sometimes mistakenly thought he was really just a burnout instead of the genius he was.

If people who didn't know Hunter sometimes had an erroneous impression of him, it was that he was not just gonzo but permanently muddled and silly. Hunter most appreciated those who understood how wrong that was and stood up for him in spite of his flaws. It didn't matter so much if someone like me understood him, but when peers such as Nicholson, Rafelson, Bill Murray, Johnny Depp, and so on did and said so, it forever endeared them to him and made him feel better about himself.

Jack spoke very spontaneously and from the heart at Hunter's first memorial. He and Sean Penn had been pacing around the crowded ballroom for a while, puffing cigars and not really talking to anyone. Finally, without introduction, Jack walked over and took the microphone when someone else was through and just started talking and shaking his head. He was obviously rattled and said that when he got the call about Hunter's suicide, he had really thought it was a joke. "You know, you people up here, it can be hard to tell sometimes," he said. It was such a shock, he continued, and he talked about how much he would miss him, how much he already did, how he always looked forward to their time together talking, and how good Hunter always was to his kids.

Hunter got to know Bill Murray through Laila and then the *Buffalo* movie, and they remained friends for more than thirty years. Bill gave him sanctuary in his apartment in New York or in L.A., they stayed in fairly regular touch, and he brought him by my place for some Nerf basketball or to borrow golf shoes. Bill and his wife, Micky, once rode into town with me to a New Year's party at Abetone's Restaurant, and he talked about Hunter's unique sense of humor and his ability to write funny. "He's so smart, but he can still make you laugh out loud. It's impressive." Considering Bill's usual level of sarcasm, that was high praise. And Hunter reciprocated.

With Hunter standing there, I asked Bill what kind of challenge it was to play Hunter in a movie. Bill just looked at me and smiled for a second. So Hunter said, "He's just another silly Irishman who thinks he can golf. You should be asking me about why Bill Murray? I hadn't seen much on TV to make me think he could act, but he's surprised the hell out of me. And the way he does my look is . . . disturbing."

When Hunter and Laila visited the Murrays' rented place in Los Angeles on their way back from Hawaii one time, they told them about all the wonderful fireworks they'd been buying on the Big Island. To demonstrate, when no one was watching, Hunter went and got one of the giant rolls of firecrackers that he liked to set off all at once, bomb style. He sabotaged me with one in his own front yard, and this time he set one off in the Murrays' entrance hall. "He was going to do it outside, in front of the big picture window we were all near," Laila said. "But when he got in the hall he decided the acoustics were better, so that's where he set it off. Insane. The door caught on fire, and Billy filled a plastic garbage can with water from the pool, twice, and threw it on the fire to put it out. Then there was firecracker paper stuck to the walls and the smell of cordite everywhere. Micky locked herself in their room and wouldn't come out. It was months later, after he wrote her this apology, before she forgave him."

That was an effect Hunter often had on wives. I gave Robin Williams's first wife a ski lesson one time, and she asked me not to mention Hunter when Robin joined us because she didn't want Robin getting involved with him again.

When Bill Murray spoke at the first memorial service he mentioned that Hunter had once tried to sell him Owl Farm when they first met. He paused and looked misty, and with his typical deadpan, said, "I could've been so fucking rich if I'd bought that ranch." Then he smiled a little sadly and went on.

As many musicians as Hunter knew well, I think he may have bonded most with Warren Zevon. Warren was married to my current wife, Harriet's, best friend from high school, and he started coming to Aspen with her so he could try to meet Hunter. It took years, and Warren and Crystal were no longer together when it finally happened. Crystal has since written a great book about Warren, *I'll Sleep When I'm Dead: The Dirty Life and Times of Warren Zevon* (New York: Ecco, 2007), with his full cooperation before he died that includes details of some of his adventures with Hunter, such as the following excerpts from Warren's diary:

July 8, 1993—Aspen

Took Ariel to the airport. . . . Then we went to Owl Farm. . . . Woody Creek. Hanging out with Hunter in the kitchen, drinking good coffee, looking at a weird letter from Clinton, perusing his new manuscript. He showed me the Epilogue—fantastic. Later he brings out his Model 29 S&W, and a .454 with a scope. We go out back to prepare for an afternoon of shooting. He's been doing artwork, shooting up huge photos; he sets up the classic Thompson for Sheriff poster & he and I shoot a happily tight group of sic shots with these two guns, then he decorates and inscribes it to me. He sets up a propane tank with detonating targets & I blast it with a .12 gauge shotgun—he hugged me—"That's shooting!" He blasts paint containers suspended over two of my posters, ties a paint thing to a mask-wearing Styrofoam head (". . . Whorehead!" he mutters. "Shithead!") What a ball! Friends are dropping by—Ed Bradley among them—Hunter's making calls trying to get me booked into the Wheeler Opera House. It's all on their video and mine. Hunter on his John Deere tractor with an inflatable [sex] doll in the scope. Hunter gets a limited edition copy of "Screwjack" and insists I give a dramatic reading. . . . We signed the "Learning to Flinch" posters, then said goodnight all around. Hunter walked us out and we're on The Lipcutter [the RV]. Said we could look at the day with "joy and confidence."

November 26, 1996—New Orleans

I called Hunter and complained about my skin and hair loss. He proposed dragging me behind a boat in the Ohio River at dawn. I told him the supposed psoriasis was affecting the "disrobing in front of strangers aspect of my career." Hunter said, "Maybe it's time to stop disrobing in front of strangers. You don't want to be a filthy, old man disrobing in front of strangers . . ." Advice on maturity from HST! <u>And he is right!</u>

Their vivid language, gambling instincts and fierce drinking habits (when Warren was off the wagon) were just a few of the things that united them, and Warren included a collaboration between him and Hunter on one of his last albums, *My Ride's Here*. Called "You're A Whole Different Person When You're Scared," it came out just before Warren was diagnosed with terminal cancer and two years before Hunter's book *Kingdom of Fear*, which the song refers to with such lyrics as

The eagle screams on Friday
The Colts are doomed this year
The fat's finally in the fire
In the Kingdom of Fear.

Hunter loved Warren, and they spent as much time together as they could in Warren's last year and talked on the phone a lot. Hunter took his death in September 2003 very hard. He lived another fifteen months, but I don't think he ever really got over losing his friend.

The great, Pulitzer Prize–winning writer William Kennedy was a good friend of Hunter's for most of his life. Hunter used to tell me that he thought Kennedy was the best writer living and that he had been one of the first editors he had applied to for work. They'd stayed in touch ever since. Kennedy's speech at the March memorial was very affecting, expressing the confusion and despair of a friend who was older than Hunter, his onetime mentor—if such a thing were possible—and one more of us for whom the suicide was totally unexpected. He loved Hunter and loved the good work he created but wasn't sure he ever completely understood him. It was a fundamental doubt shared by many. Of course, there's the old trope about who can ever really know anyone? But it's not a comfortable feeling to have about one of your best friends. Especially after he kills himself.

The other option with Hunter was the fear that maybe you *did* understand him, and it wasn't all pretty. Everyone has shortcomings, but it's hard to ask endless forbearance of your own when you make a living mocking the flaws of others. Ultimately, not even all of Hunter's self-awareness—his confessed addict's nature, his admittedly short temper, his remarkable self-absorption—could atone. Not to family, not to friends, not even to himself.

It definitely played hell with relationships of all kinds but especially those with his wives, fiancées, and girlfriends. People with Hunter's levels of addictions and his need to be the center of attention have a hard time maintaining viable long-term relationships. That never stopped him from trying, however, because Hunter was, for all of his contradictions, a true romantic, in sports, in his writing and politics, as well as his affairs of the heart. None of the former would have made any difference if he hadn't always been able to return to the latter. And it wasn't just the sex. He loved women, loved being in love, and he loved love itself, though it wasn't always easy to tell. Even if he loved you.

Hunter rarely suffered complete dingbats or mindless groupies, and never for long. Among his former long-term lovers, the levels of affection that remained varied, unless they were only assignations of convenience on both sides. In that case the women usually retained a warm place in their heart for him, the kind in which his past transgressions were largely forgotten and only the good remained, especially the more time went by.

Though there were a lot of women in Hunter's life, I think only a few had lasting significance for him. They began with his mother, Virginia, with whom he regularly stayed in touch and whose example he always respected. It wasn't unusual in discussions featuring references to all sorts of wisdom from Kant to Eldridge Cleaver, for him to mention something his mother had said. Hunter's lacerating intelligence traced directly to her genes. He knew it and always admired her and felt he had done her proud.

Hunter's first wife, Sandy, wasn't the same kind of strong woman as Virginia and she knew it. After years of what she later called almost indentured servitude, she parted ways with him, taking Juan with her, claiming she never really felt that she and Hunter had connected meaningfully during all their years together. As I watched them go through something everyone had seen coming for years, it was like the end of an era that many people were facing. All the old counterculture dreams were dying hard by the mid-1970s, and with them a lot of marriages. For some people, the party would never end, and that was a surprise to others. The notions of addictions and alcoholism had always seemed like just more misinformation we'd been fed—or signs of weak personalities, genetically poor tolerance levels, and other unfortunate personal failings—not the inevitabilities that they were becoming.

Sandy decided once and for all that Hunter was mentally ill, and she and Juan weren't as high on the list of things that deserved Hunter's attention as they should be. Hunter, for his part, was unwilling to prove otherwise. They did not part amicably and only remained in touch because of Juan.

For all that might have gone wrong from a purely logistical standpoint in raising Juan—such as Sandy taking him away from his father, Hunter not always being there a lot for him, and his being complicated when he was—Hunter always loved Juan and regarded him, instantly and always, as his peer. This may not be wholly unusual for sons and fathers, but is not always good for the sons in every way. Still, it was how Hunter treated those he respected, and he always respected his son and Juan never let him down.

In part, that was because Hunter wasn't excessively demanding in his expectations for Juan or his life and career. He believed in him implicitly and always felt strongly that he was a good and very bright kid and it was Juan's right to choose his own life. And Juan did. While he has done some writing off and on, he has always been fascinated by computers and has worked as a successful information technology consultant in Boulder since college. Hunter probably wielded as much influence with him as he could have, in the end by not trying to have much other than to raise him to understand what was right and wrong on a very fundamental level, even if Hunter's own behavior didn't always reflect that. The result, I believe, was that father and son remained good friends throughout their lives. And Hunter loved Juan's wife, Jennifer, "like a daughter" he always told her truthfully. And for his grandson, Will, it seemed he reserved his most unfettered love of all.

Laila Nabulsi was a much different woman from Sandy. Of his several serious relationships, I think this was his best matched and most compatible. She stayed good friends with him throughout the rest of his life because he wanted it that way and she was able to handle it.

"Part of my ability to stay in his life was that he kept pulling me back in," she laughs softly. "I didn't judge him. I couldn't ever go back to him the way we'd been because I wouldn't agree to living like that again. But he knew I was there for him. And he even made amends to me, finally, apologized for everything he'd put me through. I had to wait twenty years for it, but still. And that's when I began to worry about him. It wasn't that long before he died and it was so un-Hunter-like, it was like he was cleaning up some things and I began to feel like he might not live that much longer. I just didn't think he'd shoot himself. He never mentioned killing himself to me. I know other people say he talked about it, but he never did it with me."

Because she had a good career of her own, which happened to intersect Hunter's at a location he liked in the show business world, Laila came with built-in respect and a familiarity with the star syndrome that probably begat some of her take-no-shit attitude. Also, as a much younger woman than Sandy, Laila came from a different background, where being subservient and retiring weren't the way things were done. Considering her Middle Eastern heritage, this might not have been the case. But Palestinian women seem more openly aggressive and willing to take leadership roles. They are definitely less likely to be told what to do. "Certainly there was verbal abuse with Hunter, and he could be very forceful in his manner," says Laila. "But he never got physical with me. When I heard later from Sandy what she said he did, I really had to kind of wonder about it. When someone once asked me in an interview if Hunter had ever beat me I just looked at him. I said 'No. And do you think I would have stayed if he had? No!'"

When Laila did leave, it was still with all her best qualities intact, including her fondness for Hunter if not his lifestyle. She also left with the film rights to *Vegas*. Laila could hold her own, didn't mind leaving when things got too tense, and had a limit as far as how much drugs and booze she could tolerate in Hunter. Everyone did, but she got on him about it, especially after her good friend John Belushi died, and she, like everyone else, saw his similarities with Hunter. Laila was also very close to John's wife, Judy, and didn't want to end up widowed like her.

If things got too wiggy when we were around Laila would come to see Denie and me for a while. I always said that I became convinced Hunter was really losing it when he let her leave for good. She loved him, worked hard for him, and was well thought of by most of his closest friends. Tom Benton and George Stranahan (who as a minister of the same mail-order church that Tom and Hunter had joined once, actually performed a marriage ceremony between Hunter and Laila at his house), felt like she was the best of all his brides.

"In the end, we were blessed to have the time and know the person," she says wistfully. "It's hard to talk about because so few people really knew him well. I feel a little guilty about some of the interviews I've done because I think Hunter would hate it. You know how he didn't like it when you'd be in the other room talking and laughing and he could hear it but he wasn't a part of it? It feels like that."

In spite of Hunter's very real, melancholic suffering when a long relationship broke up, I never heard him play heartbreak music for days on end, as Sandy has said he did over her. And he didn't stay lonely for long. Sex wasn't something he liked to go without, and he didn't. But often he had it with old friends with no ongoing expectations, and when he was out on the road there were lots of opportunities for one-night stands

In the *Gonzo* documentary, Sandy complains about all of Hunter's groupies, citing them as one of the reasons she had to leave him. Hunter's feelings on the subject were no secret. He craved the attention, the beautiful younger women, and the sex, and that wasn't going to change.

"As Hunter went through the aging process, he was still attractive to younger women," Bob Braudis told me with a grin, "You know that. He loved it. And he loved it until the day he died." So much so that one of Bob's stories brought us both up short. "I did ask him questions that no one else had asked him," he pointed out. "Coming back from the 2000 election he of course asked me for a ride to the polling place, and he finally got dressed and was ready to roll at a quarter to seven and he had to vote at the Prince of Peace [church]. We made it by two minutes. So on the way back home I said, 'Hunter, what's the biggest regret in your life?' And he thought hard for two or three minutes and he says, 'I never came in a woman's mouth until I was thirty-five-years old. And I didn't fuck enough beautiful women in the ass until I was well into my thirties.' Then he said, 'You have a real knack for asking the hardest questions.' And I said, 'Don't worry Hunter, I'm never going to tell anyone' . . . except for Jay Cowan in 2008."

We both laughed, but it was a troubling thought to me. For a man who I know was sorry that he had never written what he considered a worthy novel, whose relationships he valued ended badly, and who felt himself brutally misunderstood by a large segment of society that viewed his life as a cartoon strip, it was a surprise to me that his biggest regret centered on not getting enough head (and tail) when he was young. "Would that be how you would feel?" I asked Bob.

"Not I," he admitted. "But maybe it was very important to him. Because he did think about the answer." We both understood that it could have just been bullshit, to gauge Bob's reaction. Or it could have been a typically macho lament, meant to turn a profound question into a man's-man banter. But it certainly reflected some of the way he lived his life and formed relationships.

Hunter's female assistants tended to be young journalism students or had worked on his speaking engagements, and many, if not all, quickly had affairs with him. Maria Khan and Hunter met in 1984 when she was twenty-three and he spoke at Arizona State University. She soon went to work for him as a researcher and fell in love. To some, Maria was similar enough to Laila to make them wonder if she wasn't just a rebound substitute. Both were exotically good looking with similar bloodlines (Maria's are Pakistani), quick wits, and a wild energy. But Maria was several years younger than Laila, enough to make me feel a little doddering at times, and I was only in my early thirties. She was less worldly and more easygoing than Laila, so their differences were substantial.

Maria got along well with Deborah and actually melded into Hunter's world fairly effortlessly. She was, as all his girlfriends were, hung up on his writing and his romantic side, and stunned about his more extreme behavioral swings. Even so, I was surprised at how well she acclimated, and I realized he had once again succeeded in attracting someone who might be too good for him. He usually sensed these things as well and tried really hard for a while.

By the time Maria arrived, Denie and I were divorced and I was spending even more time at Hunter's. Soon enough we were all plunged into trying to keep him cranking out forty to fifty columns a year for the *San Francisco Examiner* and a nationally syndicated audience. Maria hung in like a veteran and impressed everyone. Once more Hunter had a girlfriend whose tastes were closer to my own in things like music and movies, and we got along well.

To no one's huge surprise, Maria and Hunter eventually began having trouble. When they'd fight and she wanted out, to make sure she didn't just drive off in the Wagoneer or whatever else was around, he'd disconnect their starters. This particularly infuriated Maria, who was fairly knowledgeable about cars and couldn't believe he would fuck up his own cars by going so far as to sometimes slash wires just to keep her from being able to leave. This meant she had to call taxis, and it didn't take long before he'd put the damper on that with every cabbie he could threaten. Sometimes she could call a girlfriend who would risk Hunter's wrath to rescue her. Sometimes she just had to ride it out. And sometimes she'd take shelter with me.

I knew enough about Hunter and her to know that I was, by then, her last resort, and I never turned her away. Toward the end of their relationship it happened more often. She also came over to watch movies when he was out of town or before he'd get up, and we'd talk and get caught up. I helped on a number of columns and spent quite a bit of time with Hunter and her, but it was getting more difficult and I was busy on other fronts.

When it got really bad she'd have someone take her to a motel for a day or two, or she'd book a flight back home. If she stayed at my place for more than a few hours when they were fighting, Hunter would flip out and turn my water off at my pipes that ran through his basement. Eventually she'd go home just so I could have some peace.

At one point during Christmas of 1986 she spent most of a day and night at my place and then moved out and rented an apartment in Phoenix and tried to resume her pre-Hunter life. His phone calls and letters were good, but when he sent her one hundred dozen long-stemmed roses (charged on David McCumber's credit card), that turned the tide. She told David she couldn't move in her apartment without stepping on roses.

But the reunion didn't last long, and pretty soon she was back at my cabin making plans to leave for good. It was a ridiculous position to put myself in, but I was sympathetic to her situation, and I liked her. My natural allegiance would have been with my old friend and landlord, but he made it difficult. I'd been through too much of this with him. I wasn't a total shit, though, and neither was she. Nothing ever happened between us. When she was forced to spend the night, I slept on the couch. But no one believed that, including Hunter.

I knew it made him crazy to have her at my place, so I drove her to the Aspen Inn once, but he tracked her down because she'd been there before. After that she came back to my place where she talked to him on the phone for awhile and waited while he wrote her a couple of notes. She was angry and sad and running the whole depressing gamut I'd seen in Sandy and Laila and Deborah. She was tired of succumbing and returning and said that if she left the Farm this time, she'd never return. And if she didn't leave, she'd never be able to forgive herself.

I was sure he had hit her or knocked her around, and when I asked she just shrugged. I didn't want to be caught in the middle anymore. I could have been a better friend to Hunter and less of one to Maria, and I've felt bad about that at times. But it was getting hard to watch what he was doing to other people and what he was doing to himself. In the end, I didn't want to have to look for another place to live and things were pretty good most of the time. But I'd had enough.

When he turned off my water that time, I turned off his electricity at a power pole out front and we both kind of lost it. "Leave my goddamned power on or I'll blow up your natural gas tank!" he hollered over the phone.

That meant he'd also blow up my house, with us in it. "Turn on my water," I told him.

"Send her home!"

"I can't send her anywhere, and you know it. And if I could I wouldn't send her back to you in this kind of shape. She's scared of you."

"You know I'd never hurt her and so does she!"

"If either one of us knew that, she wouldn't still be here. She wants to leave. Just give her some space and maybe you can work things out."

"Not with you in the middle of it!"

He shot over the top of my house and threatened my family for generations yet unborn. I shot into the air and threatened him back. He told our friends that Maria had moved in with me, and he didn't care what happened to any of us now. It was all very juvenile, and eventually Bob Braudis showed up and lectured me and Hunter about the guns and helped Maria leave.

She had barely cleared the driveway when Hunter started shooting again, and my water never came back on so I turned off his power again. Pretty soon my phone was ringing from a variety of our mutual friends. Tom Benton was first. "Listen, Jay, he's pretty serious this time. He's threatening to blow you up and burn you to the ground. I think he means it. Maybe you should just leave until he calms down."

"I'd like nothing better. And when I go I'll stay gone. But if I leave now, I know him. I watched him burn a bunch of Sandy's things. He'll set fire to this place the second I walk out, and it has everything I own in it. All my art, all my books, all my family stuff. Everything. You know he'll do it."

"It's definitely what he's threatening, and I've never heard him this mad," said Tom. "He wants to set fire to that house so no one can ever live there again. And it *does* belong to him, he keeps pointing out. You can either be in it, or not."

At some point my water finally came back on, and the next day he had a worker on overtime from Holy Cross Electric out there installing a locked box over the power switch. And Hunter began delivering notes to me. The first had "Sunday—noon" scrawled across the top of a badly typewritten page:

Dear Jay,

ALL YOU HAD TO DO WAS CALL HER A CAB. . . . I would have paid for it myself. You could have taken it off the rent.

No doubt you had yr. own reasons—just as you did when you told me you would definitely be out of the house by the end of August.

That would be a wise & graceful move, right now. I assume you understood that.

As of now (11:45 a.m. Sunday Aug 30 '87) I figure you will want to be living somewhere else ASAP—for your own reasons—so I will think in terms of renting the house to another tenant a/o Sept. 10.

We can do a final accounting vis-a-vis rent etc, on Monday 8/31. We both understand, I think, why this should be done calmly & quietly & quickly.

If you'd had anything else in mind, you could have called her a cab. Right? Pls. correct me if I'm wrong on this.

Thanx,
Hunter

It was accompanied by a handwritten note on *Examiner* stationery:

Jay Sorry about the typos. I don't have much help these days. Give me a ring if any of this baffles + unsettles you as much as it does me.
(H)

I called him, close to tears, and explained to his answering machine that it *all* baffled and unsettled me, but that I had already found a place to rent and was moving out most of my important things to a friend's house. "So you can go ahead and burn the cabin, if that's what you have to do," I told the machine. Meanwhile, I wanted to be sure that he knew in his own mind that I couldn't call Maria a cab because none of the cabbies would come to the house after he'd shot at several who tried and had made a bunch of screeching threats to their dispatcher. Driving her off in my car had been our only option and even that hadn't worked.

Two days later, after he'd slept, I got a longer typewritten note that was even harder to handle. It had Tuesday handwritten on top.

Jay,

Sorry about the craziness last weekend. We did okay during the earlier (afternoon) phase, and I genuinely appreciated yr. help. It calmed things down and seemed to lead to a peaceful result & reasonably happy ending.

But when it blew out again (phase 2) with such a quick & brainless suddeness, I was baffled & angry and felt like a dupe for even making an effort the first time.

And I reacted more or less as we all knew I would, given her "eat shit & die" attitude and yr. firm assurance that there was nothing I could do about it, no matter how hard I tried.

That was a mistake, I think, because it cut off any hope of communication and left me with no options except cheap white trash anger. . . . Consider how you would have reacted if every time you & yr. wife had an argument she moved into my house (where I was living alone) and I refused to let you talk to her, because I felt you weren't treating her right. And it was none of your business if she wanted to sleep here. . . . And beyond that I was going to do everything in my power to get her out of town ASAP before you could talk to her.

Well . . . I can't say for sure, Jay, because that situation never came up; but if it had I suspect you would not have been happy about it, or sent me flowers the next day.

So . . . pls. accept this bottle of wine in the spirit that I offer it. We've been friends for too long to let this single-issue madness make mean fools of us. Call me or come over for a friendly talk.

Thanx,
(Hunter)

In my experience, apologies of any kind are rare to receive. I'd never really gotten one from Hunter before in so many words, and I felt bad. But it was obviously time for me to move on. Even without getting in between Hunter and Maria, I'd just had too much exposure for too long to the whole silly scene. I'd turned thirty-five a couple of days before everything went wrong. I was tired of renting and wanted to build my own house and not be at the mercy of anyone else.

Hunter came over a few days later as I was moving the last of my furniture. We shot some Nerf hoops in the empty living room where we could get a lot of good ricochet shots off the walls and ceiling. The little basket was the last thing I took down, and I gave it to him. At that point I realized I'd spent more years total in that cabin than in any home I'd ever had. Hunter was back to his good old self and told me that he didn't have the place rented if I wanted to change my mind. He apologized again, and I told him he didn't have to, that it was my fault too. Now I feel like kind of an ass about it, but I had to go and I'm glad I did.

13

Taking a Bullet

I always thought of Hunter as a candidate for taking a bullet somewhere. Taking one for the cause. Taking one from the latest girlfriend, or the girlfriend's boyfriend. Taking one from a crazed fan or a government assassin or a long list of other possible shooters. I even thought, insipidly enough, about how I probably would have taken a bullet for him. He was just that kind of person. He might not let you get by with a bad bet or lame remark, but he would have taken a bullet for a friend. Sadly, when that time came for him, in typical Hunter fashion he wouldn't let anyone help him.

Or at least that's the kind of thing you tell yourself when it happens. I've had a few other friends who killed themselves, and each time I wonder what I could have done differently. The obvious answer is to have been a better friend, and clearly that was the case with Hunter. Over the last years of his life I saw him fairly often but not like I once had. He'd call and invite me over to watch football, or to meet some ESPN people, or just to talk or have a barbecue, and I rarely made it.

I still got notes and letters from him, and I sent him clips I came across about him in unusual places, along with the occasional magazine story or unpublished novel I'd written. Any time I had political questions, he was always the first one I'd call, and he always answered or called back. I liked that a lot and still miss it. But I wasn't as close with Hunter as I once was. I'll always regret that I didn't do better by him toward the end. I'm not so crazy as to think it would have made any difference for him. It would have just made me feel better.

He used to tell me I could never write about him until after he died, so now I have. I'm getting a little tired of wallowing in the past and reliving all those days and nights, so it's good we've reached the last chapter. As Tom Petty says, "You can look back, baby, but it's best not to stare." It was a remarkable time, though, and I think Hunter epitomized it in a way no other human possibly could have: all of an era's wildness and grace, art and beauty, freedom and genius, along with its hubris, its fragility, its unfulfilled longings, and terrible tragedies.

I suppose this book will deal with the last-vestige stages of my grief but maybe not. The death of someone you love is never easy, period, but with suicide it's even less so. It feels like bad failure all the way around, even though I know taking one's own life is every person's right, and I believe in that. It was just a surprise to me because I'd never had him pull the "I'm going to kill myself" line on me, even though others apparently heard it a lot in his last years. All I knew was that he was a lot older at sixty-seven than he ever thought he'd be: he was fond of claiming he never expected to live past twenty-seven. Forty years more probably seemed like plenty. Why be greedy? he may have finally asked himself.

Certainly Hunter had written about the prospect of killing himself fairly early on. In a letter to old friend Eugene W. McGarr in 1970 that was published in *Fear and Loathing in America,* he said:

> Anyway, I figured you might like to know you aren't the only person floundering around. Kennedy's last letter was unspeakably depressing; Semonin is so weird that he won't even talk to me; Oscar is going mad because nobody will crucify him; Clancy calls at awful hours and howls about failed dreams; Hudson is doing the best metal sculpture in the country & he can't make a dime; Dennis Murphy had to be taken

> to a health farm. . . . and I'm sitting out here in the god-damn snow, trying to explain it all and not too far, on some nights, from thinking seriously about suicide.

In the story he liked to tell most frequently to Braudis and me and others, there were shades of suicide as a literary device rather than a reality, and he set it down on paper for *The Great Shark Hunt* book in 1979.

> I feel like I might as well be sitting up here carving the words for my own tombstone. . . . and when I finish, the only fitting exit will be right straight off this fucking terrace and into The Fountain, 28 stories below and at least 200 yards out in the air and across Fifth Avenue.
>
> Nobody could follow that act.
>
> Not even me. . . . and in fact the only way I can deal with this eerie situation at all is to make a conscious decision that I have already lived and finished the life I planned to live—(13 years longer, in fact)—and everything from now on will be A New Life, a different thing, a gig that ends tonight and starts tomorrow morning.
>
> So if I decide to leap for The Fountain when I finish this memo, I want to make one thing perfectly clear—I would genuinely love to make that leap, and if I don't I will always consider it a mistake and a failed opportunity, one of the very few serious mistakes of my First Life that is now ending.

Still, "death by misadventure," as coroners used to call it, is somehow the worst, the hardest, the most tragic and selfish. We blame them, we blame ourselves. We blame a cruel and often hostile world. I'd blame George W. Bush if I could just work out the details. I know it would involve a grassy knoll and a second gunman.

It's also hard with suicides when you think about everyone who wanted to live but didn't get to. My father, for example. Dead of cancer at fifty-four, but Hunter couldn't be bothered to keep going. That's a shitty way to view things, and one has nothing to do with the other, but that's still how I feel sometimes.

Another aspect of Hunter's shooting himself that I still think about was how he responded when Tom Benton once tried to do the same thing. Tom, a lapsed Catholic with an overabundance of misplaced guilt, had left his well-loved wife and the mother of his children for another woman in the mid-1970s. In the process of doing that he had crashed his motorcycle badly one night when he was fucked up, and people were worried about him. Then one night when I was still living in town, I got a call from Hunter saying that Tom's new wife, Katie, had called him over and that Tom had just tried to kill himself. I also considered Tom one of my best friends, so Hunter asked me to come and help.

Tom was in deep despair over what he'd done to his family and a fight he and Katie had been having, and had tried to end his life with a shotgun that Katie had deflected at the last minute, leaving a sizable hole in the wall. Tom and Katie were very distraught and there was an infinitely depressing Leonard Cohen record playing that Hunter and I decided had to go. I rendered it unplayable ever again, and we smiled about that. Hunter said he thought it was anyone's right to off themselves, and I agreed. But we both also felt that Tom wasn't thinking clearly. He'd been drinking, and that wasn't one of the substances he usually did or liked then, so he wasn't handling it well. Now he was embarrassed about the thwarted suicide and his friends being called in.

I told him something like, "Hey, it could easily be me any given day of the week. It's not a thing." And Hunter agreed. Just the two of us were there with them, and we stayed for a long time until Tom finally got some rest and we'd removed all the guns and knives and drugs he could possibly use against himself. When Hunter and I talked during that night, he said he always felt like he wouldn't have to kill himself because someone else, or something else, would do it for him. I've usually had the same attitude, although there have definitely been some moments in my life when I thought seriously about ending it. So, Hunter said matter-of-factly, had he. But we agreed that these were things we usually got over fairly quickly. That's what we figured would happen with Tom. And it did. He lived another thirty years—two years longer than Hunter—and died at seventy-six of cancer.

Deborah Fuller, who hadn't been at the Farm for some months, told me right before the first memorial service that she wasn't surprised Hunter shot himself, that he had mentioned it to her and she took him at his word. "As always, he controlled everything he did. The son of a bitch," she chuckled sadly, "we miss him."

This in spite of the fact that Deborah had been fired and had to later file suit after Hunter's death to receive long-deferred back wages she felt she was owed by Hunter. When Anita and estate attorney Hal Haddon offered quotes to the newspapers while the case was still being considered about the lack of merit of Deborah's claim, it seemed not only unprofessional but way off the mark for anyone who knew Deborah and her longtime association with Hunter. Numerous friends, including myself, wrote to the papers to say that she had at least one hundred thousand dollars coming (the amount she was seeking and says she had been promised), and probably deserved many times that amount.

The case also provided the first public view of the growing schism between the cobeneficiaries of the estate, Juan and Anita Thompson. Juan wrote a letter to the local Aspen newspapers agreeing that Deborah should be compensated, stating that he wanted to make his position clear. Bob Braudis later told me how happy he was I had written the letter supporting Deborah, whom he has always liked, and said, "I love Juan and Anita both. But there are problems between them." Later he told me, "I was quite shocked when Hal Haddon went on a treasure hunt inside the house for twenty minutes while I sat in the kitchen, and came into the kitchen holding the original will, saying 'I found it.' I thought there was no way Hunter had actually crafted a will. And Hal gave me the executive summary of the will: 40 percent Anita, 40 percent Juan, and 20 percent Deborah. And at that time it seemed fair. I don't think anything close to that has evolved from that written document."

Anita Thompson had been the girlfriend of one of Hunter's longtime friends when they met and she went to work as his assistant. She wasn't the first woman Hunter stole from a friend, for the night or longer. Since his death, I've spoken to some who knew Hunter and Anita and felt that she was a well-intentioned and much younger woman left stranded and looking for a way to make a living. It has been suggested that she deserves some help from the estate that she is entitled to in the will as well as for what she put up with from Hunter during their relationship.

Others might say that by writing and publishing a quick book about Hunter; suggesting at various times in the local newspapers that she might want to turn their home into a museum, à la Hemingway's in Florida; and publishing a magazine called the *Woody Creeker*, which leans heavily on Hunter's previously published and unpublished work, Anita's conduct has the look of someone trying to position herself as the Widow Thompson and make a career out of her relatively brief marriage to Hunter.

Those who knew them well had seen Hunter and Anita's relationship grow increasingly volatile. By the time he died, according to Sheriff Braudis and others, he had been in contact with divorce lawyers. Rumors have run rampant through the community following the suicide, none of which reflect well on either Hunter or Anita. "I think Hunter was trapped in a marriage and the easiest way out for him was suicide," Braudis told me. "He didn't want to deal with lawyers fighting over property, ugly testimony from both sides."

I think that another failed relationship, and an actual marriage at that, may well have been a tipping point for Hunter. But there were definitely other factors at work in his demise.

As the nineties had worn on, they had worn particularly hard on Hunter as he literally limped into the new millennium. It's clichéd, but probably no less accurate, to say that the same acute sensitivities that made him such a passionate observer and writer also made it tough for him to endure a lot of what was going on in his life at the time.

"The fact that Hunter killed himself was a huge surprise to me," Braudis told me again one day. "He and I spent a lot of time one-on-one in the months leading up to the suicide, but I never thought that he'd kill himself. In the *Gonzo* movie, almost everyone they interview, people who didn't know Hunter as well as you or I, said, 'Well I always knew he'd take his own life—he talked about it—even Steadman said Hunter never expected to live past thirty.'"

"Hunter always said that," I noted.

"I know Hunter told me he had contemplated suicide while staring out of a twenty-eighth-floor window of the Time-Life Building."

"Yeah," I said. "That was one of his favorite stories. And what rational person hasn't thought about suicide?"

"Yes," said Bob. "But Hunter had just put himself under the blade for a hip replacement, he put himself under the blade for a very complex spinal surgery, he ate a bowl of fruit every day, he tried to get some exercise. And his failing skeleton and chassis really didn't affect his computer. I think in his brain, when you could see his gears starting to mesh, you knew he was thinking about something, and when he verbalized it, more often than not it was genius."

Most of us thought he was recovering pretty well from his recent surgeries, but I believe all the treatments had depressed him to his core. He didn't like the pain and the incapacity and didn't like it when his public appearances made him appear enfeebled beyond his actual years. For his last guest shot on Conan O'Brien he was very coherent and smart, but the way he struggled on and off the stage, because of his hip and back, made him look bad. He was suddenly the kind of person even his friends didn't know if they should offer to help and risk making him look worse, or just let him do it on his own no matter how agonizingly.

An incurable bleakness about the political situation in this country he truly loved had become a regular component of Hunter's writing and his conversations. He had lived to watch the manifestly evil and morally corrupt George W. Bush be sworn in to a second presidential term that many considered stolen outright, with no salvation in sight. Our civil liberties were eroding visibly in front of us, like time-lapse photography of plants withering, and even simply engaging in the process was no longer viewed with much tolerance. "Big darkness soon come," an oft-repeated phrase of Hunter's near the end, wasn't just a clue about his own personal fate he may have already been planning but his view of the world at large. And why not? There was little to be cheery about for any of us when we turned our gaze that direction.

As Hunter wrote in *Better Than Sex*,

> Probably I was just looking for some action, but my mother diagnosed it as paranoid psychosis and said she was feeling it too. "They think we're stupid," she said. "Do you know that the suicide rate among smart people goes up like a rocket in presidential election years? It jumps about 40 percent, just like clockwork, every four years."

Many noted over the years that Hunter seemed to live every adolescent male's dream, and he did it for most of his life. As sweet as it was thought to be, though, it wasn't a situation that could last forever. "When you've lived and written about young men's pursuits, and been worshipped by succeeding generations of young, it could really make growing old a drag, I suppose," says Greg Ditrinco. Hunter still had many young friends and vacillated between identifying with them and wishing for a generation with the spine and the heart to rise up and do something to save the world before it was too late.

Hunter had run it very hard for a very long time and knew that the odds were seriously stacked against his living much longer. He had already outrun not only his own expectations but those of nearly everybody else of his vintage who had lived even half as excessively as he. Surviving their fifties was getting to be very hard for anyone I knew, and he'd sailed seven years past that rugged shoal.

The last year or two of his life wasn't easy. For part of that time he was wheelchair bound after breaking his leg in Hawaii. There were reportedly more big fights with Anita, and she even left for a while. Many thought their relationship was finished then, only shortly after they'd officially gotten married.

Hunter called his old friends regularly, right up to the end, sometimes looking for stories, sometimes just to maintain contact. Though he was considered the archetypal party monster, he had become something of a workaholic as he got older. He seemed to have a sense that he didn't have much time left and needed to get things done. "He would complain about the wasted nights when I was there the last time, and how he wasn't getting any work done," says Laila Nabulsi. "But the saddest thing was that last year, two or three months before he died, he called me, looking for a lead. Always before when he did that, we'd talk and laugh and I could hear him start to type. Then he'd ask me some more questions, say 'I got it,' and be off and running. But this last time he finally just started losing it and there was no typing. And in this voice I'd never heard before, he started repeating over and over, 'I used to know how to do this. I used to know how to do this. Why can't I do this?' It was the worst thing I'd ever heard. And I think that was the hardest thing of all for him, when he couldn't even work any more."

As with everyone who has tried to help someone get off of drugs and alcohol who doesn't really want to, Laila still feels bad about not succeeding with Hunter. But she has come to accept that it wasn't going to happen. "I try to take a Buddhist attitude about it and attribute the fact that he could never get clean and sober to his being a very high reincarnate who chose in this lifetime to go as far as he could go with no boundaries right to the end," she says. "He was never going to do rehab this time. Maybe he learned something, gained some knowledge, and he'll do better the next time."

Another aspect of his life near the end that I've been asked about more than once is did I think he was able to still get it up for sex after all of the booze and drugs he'd done. It's not something that we ever discussed, of course, so I wouldn't know. Anita has been at some pains to make sure everyone is aware that he was her lover as well as beloved. I don't know what the limits of Viagra and Cialis are, but it wouldn't surprise me if Hunter had tested them, along with all the other limits in his life. And certainly if he was having that kind of problem I think it could easily have been the last straw for him.

I can't argue with the idea that some of us just know when it's our time, or take issue with anyone's right to choose that time. In Hunter's situation, I can't say I would have done differently, and I make no predictions for myself. Retrospectively, Hunter as a suicide doesn't seem that implausible. But I still wasn't ready for it.

There has been a lot of speculation among those who still find it hard to believe. And Hunter had to know that would happen, because it happened with everything else in his life. Some wonder why Hunter would choose to shoot himself when his grandson was in the house.

Juan's son, Will, wasn't in the room with Hunter when it happened, and he was provided with immediate counseling afterward. Nevertheless, I think it was wrong on Hunter's part, but I believe he had moved way past caring at that point.

Bob Braudis thinks it was fairly basic. "As far as Juan, Jennifer, and Will being there, I think he felt that he wanted his body found by the three people that he knew loved him and that he could trust 100 percent."

Some find it unusual that a short while after the death, Juan left the house and fired multiple shotgun blasts into the sky. Juan said that after he found his father and called the sheriff's office he wanted to make some kind of tribute to Hunter and the moment, so he went outside and fired off five or six rounds in the air, the last of which was heard by an arriving deputy who was fairly concerned by it.

The fact that Anita wasn't at Owl Farm when Hunter shot himself has also been viewed askance. Anita and Hunter had been fighting fiercely and throwing things around the night before, and Juan and a neighbor had to physically separate them. That fight hadn't been resolved when she left the next day to go to the Aspen Club health and fitness center. With none of Juan's family actually in the room with him, and Anita away from the Farm altogether, it may have been the most alone Hunter thought he was going to be and the best time to get the job done without someone interfering.

Bob Baudis has also mentioned to me that, "Hunter was on the phone with Anita when he shot himself. That surprised me. And Anita didn't know what had happened."

Naturally, some people think Hunter may have been murdered. I think Hunter shot himself and knew full well what he was doing. He managed it so the bullet went through his head and into a cabinet behind him where it left a dramatic hole so neat you might think he had planned it that way. Friends have suggested as much. Giving all those lawyer friends of his one last reason for pause was the fact that he was seated in front of his typewriter with a sheet of paper in it with only one word in the center of the page: counselor.

In the end, the choice he made reminded me of a line in *Hey Rube* referring to a time when gambling debts got him in trouble: "I aged about six years in three months, and things were getting worse every day. Suicide began to look like a far, far better option than living with grief and debt forever."

The suicide of another longtime valley resident, Dick Stutsman, less than two weeks before Hunter's, may or may not have affected Hunter's timing. Dick was a popular, hardworking, fairly conservative member of a large local family that also lived in the Woody Creek area and was just five years older than Hunter when he died. Hunter used to talk about how he'd be driving home from Aspen on a lot of early mornings, just about the time that Dick and others were headed in town to work. The Stutsmans and Gerbazes and others like them had initially not been fond of Hunter or his politics when he moved to the valley, and Hunter would kind of refer to Dick Stutsman as if he were his natural antithesis. That attitude changed as time went by, and I think they both respected each other eventually. And I can't help but wonder if Hunter didn't find himself thinking, "Well, if Dick Stutsman could do it for whatever reasons he had, then I sure as hell should be able to."

The weird frenzy that followed Hunter's death I believe would have surprised and pleased even him. The level and amount of commentary about it was a testimony to his stature. The pure range of people in journalism who either knew Hunter or met him or declared themselves to have been profoundly influenced by him was, and is, remarkable. In addition to the cover and special issue on Hunter in *Rolling Stone* and memorials in the likes of *Playboy, Esquire,* and *High Times*, STARZ and the Biography channel produced shows about him, and there is now a column in the prestigious and rather formal journal *Science* called "The Gonzo Scientist." Editors and columnists from *Golf Views* to *Mountain Gazette* to scores of newspapers across the country and around the world saw fit to mention his passing, many of them at length. In the truest tribute of all, very few tried to sound like him—for a change. The king was dead.

USA Today had to run a "Corrections and Clarifications" item on February 21 admitting it had "wrongly attributed a quote to Richard Nixon as saying Hunter S. Thompson was 'that dark, venal, and incurably violent side of the American character.' It was Thompson who made the remark about Nixon." Hunter would have howled. The *New Yorker* carried a telling exchange of letters over Hunter's influences, debating whether he had mentioned writing out entire sections of Fitzgerald, or if it was Hemingway, by hand when he was young to get a sense of their rhythm and style. I heard him say he did it with both.

One of the best pieces was in David McCumber's column in the *Seattle Post Intelligencer* on February 22, 2005, where he wrote:

> As savvy and skeptical as he was as a journalist, it's easy to forget his almost boyish sense of fun. . . . Sometimes, it meant driving crazy fast through a blizzard with the top down in one of his two ancient red convertibles, negotiating four-wheel skids on icy curves while fiddling absently with the stereo, trying to get the lyrics to the Cowboy Junkies 'Where Are You Tonight?'. . . At the same time, his accomplishments as a journalist and literary lion were monumental. He will be remembered with the likes of Twain and Mencken—and should be. . . . Thanks, Hunter, for the past twenty years of friendship—and for the incredible prose that will forever define the generation that somehow lost its grip on the American Dream.

A shrine on Aspen Mountain sprung up where skiers could stop and have a puff and remember Hunter. His book sales surged, and issues of the local newspapers that came out for several days after his death are still being offered for sale on eBay. By the time his memorial service at the Hotel Jerome ballroom rolled around two weeks after his death, it had become kind of a big deal, and there was already word that it would only be the first of two. William Kennedy and others tried to think of anyone they had known who was so special he needed *two* memorial services.

In Memory of Dr. Hunter S. Thompson
July 18, 1937—February 20, 2005

> Weave a circle round him thrice,
> And close your eyes with holy dread,
> For he on honey-dew hath fed,
> And drunk the milk of Paradise.
>
> Samuel Taylor Coleridge
> Aspen, Colorado
> March 5, 2005

I liked the choice of the quotation for the invitation to the first memorial. On the front was a fine-art–style, black-and-white image of Hunter sitting at a table in a suite somewhere in his robe, eating, with white curtains blowing into the room by an open door to a deck or balcony.

Since I don't regularly attend rock star or celebrity funerals, I'm not sure what the norm is for such things. Hunter's first memorial was the only one I've ever seen so commercially staged. Several televisions with tapes and DVDs of movies about Hunter were running, and a table was set up full of odd memorabilia for the guests, including women's bikini underwear with the Gonzo emblem on them, small plastic hands with a finger you could pull to making farting noises, and reprinted contact sheets of various photos of Hunter.

The guest list was impressive and I walked straight over to Bob Braudis when we arrived. He gave me a long hug and said, "I never thought he'd cap himself. Let's talk when you get the chance." Then Harriet and I wandered around for a while, coming across a few old friends like Deborah Fuller, some of the Stranahan family, and Monty Chitty. I saw Juan Thompson for the first time in years and we talked for a while. He seemed good, if somewhat stunned by all the attention. Laila Nabulsi introduced me to John Cusack, and we all talked about how flattered Hunter would have been by the turnout. I also ran into Bill Murray and we talked with Tom Benton, who seemed as dazed as I felt. Most people looked that way, including Bob Rafelson and Craig Vetter, who just kept shaking their heads when I spoke to them. Jack Nicholson and Sean Penn rarely stopped pacing except when Jack addressed the gathering.

Just before the speeches started, a recurrent buzz in the room about Johnny Depp being there seemed amazing, given the star power of those already present. Following William Kennedy, Ralph Steadman, who looked disheveled and tipsy most of the evening, stood in front of the crowd with a drink in his hand and began by saying, "Hunter Thompson fucked up my life." It drew such a good laugh that he said it again, "Hunter Thompson fucked up my life," then wandered off into what would later become the main refrain of his book about his longtime colleague: namely, that he loved and missed Hunter but perhaps never really understood him and felt as often abused by him as appreciated. It has not been a rare lament among his friends.

Jann Wenner delivered a long but entertaining eulogy—funny and poignant, if occasionally self-serving—that for some reason surprised me, given his and Hunter's ups and downs. Only Bob Braudis and Curtis Robinson, with whom Hunter was close for the last fifteen years of his life, were selected to speak as Hunter's truly local friends. Both talked movingly and honestly about what it was like to a lose a friend and staple in their lives, not just an icon and a symbol.

Anita spoke and seemed strangely in her element, as did Sandy Thompson. Juan and his wife also got up and managed admirably. Juan said that the best times he remembered with his father were middle-of-the-night swims at a neighbor's pool when it was just him and Hunter and they'd float and talk with no one else around.

Numerous letters were read or mentioned at the service, including ones from George McGovern and a very sick Ed Bradley, who had been one of Hunter's closest confidantes, best sources, and smartest friends for more than thirty years. John Cusack and Josh Hartnett both gave readings, while Bill Murray's and Jack Nicholson's speeches were among the most touching. Johnny Depp talked about what the world had lost and also did a reading, occasionally punctuated by the shrieks of a woman who apparently couldn't believe it was really Depp. Doug Brinkley and Hal Haddon and a roster of others from the literary and legal worlds spoke and were appropriately sad and puzzled and also certain of Hunter's place in the American pantheon. An old friend of mine and Hunter's, Semmes Luckett, sidled up to me afterward and said with a chuckle, "Did you notice how the most long-winded ones were the editors?"

Once it was all said and done, I had a hard time imagining another service, let alone one as silly as what was being planned. The idea was to erect a 153-foot-high cannon shaped like the gonzo insignia and blast Hunter's ashes from it in accordance with what were supposedly Hunter's express wishes, as stated in the BBC documentary *Fear and Loathing on the Road to Hollywood*, which was made in 1978.

Obviously, Hunter made a regular practice of saying outrageous things to everyone from neighbors to friends to college audiences to people with television cameras making films about him. It was one of his trademarks, the same way he drew attention to his writing. It wasn't all meant to be taken literally, and he spent a good deal of his life making that point to anyone who asked.

While I don't dispute that Hunter had mused about having his ashes shot from a peyote-fist cannon, he also wrote about hurtling himself off the twenty-eighth floor of a New York high rise and into a big fountain on Fifth Avenue. No one later proposed doing that with his remains. I like to think that as well intentioned as Johnny Depp and Anita and others were with the cannon idea, Hunter would have squirmed in his urn over it. But he probably wouldn't have.

It seemed like the last lavish bit of self-indulgence that he could wreak, this time through his proxies. George Stranahan was quoted saying: "I am pretty sure this isn't how Hunter would have done it." But as he later told me, "He'd have probably gone even bigger."

Letters in the paper alternately damned Hunter for creating such a spectacle or praised him for his panache, even when dead. Some also complained that no matter what happened, his real fans who weren't famous or connected were going to be left out.

When Anita Thompson announced the plans for the second memorial, she first said it would be public. She also hoped to get Bob Dylan to perform for it and said that she would be giving Dylan the red IBM electronic typewriter Hunter had promised him when they first met at a Labor Day performance Dylan gave in Aspen a few months earlier. Later, after more consideration, the estate announced that the second memorial would definitely be private with full security. Naturally there were those, including close neighbors, who found a towering, double-thumbed, peyote-fist cannon in a fairly serene and rural setting somewhat incompatible with anything private.

Plans nevertheless proceeded apace, receiving the necessary clearances from several county boards and funding from Depp that was said to be good up to a million dollars. When I got my invitation I was in Montana for a couple of family birthdays and decided to pass. I heard later, even from people who had been skeptical, that it was a memorable bash. Lots of people ate mushrooms, including a well-known photographer who subsequently freaked out and had to be taken away by ambulance. A gong-and-drum Tibetan band, along with the locally based Nitty Gritty Dirt Band, provided what everyone said was amazing music, echoing between the small mesas on either side. The fireworks accompanying Hunter's ashes were, by all accounts, sensational, and I know that would have pleased him as much as anything.

A Hunter S. Thompson memorial fund to fight for civil liberties and the Fourth Amendment was started by the estate in Hunter's memory, and Depp was also reportedly a substantial contributor to that. As another fund-raiser, Ralph Steadman created a desolately sad and faintly biblical limited-edition print to sell that several of Hunter's longtime friends and family signed at the second service: Ralph, Ed Bradley, Bill Murray, Anita, Laila, Deborah, Bob Braudis, Jann Wenner, Juan, Johnny Depp, Kurt Vonnegut, and Doug Brinkley.

As part of Hunter's estate's efforts to deal with the lack of a ceremony that would include the public and Hunter's legions of fans, there was a lot of talk about a symposium of some kind in Aspen that would be combined with a concert. More than two years after Hunter's death, the first symposium of what is being considered as a possibly recurring event, was held at the Aspen Institute under the title "Politics, Truth and Justice: The Writings of Hunter Thompson." Juan Thompson was the organizer and managed to convene a number of significant personages for a discussion of Hunter's effect on political coverage in this country and to examine where his heirs and successors might be.

The panel was a good one as far as it went, including such worthies as Pulitzer Prize–winner and longtime Hunter friend Loren Jenkins, currently in charge of the international desk at National Public Radio; historian and official Hunter Thompson estate-appointed biographer Douglas Brinkley; Michael Isikoff from *Newsweek*; John Nichols from *The Nation*; journalist Carl Bernstein; and longtime Thompson attorney Gerry Goldstein. Other luminaries who might have contributed well to such a political forum included Jimmy Carter, George McGovern, Gary Hart, Bill Dixon, and Pat Buchanan, none of whom were able to make it. A special weekend edition of the *Aspen Daily News* coincided with the event, featuring all Hunter on all the pages. It was guest edited by Anita, seemingly as a response to the Juan-organized symposium, which Anita also attended.

The general conclusion seemed to be that there were so far no visible successors to Hunter, though several people mentioned Matt Taibi favorably, and the day turned into a sustained lament at having lost perhaps the last man to write honestly about politics and reach large audiences. The blame fell on the constraints of supposedly objective journalism, something that has always been tough on political correspondents and has only gotten worse in recent years. Nobody who could make a difference seems willing to step up on that front, nor could anyone probably get much coverage for doing it.

It was unusual to be at a symposium where no fewer than half a dozen of us were working on books about the subject. But it still produced some nice quotes. Loren Jenkins pointed out that "the difference between the establishment press and the genius of Hunter's reporting was to peel away the myths. . . . Hunter cut through the Kabuki Theater of American politics, which hides the reality all the time."

Carl Bernstein noted, "Hunter was amazingly open-minded. He went places we didn't go," which may have struck closer to the truth of Hunter's influence than anything else. John Nichols called Hunter "an incredibly hopeful patriot," and observed that while "Gonzo journalism didn't take, Gonzo citizenship did." Michael Isikoff allowed that he "got more mileage out of talking about my one dinner with Hunter, among my peers and colleagues, than anything else, ever."

On a personal note, Gerry Goldstein was more direct than most by saying that Hunter was a pain in the ass as a client and created crises all the time so he could be the center of attention. He also noted, "I've heard it said that Hunter was self-absorbed. Well, if that was a crime everyone at this podium would be an habitual criminal," adding that Hunter took himself seriously, and there was nothing wrong with that.

Sitting in the audience, George Stranahan may have told the best story before the symposium started. When a local journalist named John Colson walked in wearing a Gonzo Nation jean jacket, George said, "Shit, I burned all that stuff."

"No," said Colson.

"Yeah. Even the things he wrote. Who knew? He was up at the house stalking around one night around Christmas and wrote this thing for Ben [one of George's sons who was about four]. It was about this little dog, coming down the chimney and getting impaled on the andirons. And the little boy gets up and sees this drip, drip, drip."

"Ooh," Colson winced.

"Yeah. I burned it. I said 'Fuck you, Hunter.' I didn't think it was good for a four-year-old. But I should have kept it."

I feel the same way about a lot of things. I burned a bunch of stuff myself, some out of pique and some to protect us both. I still had a stack of books and several posters sitting around that I wanted Hunter to sign when I got the call about his death. Somewhere I have an autographed book cover for *Better Than Sex* that I can't find. I wish I'd picked up the phone more often for those late-night calls that finally quit coming when I never answered, and I wish I'd let him introduce me to his friends at ESPN, who I think he hoped could have given me a leg up on my career. For all of us he left owing money, it's hard not to feel as if we should have taken more advantage of him when we had the chance. But that isn't what it was about. Anyone close to Hunter paid a high price for it in the hard coin of the realm, which was blood, sweat, tears, and most of all attention. But for me it was worth it at twice the price. Up to a point.

The years of Hunter's greatest achievements coincided with that high-water mark of a generation he wrote about so eloquently. His greatest glory came well after that. I'm not really sure where Hunter was when the fun ended for him. It was a question he asked all of us at some time or another. But I think it happened for him long before he pulled the trigger. Fun is an elusive construct, but Hunter took it as his true calling. Yet he came equipped with so many gifts, including an absurdly strong constitution, that they began to seem like obstacles to be overcome, great weapons that he had to neutralize just to keep some challenge and enjoyment in the game. He managed to create his own treacherously long and vulnerable tail feathers, to publicly expose all of his weaknesses and rejigger them as displays of strength, to keep pushing on toward the next step in his own strange journey, regardless of whether it was forward, backward, or sideways, just as long as it was interesting and kept him occupied.

Much of what passed for fun in Hunter's world was different from everyone else's, and that's what made him such a unique beast. Whether he was a throwback or a too-early release of a model that was many years ahead of its time, or just some aberration that lasted forty years past its expiration date, he was not like the others. While that was exciting and stimulating, it wasn't necessarily the healthiest way to walk this world. If he had been physically a little less durable he might not have been able to abuse himself with such a crippling ferocity. If he'd been a little less bright, and a lot less sensitive, he might have been able to wander around picking up easy love and money like all the other champions of our species without much of a backward, or forward, glance.

Instead, he became a sort of repository of all that high and wild energy of a particular time and generation, wherein the seeds of something special and great resided, for whom life represented not a sentence but a huge opportunity, an open door to everything magnificent in the human spirit. Hunter certainly never viewed himself as the guide to a greatness we could all sense and feel but never quite lay our hands on. But he shared our dreams and visions, he channeled them, he understood the possibilities, and felt that extremely visceral knowledge that it was all attainable if we gave in to our best urges instead of our basest ones.

Still, it was all such a fine line to follow, and a lonely one, that in the process he became an embodiment of all the conflict and dichotomy in our nature, of the joy and confusion in our souls, of the manic, frantic dervishes we seemed destined to finally become, whirling through the darkness, trying to set fire to the heavens but really just torching ourselves until we eventually burn out. I think he lasted longer than he ever expected because he was made of sterner stuff than even he realized, and that was both his blessing and his curse.

For all of his complicated, difficult, mercurial, maddening, bipolar, kung fu kerosene-drinking, living-up-to-an-image lifestyle, he was really just as much pinned in the headlights of an onrushing doom he never understood as the rest of us. In spite of all his insider's knowledge and the dead certainty with which he conducted himself, he was really just another dazed and mortally flawed human: the true believer, the hopeful romantic, the King of Fun, the last honest man, the true sport, the guy who always bets his heart and knows it's wrong but can't stop himself.

Acknowledgments

This will seem obvious but I have to first acknowledge Hunter Thompson, not just for providing me with great material, but for taking me under his taloned and toxic wing a long time ago and thinking I had something useful to say. He may have been wrong, of course, but it meant a lot that he took the chance on me. I hope he doesn't regret it. I can't take too much more haunting.

My wife, Harriet, has also believed, when few others have, and provided more support than any reasonable human, let alone me, could have ever expected. Being wise and funny and possessed of a shrewd instinct for what works and what doesn't in my writing, and putting up with my two-year wallow for this book in a murky and testing past that didn't always help my moods, are just a few of the many reasons I love her deeply.

I don't know whether to thank or curse my mother for addicting me to reading at a very young age and always encouraging me to write. It's a poor way to make a living, I've found, but something I love enough that I don't care. Most of the time. Fortunately, my father taught me to work hard and never give up. My sister, who never had a good sibling role model, settled for me, and her example of faith has always astonished and motivated me.

Allen Jones, my generous and remarkable editor at The Lyons Press and elsewhere, was the one who asked if I had any book ideas for him. When I responded like a wolf being offered red meat, he was the one crazy enough to see merit in the possibilities of yet another book about Hunter Thompson. And he helped bring it to life. Blame him. Along with Ellen Urban, whose fine record may be tested by this project. I appreciate her taking it on.

Many of Hunter's and my mutual friends came to my assistance with stories, and some of them were even ones they hadn't shared with other authors. I've had to leave out many because there just wasn't room. Hunter generated more good stories than anyone I've ever known, enough for several lives, thirteen of his own books (and counting), and who knows how many other volumes about him, when all is said and done. I am especially indebted to Deborah Fuller, Laila Nabulsi, Bob Braudis, Monty Chitty, George Stranahan, David McCumber, Greg Ditrinco, and David Floria for their help. Maybe Hunter will trouble their sleep as well as mine for their reward.

Hunter had enough pictures taken of him to compensate for a hundred Salingers and Pynchons. Sometimes a little mystery is nice. But Alan Becker and Bob Krueger, both eminently successful photographers and longtime friends of Hunter's, were gracious enough to step forward with outstanding images for this book that portray the man and some of his best friends as well. Paul Pascarella's kind permission to use his powerful painting done in tribute to Hunter is as much appreciated as Paul and his art.

I've received significant support for this book from people who could have, and probably should have, just blown me off. Douglas Brinkley, who will likely have some of the final and choicest words on Hunter's life, and William McKeen, who has already ably weighed in on the subject, both came to my aid, for which I'm very grateful. And an accomplished writer and editor who should know better, my friend Michael Miracle, has lent me sincere encouragement from the beginning that has been singly important.

It is, by unsettling coincidence, Thanksgiving Day as I write this. Still, I can't sufficiently express my gratitude to everyone who has helped with my writing and this book. I hope I can someday be worthy and repay them.

Jay Cowan
November 2008
Snowmass, Colorado

Index